Candidate Strategies and Electoral Competition in the Russian Federation

In the early 1990s, competitive elections in the Russian Federation signaled the end to the authoritarian political system dominated by a single political party. More than ten years and many elections later, a single party led by Russian President Vladimir Putin threatens to end Russia's democratic experiment. Russia's experience with new elections is not unique but it does challenge existing theories of democratic consolidation by showing that competitive elections cannot guarantee successful democratic consolidation.

This book explores the conditions under which electoral competition contributes to democratic development. The theoretic framework focuses on the construction of infrastructure that transforms competitive elections into mechanisms of democratic development and shows how candidates for national parliamentary office systematically chose electoral strategies that undermined Russia's democratic foundation and created the conditions for a new single-party autocracy to emerge.

Regina Smyth teaches political science at Pennsylvania State University. She has written extensively on the role of political parties and elections in Russia's democratic transition. Her work appears in *Comparative Politics*, *Comparative Political Studies*, and *Politics and Society*.

Cambridge Studies in Comparative Politics

General Editor
Margaret Levi   *University of Washington, Seattle*

Assistant General Editor
Stephen Hanson   *University of Washington, Seattle*

Associate Editors
Robert H. Bates   *Harvard University*
Peter Hall   *Harvard University*
Peter Lange   *Duke University*
Helen Milner   *Columbia University*
Frances Rosenbluth   *Yale University*
Susan Stokes   *University of Chicago*
Sidney Tarrow   *Cornell University*

Other Books in the Series
Lisa Baldez, *Why Women Protest: Women's Movements in Chile*
Stefano Bartolini, *The Political Mobilization of the European Left, 1860–1980: The Class Cleavage*
Mark Beissinger, *Nationalist Mobilization and the Collapse of the Soviet State*
Nancy Bermeo, ed., *Unemployment in the New Europe*
Carles Boix, *Democracy and Redistribution*
Carles Boix, *Political Parties, Growth, and Equality: Conservative and Social Democratic Economic Strategies in the World Economy*
Catherine Boone, *Merchant Capital and the Roots of State Power in Senegal, 1930–1985*
Catherine Boone, *Political Topographies of the African State: Territorial Authority and Institutional Change*
Michael Bratton and Nicolas van de Walle, *Democratic Experiments in Africa: Regime Transitions in Comparative Perspective*
Michael Bratton, Robert Mattes, and E. Gyimah-Boadi, *Public Opinion, Democracy, and Market Reform in Africa*

Continued after the index

Candidate Strategies and Electoral Competition in the Russian Federation

DEMOCRACY WITHOUT FOUNDATION

REGINA SMYTH
Pennsylvania State University

CAMBRIDGE UNIVERSITY PRESS
Cambridge, New York, Melbourne, Madrid, Cape Town, Singapore, São Paulo

Cambridge University Press
40 West 20th Street, New York, NY 10011-4211, USA

www.cambridge.org
Information on this title: www.cambridge.org/9780521846905

© Regina Smyth 2006

This publication is in copyright. Subject to statutory exception
and to the provisions of relevant collective licensing agreements,
no reproduction of any part may take place without
the written permission of Cambridge University Press.

First published 2006

Printed in the United States of America

A catalog record for this publication is available from the British Library.

Library of Congress Cataloging in Publication Data

Smyth, Regina, 1961–
Candidate strategies and electoral competition in the Russian Federation :
democracy without foundation / Regina Smyth.
   p.   cm. – (Cambridge studies in comparative politics)
Includes bibliographical references and index.
ISBN 0-521-84690-0 (hardback)
1. Elections – Russia (Federation)   2. Politics, Political – Russia (Federation)
3. Political candidates – Russia (Federation)   4. Democracy – Russia (Federation)
I. Title.   II. Series.
JN6699.A5S29   2006
324.7′0947–dc22   2005010533

ISBN-13   978-0-521-84690-5 hardback
ISBN-10   0-521-84690-0 hardback

Cambridge University Press has no responsibility for
the persistence or accuracy of URLs for external or
third-party Internet Web sites referred to in this publication
and does not guarantee that any content on such
Web sites is, or will remain, accurate or appropriate.

Contents

1	ELECTIONS AND THE DEVELOPMENT OF DEMOCRATIC CAPACITY	page 1
2	ONE STEP FORWARD, TWO STEPS BACK: RUSSIA'S FAILED CONSOLIDATION IN COMPARATIVE CONTEXT	14
3	THE MICROFOUNDATIONS OF DEMOCRATIC RESPONSIVENESS: CANDIDATE STRATEGIES AND ELECTORAL INFRASTRUCTURE	43
4	MANY CANDIDATES, FEW CHOICES	71
5	TO JOIN OR NOT TO JOIN: CANDIDATE AFFILIATION IN TRANSITIONAL RUSSIA	102
6	FINDING FIT: CANDIDATES AND THEIR DISTRICTS	131
7	CAMPAIGNING FOR THE DUMA: MIXED MARKETS, MIXED MESSAGES	165
8	DEMOCRATS, DEMOCRATIC TRANSITIONS, AND RUSSIAN DEMOCRACY	197
Appendix A	*The Sample*	213
Appendix B	*The Candidate Survey*	215
Appendix C	*Variables Constructed from Survey Data*	223
Appendix D	*Sample and Variable Construction for Analysis in Chapter 2*	229
Works Cited		233
Index		245

1

Elections and the Development of Democratic Capacity

Elections and representation are two different institutions.
    Yury Sharandin, chair of the Constitutional Legislation Committee of the Federation Council[1]

In describing the third wave of democratic transitions, Samuel Huntington (1991) wrote that the introduction of elections signals the death of authoritarian systems. Subsequent developments have demonstrated that the relationship between elections and regime change is much more complicated. Yes, the critical event in the consolidation period is the introduction of competitive elections. However, electoral competition does not always mark the death of an authoritarian regime. Rather, it signals the beginning of building a new regime while grappling with the vestiges of the old, a process that can end in a range of outcomes from stable, responsive, and accountable democracy to authoritarian revival.

This book explores the role that electoral competition plays in the evolution of transitional regimes. Its premise is that understanding how individual politicians respond to incentives in the newly established electoral arena helps to explain the success or failure of democratic consolidation. While the empirical focus of this book is largely on the Russian Federation, the theoretic framework illuminates the broader implications of electoral politics in new democracies.

As Russia emerged from its democratization period and undertook competitive elections in 1993, optimism about the country's chances of achieving democratic goals was boundless. Analysts declared that the Communist Party – and by implication the authoritarian regime – was over. Elections,

---

[1] Ratiani, Natalia, and Olga Tropkina. "Senators May Be Elected Soon: The Federation Council Is on the Threshold of Crucial Reforms," *Izvestiya*, June 22, 2004, p. 1.

they argued, had supplanted both the party and authoritarian rule, and would serve as the basis for a stable democracy. As time went on, early optimism waned. Russianists noted with alarm that President Vladimir Putin revived an old Soviet phrase, "managed democracy," to describe his vision of Russian politics (Colton and McFaul 2003a: 10–11). By 2003, it was impossible to ignore the growing use of coercion to win voter support. Not only were elections a false measure of democracy in Russia, repeated elections had not fulfilled their mandate of pushing (or pulling) Russia toward democratic governance.

These outcomes place Russia in a growing set of democratic regimes that are either incapable or unwilling to generate democratic responsiveness in the face of competitive elections.[2] The cases raise an important set of questions for comparative politics and, in particular, for the study of democratic consolidation. When does electoral competition provoke and structure elite investment in democratic regime structures and behaviors that transform elections into mechanisms of representation and accountability? Conversely, what conditions lead elite politicians to choose strategies that consciously or unconsciously undermine democratic development?

This study argues that it is no surprise that competitive elections did not produce an effective and accountable democracy in Russia.[3] Starting with the founding elections in 1993, it was clear that assumptions about the building blocks of democratic governance that underpin theories of democratic consolidation did not apply to this case. Outside of Moscow, the harbingers of democratic development, political parties, were almost invisible to voters. Sitting around in late-night meetings, regional party leaders struggled to feed themselves, pooled their money to buy vodka, and lamented that while everyone was talking about elections, very few seemed to be paying attention to the campaign. They gossiped about their

---

[2] *Journal of Democracy* provided a venue for debates over the relationship between elections and democracy. Guillermo O'Donnell's work, aptly titled "Illusions About Consolidation," 1996, has been a catalyst for this debate. Thomas Carothers prompted a lively discussion in January 2002 that involved responses from policy makers and prominent scholars; see Carothers, 2002: 5–21.

[3] Przeworski et al. define competitive elections as ones in which the opposition has some chance to win given 1) ex ante uncertainty about the incumbents' chances of maintaining office; 2) ex post irreversibility (winners take office); and 3) repeatability (strong expectations that future elections will occur). See Przeworski et al., 2000: 3.

Elections and Development of Democratic Capacity

rivals' ties to business or the governor, grumbled about the role of Kremlin resources in the campaign, and complained about the lack of enforcement of electoral regulations. Only the Communists seemed to know how to reach their voters through door-to-door campaigns built on the vestiges of the Soviet-era party. Conflict among candidates and within parties was ubiquitous. No one, not even the Communists, seemed to be able to work together in pursuit of common goals. Universally, party leaders worked to broker deals among like-minded organizations, but ultimately failed to reach agreements.

These examples illustrate a central finding of this work. Russia lacked the formal and informal structures and patterns of behavior that secure democracy at the point of founding elections. There is no question that Russian elections changed the strategies of prominent politicians. However, factors such as institutions that privileged individual politicians over collective actors, the diffusion of political resources, and the profound level of uncertainty that surrounded the electoral process led politicians away from behaviors that would help to create an accountable, efficient, or responsive government.

Events in Russia demonstrate that repeated electoral competition is not equal to democratic governance, nor is it likely to produce democracy any time soon. In fact, with each election, Russia has moved further from norms of free and fair elections.[4] Rather than generating strong and consistent coalitions of politicians and voters, each contest triggered a seismic reorganization of alliances and organizations. Between elections, the weak systems of checks and balances ensconced in the constitution coupled with the lack of a viable opposition have proved unable to check the growing power of the president.

This book explains Russia's political evolution with a theory of the relationship between electoral competition and democratic development. The logic of the explanation reasons from the actions of individual candidates and party leaders to national-level outcomes. The two levels of analysis are linked by the concept of electoral infrastructure – the political information and patterns of political coordination and cooperation that are necessary for

---

[4] The Organization for Security and Cooperation in Europe (OSCE) report listing Russia's violations in the 2003 parliamentary election can be found at http://www.osce.org/documents/odihr/2004/01/1947_en.pdf, accessed October 21, 2003. A comprehensive analysis of election and post-election developments can be found at Freedom House Reports, www.freedomhouse.org, accessed June 12, 2004.

a regime to fulfill procedural and normative criteria of democratic governance. The analysis shows that in transitions that are marked by uncertainty, in which candidates and party leaders have a very weak sense of what voters want from government, institutions and resource distributions that enable candidates to compete independently can derail democratic development. The argument is developed and tested using data from Russian elections, but is not a Russia-specific argument. The model and approach are applicable to a range of consolidating regimes to explain variation in both the timing and the outcome of democratic consolidation efforts.

This introduction sets out the analytic framework in broad strokes, establishing a connection between candidates' decisions in response to competitive elections and the capacity for democratic governance. The discussion proceeds by placing Russia within the broader context of postcommunist states and underscoring that elites' actions are an important element in the explanation of the range of outcomes that these states experienced following their founding elections. I then describe the development and test of the theory that is laid out in the remaining chapters of this book.

Why Study Russia?

The empirical focus of this book is squarely on the evolution of the new regime in the Russian Federation for a number of reasons. The first reason is a purely practical consideration. The importance of the Soviet Union in the global security environment led to disproportionate focus on Russia's transition. As a result, the scholarly and policy community compiled enormous data on almost all aspects of Russian political, social, and economic structures. This rich pool of information provides an excellent backdrop to this book.

Theoretically, the Russian example highlights a crucial flaw in the concept of democratic consolidation. The expectation that the natural and even inevitable progress of development will be a linear evolution toward a single endpoint, democracy, taints the consolidation framework. The data I present in Chapter 2 show that the period after founding elections can be marked by democratic deepening, as in Estonia, or by decline, as in Russia. These developments can be roughly linear, as in the case of Romania, or progress in fits and starts, as in Ukraine and Georgia. By any measure, the reality of the postcommunist transitions is that the consolidation period produced a range of outcomes, from democracy to authoritarianism and a number of variations in between. More importantly, these cases strongly

Elections and Development of Democratic Capacity

suggest that consolidation need not end in democracy. Hungary, Poland, and Latvia made significant strides toward democracy, while Kazakhstan and Belarus have made little or no progress. Turkmenistan began the process as a brutal dictatorship and that has not changed.

Although prominent in the literature and in the policy world, Russia's experience is not unique. The high levels of political uncertainty, weakly organized civil society, and dispersed set of political resources that marked conditions in Russia at the point of the founding elections characterize a number of consolidating regimes in Latin America, Africa, Asia, and even the Middle East. Works surveying the democratic transitions in the third wave of democratization demonstrate that while competitive elections are essential to democratic regimes, electoral competition is not sufficient to ensure successful consolidation.[5] The demise of fledgling democracies across these regions underscores the fact that simply convening competitive elections is not tantamount to democracy. Recent evidence from across the globe points to the unhappy truth that not all transitional regimes, even those that make a good-faith effort at competitive elections, culminate in representative democracies (Bratton 1997; Karl 1995; Levitsky and Way 2002; O'Donnell 1994; Rose and Munro 2003; Zakaria 1997).

In response to this new understanding of political realities, scholars began to explore the meaning of elections in new democracies.[6] This book enters into the debate about the origins and durability of semi-authoritarian regimes by linking the strategic choices of key actors in the electoral process, candidates and party leaders, to the national-level outcomes – democracy or not. I argue that politicians' choices can produce electoral infrastructure in the form of information, patterns of coordination and cooperation that transform elections into mechanisms of democratic governance. Yet, the accumulation of infrastructure is not the inevitable byproduct of electoral competition. The Russian case clearly shows that under conditions of uncertainty, permissive institutions, and dispersed electoral resources, candidates will choose campaign strategies that perpetuate uncertainty, undermine coordinated action, and shape very weak and underinstitutionalized parties.

---

[5] This book contributes to a growing set of studies focused on the mechanisms of semi-authoritarianism in postcommunist states. For example, the framework developed by O'Donnell 1994; 1998, has been applied to understand post-Soviet cases; see Kubicek 1994: 423; Tsygankov 1998: 329.

[6] For examples of the discussion of elections and democratic development in postcommunist cases, see Clark 2000; Hale 2000: 123.

A Strategy for Theory Development: Linking Individual Behavior, Elections, and System-Level Outcomes

Much of the contention in the consolidation literature centers on defining the endpoint of democratization: How do we know when an authoritarian regime is transformed into a consolidated democracy? Minimal definitions (e.g., Dahl 1971) focus on the procedures that enable democratic governance. For example, Adam Przeworski (1986) stresses elite support for the regime or contingent consent as a test of consolidation, relegating any regime that does not meet this test to a residual authoritarian category. Maximal definitions focus on behavior or norms. A number of scholars combine these two concepts, defining consolidation as an endgame of the democratic transition that is marked by a decline in political uncertainty (Alexander 2001; Bunce and Csanadi 1993; Przeworski 1986; Schedler 2001; Schmitter 2001). As Phillippe Schmitter writes:

Consolidation could be defined as the process of transforming the accidental arrangements, prudential norms, and contingent solutions that have emerged during the transition into relations of cooperation and competition that are reliably known, regularly practiced, and voluntarily accepted by those persons or collectivities – that is, politicians and citizens – that participate in democratic governance (Schmitter 2001: 68).

This definition stresses the very concepts that are at the heart of this study – information and coordination in electoral competition – and defines them as important measurements or landmarks of successful consolidation. Yet Schmitter's conception of consolidation straddles the minimalist and maximalist camps in that it does not get at the qualitative aspects of democracy or core democratic norms. It falls short of the very rigorous definition offered by Juan Linz and Alfred Stepan (1996: 5–7), who focus on the deepening of democracy in terms of representation, accountability, and effectiveness. Taking this definition one step further, Larry Diamond (1999: 65) combines deepening with the idea of elite commitment, focusing on "broad and deep legitimation" that represents "a shift in political culture."

The definitional debate is undeniably important to the understanding of regime change but it obscures a number of critical concerns. As discussed previously, debates over whether to define democratic consolidation in minimal (procedural) terms or maximal (quality of democracy) terms do not capture the variation in the outcomes of the consolidation period. Moreover, the debates over endpoints do not address the range of variation in the process of consolidation, the obstacles that new democracies face as they attempt to consolidate, or the temporal variation in the trajectories of political development.

To address these concerns, the theoretic framework developed in this book describes consolidation as a process that begins with founding elections and culminates in a range of outcomes from functioning democracy to authoritarianism. This approach concentrates on the effect of a critical political change – the introduction of competitive elections – on the movement toward or away from democracy. The dependent variable is the degree to which candidates' strategies do, or do not, generate and sustain the key electoral and representative institutions of democracy and lay the groundwork for democratic deepening.

Viewed from this perspective, competing definitions of consolidation are not mutually exclusive but provide the outlines of a model of political development in which the imposition of new procedures, elite commitment, and democratic deepening are key landmarks. A democratic regime structure is a necessary condition for any democracy. Elites must commit to competing for power through the new institutions. In turn, this competition can prompt the creation of new political norms and institutions that generate the capacity for citizens to hold their elected representatives responsible for their actions in office. However, there is no guarantee that elections will have this effect. In short, elections are the causal engine of this process, but they can steer the regime in multiple directions.

There is no doubt that elections signal a break with the old regime. They don't simply replicate the past nor do they mirror the forces that put them in place (Alexander 2001; Ames 2001; Jones Luong 2002; Kitschelt et al. 1999; Kitschelt and Smyth 2002). Time and again, authoritarian leaders as disparate as Mikhail Gorbachev and Augusto Pinochet have introduced competitive elections that escaped their control and led to their demise. Electoral competition can transform existing social forces, institutional actors, and individual elites. Poland's mighty Solidarity movement was undone by electoral competition, as were the national fronts that led the way to independence in the Baltic states. Boris Yeltsin used elections to revive his flagging political career and challenge Gorbachev's national leadership. The previously unheralded Liberal Democratic Party of Russia and its volatile leader, Vladimir Zhirinovsky, emerged as a permanent fixture in national politics after its startling showing in the 1993 elections.

At the same time, elections cannot shut the door on the past as the wide-ranging legacy of the old communist regimes continues to influence politics under new rules in many states. Personalities, reputations, skills, and resources drawn from the old system can profoundly influence the successes and failures of vestigial parties, new party organizations and non-partisan candidates. In East Europe, some communist successor parties used effective strategies to achieve remarkable and unpredicted success while others foundered (Grzymala-Busse 2002; Ishiyama 2000; Ishiyama and Shafqat 2000). Some of these organizations used electoral competition as a mechanism to adapt to the new environment, while others clung stubbornly to entrenched ideas and patterns of behavior.

A good starting point for understanding elections as a catalyst for democratic development is to distinguish among the roles that elections play in new and established systems. In established systems, elections fulfill a long laundry list of functions: generating and maintaining party systems, engendering equality, legitimizing regimes, installing governing officials, presenting citizens with choices, building communities, involving and educating citizens, preventing tyranny, enabling representation, and provoking accountability and responsiveness (Katz 1997). In contrast, studies of the role of elections in new democracies point to two overarching processes or functions that are integral to democratic deepening: elite incorporation and mass interest aggregation (Aldrich 1995; Kitschelt et al. 1999).

Integration or incorporation of elites into the electoral arena in new democracies is usually but not exclusively accomplished through political parties. Widespread elite incorporation enables party organizations to fulfill a number of important roles in the new democratic systems. First, incorporation cements the contingent consent bargain that elites broker in the democratization phase (Przeworski 1991). Second, it forges increased capacity for governance by solving social choice and collective action problems in government (Aldrich 1995; Cox and McCubbins 1993). Elite incorporation also structures the choices presented to voters on the ballot and links voters and government to enable responsiveness and accountability.

The analysis of the postcommunist cases in the next chapter shows that the level of elite incorporation at the point of founding elections is not uniform across the cases. An important implication is that elections are tasked with different burdens in different contexts. In some cases, elections are important mechanisms for incorporating elites; in others, this process is already complete when electoral competition begins.[7] Chapter 2

---

[7] It is beyond the scope of this work to explain this variation, but authors cite the nature of the authoritarian regime, mode of transition, and level of political organization at the point of founding as key factors. For a more complete discussion see Munck and Leff 1997.

Elections and Development of Democratic Capacity

demonstrates that in cases where elections must provoke incorporation, they may or may not succeed depending on conditions at the point of founding elections, institutional structures, time, and international context. Moreover, as the subsequent investigation of the Russian case shows, elites within new regimes do not respond uniformly to the opportunities offered by electoral competition, as some elites choose strategies that engender coordination and cooperation and others do not.

In the next stage, elite incorporation is critical because it drives the process of democratic deepening identified by scholars focused on normative democratic goals such as accountability and representation. Once committed to the electoral process, elites face significant incentives to forge ties to mass voters and solidify those ties within political institutions to ensure that their mass followings remain loyal. As such, elites are likely to reach out to voters in order to channel their demands through the electoral process and avoid the instability wrought by out-of-system behavior (Huntington 1968). Elites also shape voters' demands and their propensity to work together to pursue common goals. The need to solidify support to win elections generates strong incentives for candidates and party leaders to ensure participation and turnout through voter registration drives and education programs. The motivation for doing so is not an altruistic tendency to cultivate social capital but a need to ensure that the candidates' voters show up at the polls and cast their votes correctly. All of these activities may extend beyond the electoral arena and between contests, shoring up democratic deepening.

While elite integration facilitates this process of democratic deepening, it does not make it inevitable.[8] Interest aggregation is likely to be the result of experimentation and learning as candidates and parties try out different appeals and discern the preferences of potential supporters. This protracted process leaves the new regime vulnerable to exogenous shocks, crises, and scandals that sharply reorder politics and generate instability. Moreover, as the evidence presented later will show, even elites who support democratic goals may not adopt strategies to shore up democratic deepening.

Finally, not all voters will respond to elites' actions in the same manner. Both Diamond (1999) and Linz and Stepan (1996) argue that some polities may resist elites' efforts to mobilize existing interests in support of their cause. Scholars often cite Poland as an example of a new electorate whose

---

[8] For example, Grzegorz Ekiert and Jan Kubik (1998: 574) find that in Hungary and Slovakia, two successful consolidators, party organizations are the lead instigators of protest activity.

norms and existing organizations generated resistance to elites' efforts to forge stable ties to voters early on in the transition, generating prolonged electoral volatility.[9] My own work on Russian party organizations demonstrates that parties' campaign strategies can hinder the emergence of durable ties between voters and organizations (Smyth forthcoming). The implication is that not all elites will adopt strategies that further democratic deepening and not all voters will embrace their efforts.

To explain this variation in elites' strategies, the empirical chapters of this work show how uncertainty about voters' preferences, electoral institutions that privilege individuals over organizations, and diverse resource distributions lead candidates with disparate goals to choose electoral strategies that short circuit patterns of incorporation and interest aggregation. The evidence reveals how these conditions produce four patterns of behavior that, while individually rational, work to undermine democratic infrastructure: Too many candidates choose to run in every election; too few candidates choose to tie themselves to political parties; most candidates do not establish strong electoral connections to their constituencies; and candidates do not invest in campaigns that generate reliable information to guide voters' choices, future government actions, or future campaigns.

The Plan of the Book

The preceding framework establishes the two major tasks of the book. The first task is to show that candidates' responses to competitive elections matter for the outcome of democratic development, and that their impact on outcomes is felt both in the incorporation of political elites into the new regime and the development of stable linkages between and among candidates and voters. In other words, to prove the theory to be right, I must show that the variation in the level of democratic capacity across postcommunist countries is at least partially dependent on elite actions.

Chapter 2 shows that prior degrees of elite commitment to democracy, combined with the prospect of eventual EU membership and constitutional structures, have worked to decrease political uncertainty and to increase reliable information in most of the postcommunist democracies of Eastern and Central Europe. In contrast, none of these factors operates in the Russian Federation, generating the particularly extreme form of electoral

---

[9] See Ekiert and Kubik 1998: 477. For a theoretic discussion, see also Diamond 1999: 218–60.

Elections and Development of Democratic Capacity

and informational uncertainty uncovered by my research on candidates' strategies. To show the importance of elites' responses to electoral competition as a critical causal variable in the larger process of democratic consolidation, the chapter incorporates elite commitment into an empirical analysis of the developments in postcommunist cases from the period of the founding elections to the present. The chapter surveys the postcommunist cases to show that elite responses matter, even when we control for competing explanations of the outcomes of consolidation. Finally, the discussion develops the three-pronged concept of electoral infrastructure to measure key variation across the postcommunist cases.

The second goal of the work is to develop and test an individual-level theory that explains the variation in elites' responses to the introduction of competitive elections. Toward this end, Chapter 3 sets out an individual-level model that explains candidates' decisions at critical points in the electoral process: entry, partisan affiliation, district selection, and campaign strategy. I draw the explanatory variables – institutions, goals, resources, and information – from Western studies of candidate behavior, and modify them to reflect the reality of Russia's transitional context.

The remainder of the book focuses on theory testing, using data from Russian elections. The empirical core of this work is a pair of surveys of candidates for national parliamentary office in 1995 and 1999, the second and third post-Soviet elections. I use this evidence, augmented with aggregate candidate data from 1993 and 2003, to analyze candidates' decisions to run for office, district choices, partisan affiliations, and campaign strategies, as well as the wider implications of these decisions for democratic consolidation. The data show that competitors adopt very different strategies to meet the challenges posed by new elections and that these strategies have very different implications for their success in winning votes and for the consolidation of institutions that support democratic development. Following this line of reasoning, my work focuses on the strategic choices of electoral contestants throughout the electoral cycle, from the decision to enter the race to the campaign strategies that they adopt to convince voters to turn out and support them.

Chapter 4 examines candidates' entry patterns. Mindful that the available data do not include those candidates who considered running but gave up, the chapter examines the causes for the large numbers of candidates who run in every race. The study compares entry patterns across regions and examines the behavior of candidates who ran in one race but didn't run in the others. Finally, the chapter discusses the implications of candidate and party proliferation on the accumulation of democratic infrastructure, highlighting the effect of candidate proliferation on information accumulation.

Chapter 5 looks at candidates' propensities to affiliate with party organizations and explains why some candidates run with the Communists while others join Fatherland–All Russia, Yabloko, the more obscure Social Democrats, or even run as independents. By looking at the reciprocal relationship between candidates and parties and characterizing the types of candidates who join party organizations, the data generate a new perspective on party development from inside the organization. The chapter then turns to the question of electoral infrastructure and presents clear evidence of the different forms of constituency ties that are emerging from the electoral process. Moreover, the analysis shows how the growing strength of the president's United Russia Party influenced individual decisions to change the dynamic of elections in 2003.

Chapter 6 examines how candidates choose their districts. Do candidates choose districts based on where they can win? Do they choose districts based on knowledge of a preexisting constituency? Given Russia's mixed electoral law, these decisions are complicated choices. Absent a residency requirement, candidates can run in any one of 225 single-member districts, on a central party list, on a regional party list, or on both a list and in a district. I find that two sets of factors drive candidates toward or away from particular districts: candidate-specific factors such as goals, information, and resources, and exogenous forces such as central party bosses, regional party bosses, and regional officials. This analysis of district choice provides more clues about the types of linkages that candidates seek to build with potential constituents.

Chapter 7 looks at candidate strategies during the campaign period. These choices are divided into two categories: the type of organizational structures that candidates rely on during the campaign period, and the types of messages they use to attract and mobilize constituencies. All candidates, even partisans, face the choice of developing individual organizations and candidate-centered messages or relying on party organizations and party platforms. The chapter relies on the survey data to examine both aspects of campaigning. These data, together with analysis of a hypothetical spatial model of electoral competition, suggest why the accumulation of electoral infrastructure is not inevitable or at the very least may occur only over a long time period or in a response to an exogenous shock. Focusing on campaign structures and messages also reveals some of the profound weaknesses of

Elections and Development of Democratic Capacity

party organizations in Russia and explains why they have not had much influence beyond the party list race for legislative seats.

The final chapter explores the implications of this study for other cases of transition. The discussion highlights lessons learned from Russia's experience in the consolidation period. Placed in a comparative context, Russia's trajectory is not unique in the process of transition. The results presented here can inform our comparative understanding of the role played by elections in the evolution of transitional political systems, as well as the advantages of focusing on candidates and the impact of their behavior on electoral infrastructure.

2

One Step Forward, Two Steps Back

RUSSIA'S FAILED CONSOLIDATION
IN COMPARATIVE CONTEXT

Nothing is less real than realism. Details are confusing. It is only by selection, by emphasis that we get at the real meaning of things.

Georgia O'Keeffe, 1922[1]

Until the 2003 election, students of Russian politics were deeply divided in their assessments of Russian democracy. The outcome of this election, and the subsequent emergence of a dominant political party in Russia, United Russia (UR), led a majority of scholars and policy analysts to conclude that Russia's nascent democracy was in crisis. As Vladimir Putin strengthened executive control over all aspects of governance in the wake of terrorist attacks in Moscow and in the Caucuses, there was growing concern that Russia's democratic experiment was over. Reflecting these concerns, in late 2004 Freedom House downgraded its assessment of Russian democracy.

The arguments presented here suggest that these changes were neither sudden nor should they have been unexpected. The imposition of proportional representation, the appointment of regional governors, and the abolition of term limits are consistent with, but not the inevitable consequence of, the actions of individual politicians taken in response to competitive elections, and were shaped by the political, social, and economic context of the Russian transition.

Recent scholarship sums up the paradox that marks Russia's political process: recurring competitive elections that propel the regime away from democracy by diminishing the capacity for organized opposition to a ruling party (Colton and Hale 2004; Colton and McFaul 2003a, b; Rose and Munro 2003). This puzzle is not only relevant for Russia. Uzbekistan, Moldova,

---

[1] Lippard, Lucy. *Portrait of an Artist: A Biography of Georgia O'Keeffe*. New York: Seaview 1981.

and Belarus experienced similar outcomes. In these cases, repeated elections were insufficient to ensure successful consolidation and, moreover, actually coexisted with a decline in the quality of democracy.

Placing the Russian experience within the context of other postcommunist cases highlights the shortcomings inherent in the assumptions of the consolidation framework. The impact of elections on Russia's political development raises the need to investigate the conditions under which democratic transitions move toward full democracy. Many post-Soviet states lag behind the East Central European states, yet they exhibit widely divergent levels of economic growth, corruption, support for authoritarianism, and international engagement. In theoretic terms, these cases challenge consolidation theories that rest on a single set of structural explanatory variables, since the theories fail to predict critical cases, cannot account for the nonlinear developments, and posit weak causal mechanisms to explain the observed relationships.

To address this gap, it is essential to compare relative power of different explanations while working to understand how key actors – partisan and independent candidates – respond to the introduction of electoral competition. I propose to abandon the consolidation framework in favor of a model that incorporates the role of elite strategies, including efforts to mobilize and bind potential voters, into analyses of political development. Elections are critical points for a number of reasons. Elections can serve as a focal point of political action. They can reveal important information about the value of political resources, clarifying the relative influence of different actors. Finally, elections can provide a catalyst to generate new institutions and norms that link voters and representatives, citizens and government. Or elections can do none of these things. In this light, the theory-building goal of post-election research should be to understand when elections induce political actors – from presidents to voters – to engage in strategies that support democratic development and when they do not.

The first section of the chapter outlines a framework to test competing theories of political development across the postcommunist cases. The statistical analysis reveals two new insights: Elite actions are critical to explaining increased democratic capacity, and Russia represents an important but not unique challenge to theories of political development following founding elections. However, the analysis is limited by its use of existing measures of democratic capacity. Although these measures capture variation in procedures and elite commitment, they omit other critical influences on democratic transitions, most especially the incentives faced by candidate and other political elites. To capture and explain the variation in these incentives, the last section of the chapter expands the discussion of the three elements of electoral infrastructure: information, coordination, and cooperation.

Defining and Measuring Democratic Consolidation in the Postcommunist Context

Despite debates surrounding definitions of consolidation and the viability of the consolidation framework, there is significant agreement on measurement. The most common measure for all of these definitions of democracy centers on regime durability – or government turnover – usually over the course of two or three election cycles.

This measurement is vulnerable to two related critiques that mirror comments aimed at procedural definitions of democracy discussed in the first chapter. First, democratic regimes may endure without fulfilling the goals of democracy. Second, I would argue that absent good measures of democratic deepening, two elections do not provide sufficient proof that the battle for democracy is over, particularly if our central concern is the capacity of citizens to use the levers of elections to demand responsiveness, representation, or efficiency from their government or to hold their representatives accountable for their actions in office. By imposing these limited time constraints within the consolidation framework, it is possible that we will miss the development of institutions and norms that ensure long-term democratic stability.

An alternative measure for procedural and elite commitment definitions of democracy is to compare democracy scores such as Polity or Freedom House (FH) at different points in time. For that exercise to be meaningful, it is critical to clarify what these scores actually measure. One tactic is to focus on the degree to which these scores correspond to minimal or maximal definitions of democracy. Polity scores focus more on formal rules – for example, measuring a regime's capacity for protection of civil rights rather than actual rights.[2]

---

[2] The analysis presented in this chapter was run with both Polity and FH scores, and the results did not change. While there is significant disagreement on the scores of particular cases (notably Russia and Romania), there is a high correlation in the set of countries that are defined as consolidated or not.

One Step Forward, Two Steps Back

In contrast, FH scores incorporate important elements of a behavioral-based definition of democracy, including measures of political parties and effective opposition.[3] In concrete terms, Freedom House scores range from one to seven – consolidated democracies score between one and two, while authoritarian systems receive between a six and a seven. FH measures are extremely effective measures of procedural regularity and elite commitment. Still, they fall short of capturing the full range of variation in the quality of democracy across states that are deemed consolidated. This point is evident if we examine an alternate set of measures available from Freedom House dedicated to elucidating differences across the postcommunist cases. (These scores are not used in the later analysis because they are available for a much shorter time period.) These more detailed scores illustrate persistent differences between overall scores or the electoral process score and the governance scores that reflect effectiveness, stability, and legislative capacity at all levels of government.

Using the FH scores, we can describe the variation in postcommunist development in two ways. The first is to examine the differences in scores across countries. As of 2003, only nine of the twenty-nine postcommunist cases were considered consolidated, yielding an FH score of two or less. Yet, ratings in a single year mask a great deal of variation in the path that brought different countries to that point. To examine this variation, Figure 2.1 shows the change in Freedom House scores between founding elections and 2003. Negative numbers indicate democratic deepening while positive numbers indicate decline. These scores show that while most postcommunist cases have made some progress toward democracy, four cases, including that of Russia, lost ground. The finding provides a starting point for the project: How can we explain Russia's poor performance relative to other cases?

To provide even more information, Figure 2.2 plots the change in FH scores relative to the countries' scores in the years after founding elections. This figure reveals that countries that start with low scores (strong democratic practices) rarely lose ground. Conversely, with the exception of Romania and Albania, countries that begin with very high scores most often make little or no progress. In contrast, countries with middle-range scores exhibit a high level of variation, both in the magnitude and in the

---

[3] Full Freedom House data are available at www.freedomhouse.org. A second set of detailed scores that are focused solely on postcommunist cases is not available for the entire period. These scores are highly correlated with Freedom Scores; see http://www.freedomhouse.org/research/nattransit.htm.

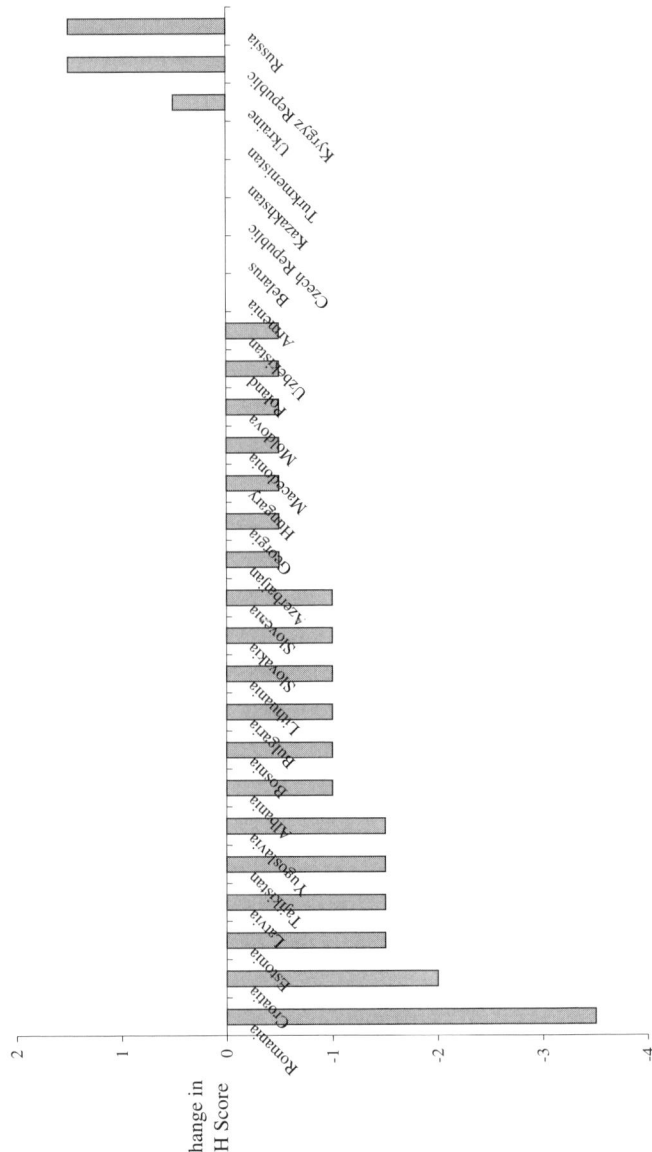

Figure 2.1. Change in Freedom House Score, from Founding Election Through 2003

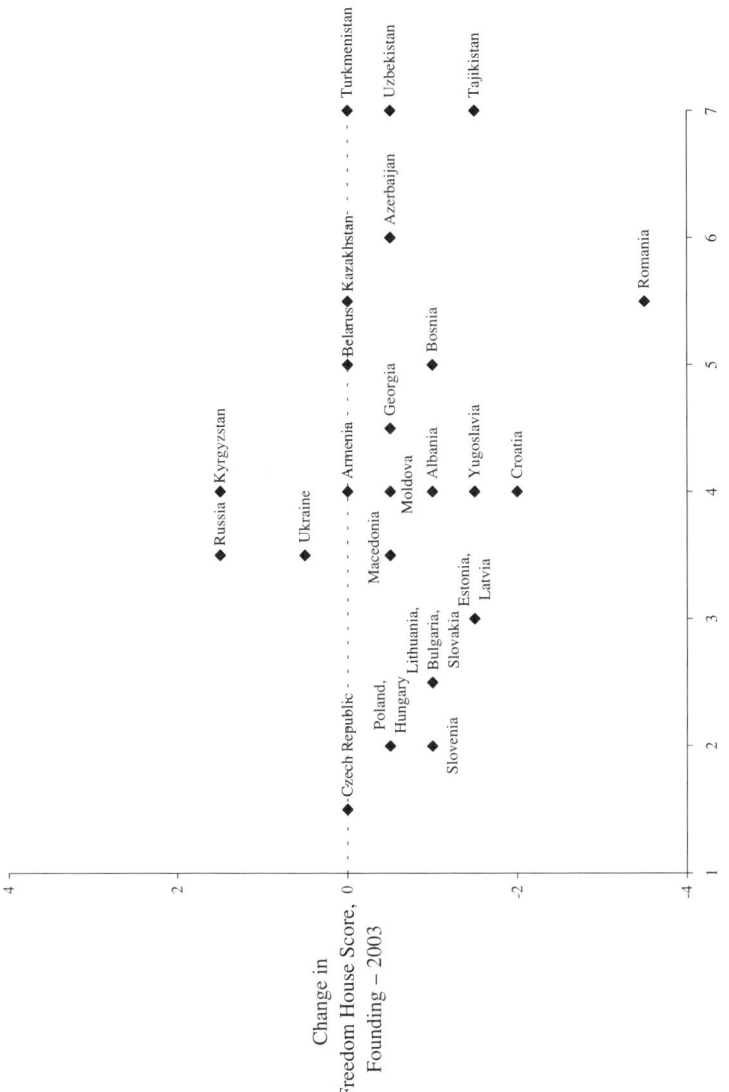

Figure 2.2. The Impact of Starting Position on Change in Consolidation Scores

direction of movement during this period. This figure strongly suggests that the starting point of consolidation matters for the ultimate endpoint and for the time that it takes to reach that point. In other words, not all consolidation processes are the same. Countries that hold founding elections with significant elite commitment to the regime move toward democracy despite significant volatility in their party systems, party organizations, and linkages between mass and elite actors.

Figure 2.2 also reveals four general patterns or consolidation trajectories. Hungary and Poland exemplify the first and most successful path: countries that begin and end the consolidation period with a low (consolidated) democratization score. These countries are currently considered consolidated democracies. The Central Asian states are antitheses of these success stories. These countries began the consolidation period as authoritarian states and did not progress. In the middle are cases where new regimes began on shaky ground and followed divergent paths. For example, Russia's democracy scores fell and then rose, stabilizing above the starting point, whereas Romania and Albania both moved toward democratic goals.

These patterns raise the more general question of what factors explain the variation in democratic development after the introduction of competitive elections. The picture of the relationship between elections and democratic consolidation that emerges from these simple descriptions of postcommunist cases is more complicated than suggested by Samuel Huntington (1991) and other democratization theorists. Not only are the trajectories and levels of progress different across cases, it also appears that the starting points are radically different.

Considered together, Figures 2.1 and 2.2 highlight a theoretical gap in our understanding of the processes of democratic consolidation and demand a theory that links the role of elections and consolidation. These figures suggest that successful democratic consolidation encompasses all three components of competing definitions of consolidation – institutional structure, elite commitment, and democratic norms – and that these elements constitute stages or markers of a developmental model of consolidation that can go off track and undermine progress toward democracy.

Elections and Democratic Consolidation: Promoting Elite Commitment and Interest Aggregation

The basic mechanisms of an electoral democracy are very simple. Elections are called, and candidates, either within party organizations or as individuals, stand for office. During the campaign period, these candidates try to persuade voters to support them. Voters choose among the contestants, electing their representatives. After a term of office, the process is repeated, providing voters the opportunity to assess the performance of incumbents and renew their support or punish them by electing opposition candidates. While we know that there are any number of ways in which this model does not accurately describe developed democracies, we have not thought systematically about how the same shortcomings can thwart accountability, representation, and stability in new regimes.

A good starting point in addressing the role of elections in new democracies is to distinguish among the roles that elections play in new and established systems. As noted in Chapter 1, in established systems elections can fulfill many functions such as maintaining party systems, generating equality, legitimizing regimes, installing governing officials, presenting citizens with choices, building communities, involving and educating citizens, preventing tyranny, enabling representation, and provoking accountability and responsiveness (Katz 1997: 100–7). In contrast, studies of the role of elections in new democracies point to two overarching processes or functions that are integral to democratic development: elite incorporation and mass interest aggregation.[4] Political parties are typically assumed to be the vehicle for elite incorporation. Such incorporation cements the contingent consent bargain that elites broker in the democratization phase (Przeworski 1991), aids in the solution of social choice and collective action problems within parties and in the legislature, and structures the choices presented to voters on the ballot. Overall, this concept of elite incorporation maps to procedural and contingent consent definitions of democracy.

Elite incorporation through elections provides a crucial mechanism for democratic deepening in new democracies. Insofar as incorporation occurs, elections afford voters opportunities to assess an incumbent relative to her campaign promises and actions in office and either withdraw their support or reelect her. This constant reevaluation provokes strong incentives for candidates to anticipate voters' demands and for incumbents to respond to those demands. Voters can also use elections to hold incumbents accountable for their actions in office – to "throw the bums out" if they do not act in accordance with voters' expectations and preferences.

---

[4] There is a wide literature on the role of parties and party systems in consolidation since these institutions often stand in as a proxy for elections. John Aldrich (1995) expands on this model in his study of the emergence of U.S. parties. See also Mainwaring and Scully 1995; Randall and Svasand 2002: 5–6.

The impact of elite incorporation extends beyond elections. Differences across the level of cooperation and coordination within parties also influence the trajectory of political development. Disciplined centrist parties produce more effective governments than those built on loosely organized, fragmented, or polarized party organizations. Likewise, patterns of cooperation among individuals and between party organizations influence government efficiency.

In the broader picture, repeated elections offer an opportunity for elites and voters to reach consensus over governmental and electoral institutions and to define national priorities. This process involves forging an acceptable definition of the ruling majority as well as the relationship between the majority and minority social groups. Clearly, when elections do not yield information, cooperation, and coordination within the context of institutionalized political parties, the process of forging consensus and social peace becomes much more difficult.

The introduction of competitive elections is the hallmark of consolidating systems. The responses of leaders and voters to the opportunities presented in elections vary widely from country to country. The previous discussion posits that elite commitment to the new system shapes the trajectory of political development after founding elections. This argument suggests that if elite commitment matters for political development, then it should emerge as significant in an analysis after controls are put in place for other factors that are critical to successful consolidation. The next section defines these alternative explanations and develops a framework to test competing explanations.

Structure and Agency: Explaining Different Trajectories of Democratic Development

Theories of democratic consolidation generally fall into two broad categories: structural explanations that center on social divisions, economic structures, or institutions, and actor-centric explanations that stress political interactions or strategies. Each of these approaches yields very different predictions about Russia's success relative to other postcommunist cases. As a prelude to quantitative analysis, the next sections draw out implications from each of these structural categories and identify the causal mechanisms that link a factor or set of factors to political development, framing these mechanisms in terms of hypothesis that summarize conventional wisdom or points of conflict in the existing literature on democratic consolidation (Aldrich 1995: 29–45; Cox and McCubbins 1993: 107–36).

Civic Culture Versus Political Cleavages

Despite the range of potential legacy effects, two arguments stand out: the uniqueness of post-Soviet states, and the role of popular attitudes, toward democracy. Based on the notion of a civic culture, authors argued that it is citizens' attitudes, and not the structure of politics or the choices of key actors, that shape democratic consolidation (Almond and Verba 1965). The implication is that if citizens do not hold democratic values or support democratic development, then consolidation would be difficult. This hypothesis produced a stream of single-country studies that revealed that Russians show unexpected support for democracy.[5] The comparative evidence is less convincing. Both Juan Linz and Alfred Stepan (1996) and Richard Rose, William Mishler, and Christian Haerpfer (1998) find that Russians (along with Belorussians and Ukrainians) are much less likely to reject authoritarian rule than their counterparts in East Central Europe. These studies yield the following proposition:

> H1: Strong antidemocratic sentiment is likely to undermine democracy.

In contrast, Geoffrey Evans and Stephen Whitefield (1998) turn the civic culture thesis on its head, arguing that in lieu of traditional cleavage structures, political cleavages may well help to define political interests and act as a catalyst for political organization, overcoming any disadvantage of nostalgia for the old regime (Evans and Whitefield 1993 and 1998). From this perspective, strong antidemocratic sentiment generates clear political divisions that act as a catalyst for political organization and may aid consolidation.

Post-Soviet Versus Postcommunist

The elite character of the transformation across the postcommunist cases rendered them distinct from previous transitions.[6] Yet, the absence of

---

[5] Contrary to expectations, early studies showed remarkable support for democratic and market norms in Russia. See, for example, Bahry, Boaz, and Gordon 1997; Gibson 2001; Reisinger, Miller, Hesli, and Maher 1994. Moreover, Russian citizens' support for democracy is not limited to abstractions. Reisinger, Miller, and Hesli 1995b.

[6] For example, the relative lack of social organization or existing cleavage structure distinguished these cases from the European and Latin American transitions. See Collier 1999.

well-organized civil society and mobilized cleavage structures did not flatten the political landscapes of the new regimes. Proponents of the importance of the Leninist legacy quickly rejected the idea that all states shared the same legacy, and moved to examine the diversity of Leninism across the bloc. This variation in legacies makes it very difficult to generalize about their effects. Analysts alternatively characterized legacies, norms of behavior, beliefs, and cognitive frameworks that guide the behaviors of postcommunist citizens or patterns of social or political organization (Ekiert and Hanson 2003; Jowitt 1996; Kitschelt et al. 1999; Lijphart and Crawford 1997; Linz and Stepan 1996).

A variation of this legacy argument focuses on the distinctions between post-Soviet countries and other postcommunist cases. The scores of post-Soviet states, excluding the Baltic nations, were substantially higher (average FH score 5.66) than those of the East Central European states. More importantly, the average post-Soviet score increased over time while the ECE score dropped. A number of causal mechanisms may generate this difference in consolidation trajectory over time. The first is the longer period of time that the Soviet states endured communist rule or the positive experience that a number of the European cases had with democracy in the interwar period. In addition, scholars often cite the variables that are included in this study – popular attitudes, economic conditions, and social and political organization at the point of founding elections – as the root cause of this difference (Linz and Stepan 1996). Alternatively, Alexander Motyl (1997) argues post-Soviet states were disadvantaged by the structure of the elite and their low capacity to affect revolutionary change. It is not clear whether or not these factors account for the differences across groups of cases or if there is truly something unique about the post-Soviet experience – such as the nature of the authoritarian regime – the other variables do not capture (Bunce 1998 and 2000). The debate suggests a second proposition:

> H2: All things being equal, post-Soviet states should consolidate more slowly than their European counterparts.

Economic Explanations

Seymour Martin Lipset (1959) touched off a protracted debate when he argued that rich countries are better able to sustain democracy than poor ones. Adam Przeworski and his coauthors (2000: 101–3) provide rigorous support for this proposition, showing that democracies with per capita income over $6,000 are remarkably durable. They demonstrate the proposition that countries with rapid growth and relatively low inflation are also more likely to sustain democracy. However, these studies do not yield a clear prediction about the relationship between economic conditions and democratic consolidation.

The intuitively appealing modernization arguments – that economic wealth or economic development should foster democratization – have not been consistently born out. In an extensive empirical study, Przeworski and Fernando Limongi (1997) show that economic prosperity does not increase the likelihood of democratic transition. Likewise, looking at survey data, Linz and Stepan (1996) find that popular perceptions of economic conditions do not undermine regime support although they may influence attitudes about incumbent governments. Overall, the findings about the relationship between economic prosperity and consolidation suggest that the relationship is complex and may depend on other factors such as international involvement (Colaresi and Thompson 2003). Ambiguities in the overall findings suggest the following proposition:

> H3: A regime's economic health will not be a critical factor in democratic consolidation.

International Influences

There is little doubt that international forces or diffusion influence democratic consolidation. In studies of postcommunist consolidation, a number of scholars found that the distance between a country's capital from Vienna is a significant factor in explaining a range of outcomes (Kopstein and Reilly 2000). Stephen Levitsky and Lucan Way (2002b) find that the patterns of international aid also influence democratic development. Yet, it remains unclear how these mechanisms work, particularly since states such as Russia received tremendous international assistance but failed to consolidate. Likewise, the growing linkages between the United States and the Central Asian states appear to bolster authoritarianism rather than democracy.

To begin to explore the relationship between international factors and democratic consolidation, I focus on the role of the European Union (EU). The benefits of future EU membership provide elites with strong incentives to maintain democratic regimes, particularly in a period when mass support for EU membership was quite high.[7]

H4: Candidate members of the EU should consolidate faster and more completely than non-candidate members.

Institutional Explanations: Majoritarian Versus Proportional Structures

With the third wave of democratization, scholars and policy makers began to assess how institutions influence consolidation. Scholars wrote of democracy creation, institutional architecture, and institutional engineering. Across these studies, the overriding notion was that structural factors such as legacy, cleavages, and economics could be reshaped with the "right" kind of institutional structure (DiPalma 1990; Elster, Offe, and Preuss 1998; Lijphart and Waisman 1996).

The growing literature on the effects of specific regime types and institutional structures on democratic durability centers on the role of majoritarian versus consensual distinctions. The centerpiece of this debate is the conflict over whether or not presidential regimes are less conducive to democratic durability than parliamentary regimes (Linz 1990; Linz and Valenzuela 1994; Mainwaring 1993; Mainwaring and Shugart 1997a, b; Przeworski et al. 2000; Stepan and Skach 1993). The answer is a qualified yes. Assessing the impact of presidentialism is complex because this institution interacts with other institutional features, such as fragmented party systems and internal legislative structure, that promote deadlock at the national level (Mainwaring 1993; Stepan and Skach 1993).[8] Still, there is growing evidence that strong presidential institutions exert a significant impact on the patterns and level of elite coordination and cooperation, suggesting that the presence or absence of this institution would help to explain elite responses

---

[7] Again, time will show what the long-term effect of EU membership is on democratic development as mass support declines. Grzymala-Busse and Innes (2003) argue that EU membership has already generated deleterious effects for some political parties. In the context of this argument, changing attitudes toward the EU may have disrupted the process institutionalizing of mass–elite linkage structures. See Grzymala-Busse and Innes 2003.

[8] The Russian case is telling on this point since the contrast between Presidents Yeltsin and Putin has been enormous without a concurrent change in regime structure. Increased informal presidential powers resulting from the success of the Kremlin-sponsored United Russia (UR) Party ended the gridlock within the parliament and between parliament and executive. The UR majority in the State Duma dominated legislative committees, establishing them as gatekeepers for the legislative process and initiating a norm of quick passage of Kremlin-sponsored legislation.

to electoral competition as well as the distribution of collective goods produced by the regime (Samuels and Shugart 2003; Shugart 1998). I frame this assertion as a hypothesis:

> H5: Presidential regimes are more likely to hinder democratic development than parliamentary regimes.

Strategy and Choice: The Primacy of Actions in Consolidation

A rival set of theories that emerged from the analyses of the third wave of democratization in Latin America and Southern Europe posits that the strategic choices of political actors and not the existing preconditions determine whether democracy succeeds or fails. The approach is rooted in micropolitical economy or rational choice paradigm that reasons group- or system-level outcomes from individual-level behaviors. A number of studies use this approach to understand institutional selection in the post-Soviet context (Frye 1997; Jones Luong 2002; McFaul 2001). These studies underscore how a variety of factors, ranging from institutional to cultural factors, shape elites' preferences over different regime types or institutional structures, including electoral rules, constitutional structures, and financial institutions. Yet, the process-based or strategic actor approach is less frequently used to examine political behavior in the consolidation period – or, more specifically, to understand how the introduction of competitive elections alters the strategic choices of political elites.[9]

The comparison of FH scores at the start of the consolidation period underscores the wide differences in starting points across the post-Soviet cases, particularly in terms of elite incorporation into the new regimes. Some transitions feature high levels of elite incorporation at the time that founding elections are introduced, while in others incorporation is largely nonexistent. When incorporation occurs before political competition begins, elections provide elite actors with strong incentives to build stable ties to constituencies in order to capture office or influence the national policy agenda. In other cases, defined by middle- to high-range scores, elections are tasked with providing incentives for incorporation, to

---

[9] The growing middle-range literature on postcommunist party development is an exception. For excellent studies in a number of countries, see Grzymala-Busse 2002; Hanson 1995; Kitschelt et al. 1999. These studies provide an important start to understanding the link between elections and democratic consolidation, particularly because they look inside party organizations to assess the capacity of parties to influence political behavior and outcomes.

motivate elites to invest in the process. As noted earlier, in many cases elections apparently do not have this effect. The trajectories of different states suggest the need to understand the factors that shape the critical decisions of elite actors in response to competitive elections, as per this hypothesis:

> H6: Democratic deepening is more likely insofar as elites are incorporated into the political regime at the point of founding elections.

When elite actors are not incorporated into the regime at the point of founding elections, incorporation is likely to take time, as elections become central to governance. As the Russian case illustrates, the amount of time may be substantial. In 1999, McFaul argued that a protracted transition in Russia was likely to fail. Yet, democratic transitions in cases such as Slovakia and Albania faltered in the late 1990s only to regain their momentum toward democracy. Recent events suggest a similar process may be occurring in Ukraine. At the same time, Russia and Belarus continue to struggle. This comparison suggests that under some circumstances, time is an important catalyst for democratic development, while in others it signals regime weakness and vulnerability. Yet, if we conceptualize consolidation as a process rather than an endpoint, then time may well play a role in the explanation.[10] This conjecture yields another proposition:

> H7: All other things being equal, time should foster democratic development.

Testing Theories of Consolidation: Model and Results

The hypotheses discussed previously pit structural explanations against actorcentric explanations. They also provide clear tests of individual theories. To understand how these variables jointly shape postcommunist trajectories, it is essential to test them within the framework of a single model:

$$FH\ 2003 = \beta_1(\text{Constant}) + \beta_2(\text{Oldregime}) + \beta_3(\text{Postsov}) \\ + \beta_4(\text{Growth}) + \beta_5(\text{EUcandidate}) + \beta_6(\text{PPI}) \\ + \beta_7(\text{PRfounding}) + \beta_8(\text{Time}) + v_1$$

---

[10] This model specifies time as a linear variable. However, there is reason to believe that the effect of time may not be linear. To examine this possibility, I used alternative specifications to change the functional form of the variable. These measures did not change the results. I present the simplest conceptualization parameter with the caveat that as time goes on, the parameter may no longer influence movement toward consolidation.

One Step Forward, Two Steps Back

Table 2.1. *Variable Definitions*

Variables		Descriptions
Dependent Variable	FH2003	Country's FH score in 2003
Independent Variables	Oldregime	The percent of the population that supports a return to the communist regime
	Postsov	Whether the country is a former Soviet republic
	Growth	Average real GDP growth from founding elections to 2002
	EUcandidate	Whether the country is an EU candidate member (or full member after 2003)
	PPI	Presidential Power Index
	PRfounding	Country's FH political rights score at the point of founding elections
	Time	Number of years since founding elections

Appendix A describes the details of the variables, and a short description Table 2.1 provides. The dependent variable is the country's FH score in 2003. A number of different specifications were used in the regression but none altered the results. The independent variables correspond to the theories described previously. Two of these variables warrant additional explanation. The PRfounding variable uses the political rights component of the FH measure to capture the level of elite commitment and procedural regularity at the point of founding elections. The measurement of this variable corresponds to FH scores: The higher the PR score, the fewer rights exist in the system. However, it is important to note that the FH PR score is not equivalent to the more complex FH score, which also measures civil liberties in addition to political rights. The cultural variable measures mass support for the former (communist) regime using the World Values Survey, supplemented by a comparable survey in Central Asia. I rely on this measure because I do not want to risk conflating attitudes toward the democratic regime with attitudes toward the current government.

The hypotheses yield the following predictions about the parameters in the equation:

β_2: If the civic culture argument (H1) is correct, then we would expect the parameter to be positive and significant. A negative parameter would support the political cleavages argument.

Candidate Strategies and Electoral Competition

β_3: Post-Soviet states should be less likely to consolidate (H2). The parameter should be positive and significant.

β_4: Economic growth (H3) should not be significant.

β_5: Being a candidate member of the EU should push a country toward consolidation (H4). The parameter should be negative and significant.

β_6: Higher levels of presidential power should discourage consolidation (H5) and the parameter should be positive and significant.

β_7: If the incorporation of political elites matters at the point of founding elections (H6), then this parameter should be positive and significant.

β_8: If consolidation is a process of experimentation (H7), then time should be negative and significant.

The actual results of the regression are reported in Table 2.2.[11] The F-test and R^2 values indicate that the model does a remarkably good job of explaining variation in democratic development from the point of founding elections, with the caveat that the analysis is based on a relatively small number of cases. The interpretation of the parameter estimates is supported by standard regression diagnostics (jackknife analysis and colinearity tests).

The cultural and economic structural variables are not significant. Neither mass support for the old regime nor economic growth generates democratic consolidation across these cases. Likewise, the post-Soviet variable is not significant. In other words, when we control for factors frequently cited as crucial for transition outcomes, post-Soviet exceptionalism disappears.

In contrast to these negative findings, the presidential power index is strongly significant. At least in the postcommunist cases, strong presidents discourage democratic development once electoral competition is introduced. Finally, the EU candidate variable is also strongly significant, underscoring the important role that the EU plays in maintaining democratic development in postcommunist Europe.

In terms of procedural variables, the parameters reveal that the level of elite commitment and procedural regularity at the point of founding elections is directly correlated with the overall level of democracy in 2003. The higher the score at the founding, the higher the overall FH score is likely to

---

[11] The small number of cases included in the analysis raises questions about the impact of outliers on the parameter estimates and the validity of hypotheses tests. To control for these problems, I reestimated the parameters using a jackknife technique. The jackknife results are virtually identical to the results presented here, confirming that the parameters in Table 2.2 can be interpreted in a straightforward manner.

One Step Forward, Two Steps Back

Table 2.2. *Explaining Development in Postcommunist Countries After Founding Elections*

Variable	Coefficient (Robust s.e.)
Oldregime	−.007
	(.01)
Postsov	.016
	(.18)
Growth	.0008
	(.002)
PPI	.10***
	(.02)
EUCandidate	−1.6***
	(.19)
PRfounding	.14**
	(.08)
Time	−.13**
	(.07)
Constant	3.45
	(.80)
N	22
F	58.19
R^2	.95

One-tail significance levels are denoted as * = .10, ** = .05, and *** = .01.

be at the end of the period. Finally, the passage of time between the point of founding elections and 2003 does seem to provide states the opportunity to move toward consolidation, although a more complete analysis awaits the assessment of adjusted impact that follows.

We can produce a more nuanced picture of the impact of each factor on consolidation by multiplying the parameter by the range of each variable in the data set. This transformation shows the potential impact of each explanatory factor by controlling for the fact that some factors vary over a wide range and others do not. Table 2.3 reports the adjusted impacts of significant variables.

These scores show that two structural variables, presidentialism and EU candidacy, have the greatest potential effect on consolidation trajectories. These findings are consistent with the arguments presented earlier and point to the strong incentives that each of these factors provide for elite actors. The prize of EU membership prompts compliance with democratic

Table 2.3. *Impact of Significant Independent Variables*

Variable (range)	Adjusted Impact (parameter range)
PRfounding (1–7)	.98
PPI (3–23)	2.0
EUcandidate (0–1)	–1.6
Time (7–13)	–.78

procedures, whereas presidential systems discourage elite coordination and cooperation in pursuit of office. Table 2.3 also shows that elites' commitment to procedure at the point of founding elections also influences democratic trajectory, but does not preordain an outcome. That is, other conditions that affect elite behavior can undermine or reinforce procedural certainty. Finally, time has the smallest adjusted impact of all of the significant parameters. Also, given that these parameters measure effects "on average" across a small number of cases, it is quite possible that the impact of time is positive in some cases and negative in others.

Interpreting the Results

The quantitative analysis supports the proposition that elections matter in the process of political transitions and that political actors often need time to adjust to the new rules and procedures. The findings confirm previous work that suggests that post-election political developments are strongly conditioned by the two structural variables that provide clear incentives for elite behavior in elections, and elite commitment to democracy in the first rounds of elections.

This analysis also shows that the exceptionalism of post-Soviet cases is not apparent when other variables are included in the explanation. In part, this effect is a function of the sample that does not include two clear failures in the post-Soviet column but does include the successes in the Baltic states. However, there is also a theoretic reason to expect that other variables will wash out the post-Soviet effect. Valerie Bunce (1998) argues that critical differences across these cases are rooted in the structure of the authoritarian systems and that these differences are manifested in the democratization phase of transition. This legacy effect may be captured either in the predispositions of political elites or in the selection of strong presidential institutions, or in both factors. In the data used here, both variables are positively correlated with the variable that identifies former Soviet states.[12]

The direct effect of founding conditions suggests that countries that start with low levels of elite commitment and procedural certainty are less likely to gain ground toward democracy, at least over the time captured in this analysis. The analysis also underscores that elections do not inevitably produce behavior consistent with democratic development, at least in the short term. This finding raises important questions at the core of the empirical chapters of this study: What are the set of elite strategies that foster democratic development, and what factors prompt elites to choose that set of strategies over others that might weaken, stall, or stop democratic development?

These results point to some of the conditions that are likely to preclude elite incorporation once elections are introduced. The incentives generated by majoritarian systems marked by strong presidential institutions appear to undermine democratic procedures and elite commitments to the new regime. In contrast, EU candidacy does appear to provide incentives for elites to play by the rules of the game regardless of the starting point. Finally, while time fosters democratic development on average, it is not a panacea for all systems. The direct effect of the variable is quite modest and operates at the margin of all other effects. It is entirely plausible that the failure to provoke elite commitment in the short term leaves such countries vulnerable to decline in the longer term.

Elite commitment to democratic procedures is only the first step in activating elections as mechanisms of popular control of government. For democratic deepening to occur, elite and mass actors must choose strategies that forge stable patterns of interest aggregation and representation that embody societal consensus over democratic goals and across trade-offs from efficiency to representation. Where these priorities are not established during the democratization phase of transitions, competitive elections can provoke a process of experimentation to define them. This process may be successful or not. It may happen quickly, as in a number of the West European democracies, or slowly, as in the case of the United States. This variation raises important questions about the factors that influence the pace, structure, and success of interest accumulation and the best way to

---

[12] The correlation for Postsov and PPI is .56, and the correlation for Postsov and PRfounding is .44. For explanations of the post-Soviet propensity toward strong presidential institutions, see Easter (1997) and Frye (1997).

measure these phenomena. The next section begins the task of specifying these factors.

Democratic Deepening: Forging Linkages and Defining Priorities

There is no question that democracy is a very difficult concept to measure. Direct measures require a tremendous amount of information about the true preferences of voters, the actions of representatives, their campaign pledges, and their responsibility for the policies that emerge while they are in office. The few attempts that have been made at such measures have focused on well-established democracies, where such information is readily available.

In new democracies, where such information is generally unavailable to citizens or to scholars studying the democratic transition, democratic capacity is most often defined in terms of political parties, or more precisely, political party systems. The effective number of parties has stood in as an important measure of consolidation. The thesis is that as the numbers of parties decline, the capacity for governance becomes greater and bonds between voters and parties become stronger. The postcommunist comparison demonstrates that even this measure can be misleading without detailed information about the forces that have influenced the winnowing of party organization. For example, a comparison of the decline in the effective number of political parties in Poland and Russia shows very similar patterns. Both start with high effective numbers of parties and both see a significant decline over four election cycles and end about the same place. Yet, by their FH measures, Poland is a consolidated democracy while Russia hovers on the brink of authoritarianism. The difference in the two systems is that in Poland the decline in the effective number of parties captures a process of interest aggregation that introduced some stability into the system. In contrast, in Russia, the impetus for the decline is the growing monopoly of electoral resources by the state.

This statement should not negate all studies of party development. Some basic facts about party organizations reveal much about the quality of democracy in a country. In his examination of southern politics in the United States, V. O. Key (1949) argued that when the numbers of competitive parties fall below two, critical decisions are made by a subset of the population, which he argued was undemocratic. We know that party system fragmentation and polarization lead to instability and inefficiency

(Frye 2003). Yet, we need to know something about what is going on within political parties in order to assess whether or not they embody the capacity to promote democratic consolidation or if they are a useful indicator of democratic deepening.

Absent good information about the nature of the relationships among candidates, leaders, and voters within party organizations, summary measures of parties or the structure of the party system can overstate democratic development. It is not the presence or absence of parties that matters for a state's democratic capacity, it is the ability of those organizations to constrain individuals, from party leaders to voters. In early stages of development, political parties are often more analogous to holding companies that lack the capacity to constrain behavior, channel resources and interests, or even attract loyal followings. In new democracies where candidates can run as independents, the reliance on parties as the sole measure of development may totally obscure the important role of these independent candidates in shaping political development. To assess the capacity for governance more accurately, it is essential to look beyond parties to account for the role of independent candidates and the nature of the relationship between parties and individual members, from candidates to leaders.

Looking Beyond Political Parties: The Role of Infrastructure

The three components of electoral infrastructure – information, coordination, and cooperation – provide a new and important measure of democratic capacity. A wide range of theoretic studies show that the behaviors captured by this concept are essential to transforming competition elections into mechanisms of democratic accountability, responsiveness, and representation (Aldrich 1995; Cox 1997; Katz 1997; Kitschelt 2000; Przeworski, Stokes, and Manin 1999). In established democracies, political parties often provide an excellent summary of the polity's capacity for democracy. However, in new systems, it is important to look at each component to assess the health of the new regime.

Information. The concept of information as an element of electoral infrastructure focuses on the persistence of uncertainty in new democratic regimes. This section asks a simple question: What auxiliary assumptions about information and behavior support the electoral model of democratic governance? I argue that this seemingly simple model of responsiveness rests on a number of profound assumptions about electoral infrastructure:

the information available to candidates and voters, and the behaviors engendered by this information. However, electoral infrastructure does not always exist at the point of founding elections, and it is not likely to emerge unless it is in the candidates' best interests to build it.

Information is a two-edged sword in democratic elections. On one hand, uncertainty about likely winners and losers over time is a critical element of democracy. The specter of future loss provides healthy incentives for competitors to play by the rules lest they be treated unfairly in the future (Dahl 1971; Przeworski 1986). On the other hand, the lack of shared information about contestants' chances undermines elections as mechanisms to generate and sustain democracy. The lack of consensus is likely to persist if the disagreement is rooted in politicians and voters holding fundamentally different assessments of the state of the world. Existing attitudes will condition the interpretation and meaning of new information, perpetuating incongruities.

Przeworski and Limongi (1997) clarify this distinction by drawing a line between uncertainty, or the chance that a member of the governing coalition could lose now or in the future, and unpredictability, or how many votes such contestants will win. In most established democracies, candidates and party leaders share a good sense of candidates' chances of winning office, although considerable unpredictability remains, particularly if you look over time. This shared assessment of a candidate's or a party's capacity to win votes provides a basis for the strategic calculations that lead to coordination and cooperation.

The link between information and strategic choice can be seen at each phase of the election contest. There are two central questions in the entry phase of election: What are my chances of winning, and how can I improve those chances? These questions are not easy for any candidate to answer. Calculations about the viability of electoral platforms or the number of votes a candidate needs to win a seat in parliament are extremely complex. Institutional structure, such as district magnitude or electoral threshold, conveys a good deal of information about candidate viability but also the impact of the rules is impossible to assess without clear information about voters' preferences.

Candidate success also hinges on non-institutional factors such as the number of candidates in the race and the basis of their electoral appeals. This observation raises a host of additional questions that potential candidates and party leaders must answer to make effective strategic choices. What do voters want from government? What criteria will they use to assess the candidates running for office? How will these criteria play out in terms of support for different candidates? And what platforms are other candidates likely to choose?

Information problems become even more complicated if a candidate considers affiliating with a political party. What is the underlying support for the party in the district, both currently and in the future? To what extent does the party label constrain a candidate's choice of a platform, both now and in the future? How much competition is there for the party's nomination? To what extent is the party viable as a coordination mechanism in the legislature?[13] This information may not be readily available at the point that the candidates need to begin the ballot registration process, leading potential contestants to miscalculate their chances.

Finally, contestants' actions shape the information available to voters. Campaigns are rich sources of information about incumbents' performances. Parties can provide critical information shortcuts for voters by signaling the positions of candidates who affiliate with the party. Campaign promises can provide yardsticks for future actions. Yet, none of this information is automatically available, in Russia or elsewhere. Nor is it inevitable that the electoral process will generate information that can be used in future elections. The empirical chapters of this study assess fundamental questions: What information do Russian candidates have, and how does it influence their strategic choices? To what extent do Russian candidates behave in ways that generate information, both for other candidates and for the electorate? And insofar as they are not choosing strategies that produce good information, what are the consequences of this behavior, both for responsiveness and for other political outcomes?

Coordination. One of the clear costs of uncertainty in elections is that it inhibits the coordination and cooperation among contestants that are essential for elections to act as mechanisms of responsiveness and accountability (Cox 1997). The essence of coordination is that individuals' self-interest will lead them to converge on behaviors that are mutually beneficial. Importantly, coordination is atomistic behavior; it is not based on an exchange of benefits or resources. Nor does coordination require actors to interact or work together, incur costs, or build an enforcing mechanism. The absolute

---

[13] This book focuses almost exclusively on the election period and not on the effects of activity in the legislature. For discussion of coordination and cooperation within the legislature, see Ostrow 2000 and 2002; Remington 2001a; Smith and Remington 2001; Smyth 2002.

or relative benefits of coordination need not be the same for all actors for it to occur.

Candidates and party organizations have numerous opportunities to coordinate throughout the election cycle. The most studied type of candidate coordination is strategic entry, where potential candidates decide to compete based on their chances of winning (Cox 1997; Downs 1957; Herron 2002; Riker 1982). Given good information, sure losers will not want to embark on the costly endeavor of running for office and sink resources into a hopeless cause. Stronger candidates gain from this behavior, because their chances of winning improve as hopeless candidates decline to participate. The number of candidates who run in each district should be a significant indicator of levels of coordination and, in turn, of democratic deepening.

If the campaign period reveals information about the viability of the candidates, coordination may also occur as like-minded candidates come to understand that if they both run for office, their choices will ensure the victory of a third, less-appealing candidate. In this case of strategic withdrawal, the payoff to the candidate who remains in the race is far greater than the benefit to the candidate who withdraws. Again, elites' failures to coordinate can have profound impact, as they make coordination among voters essentially impossible (Cox 1997).

As with the accumulation of information, none of these forms of coordination are inevitable. Institutions, actors' goals, information, and existing resources all condition individuals' choices to coordinate behavior. The complex relationship between coordination and information renders it a chicken and egg problem. For voters, candidates' coordination failures complicate their vote decisions by magnifying the costs of voting, increasing their uncertainty, and, moreover, making coordination in the form of strategic voting more complicated. When coordination does not occur, voters need to collect information on more candidates. They may face very different types of information and appeals that are difficult to weigh against each other.

The focus on the relationship between information and coordination is a precursor to addressing the most commonly studied element of electoral infrastructure: political parties. In their ideal types, parties and their brand names embody high levels of information and coordination. Yet, parties often fall short of this ideal in significant ways. The information carried by a party label in the United States is significantly different from the information carried by party labels across Europe. In new democracies, parties may not even convey reliable information about what their candidates are likely to do in office or their prospects for winning voter support. Parties may not have the wherewithal to motivate strategic entry or strategic voting. To clarify the role of political parties, it is critical to look inside party organizations and examine candidates' strategies in relation to parties' goals.

Cooperation. Political parties are examples of cooperation among individuals. In contrast to coordination, cooperation is best described as a trade of resources or a mutually beneficial but costly bargain. Cooperation can also take the form of mutual investment in behaviors that yield a collective good. Both types of cooperation are present in the electoral arena. For example, like-minded parties may bargain over placing candidates in districts where they are likely to split the vote and elect an undesirable opponent. Likewise, candidates and other elites may participate in building party organizations, sharing resources, and developing a common platform. In each case, the party organization enforces the bargains among individuals.

In his famous quote, E. E. Schattschneider argued that, "political parties created modern democracy... and democracy is unthinkable save in terms of parties" (1942: 1). John Aldrich opened his seminal work by describing democracy as "unworkable" absent parties (1995: 3). This strong belief in the centrality of parties in democratic governance propelled the most extensive strand of inquiry into the accumulation of electoral infrastructure.[14] The postcommunist cases strongly demonstrate that not all parties are created equal and not all parties make democracy workable. A growing literature recognizes significant differences in the structures of party organizations and the functions they play in electoral democracy (Diamond and Gunther 2001; Kitschelt 2000; Mainwaring and Scully 1995). Although political parties and party systems populate all successful democracies, not all countries that build parties and party systems evolve into successful democracies. This anomaly raises the question of which types of parties and party systems support democratic development and which do not.

---

[14] It is impossible to do justice to this rapidly expanding literature. For general studies, see Diamond and Gunther 2001; Mainwaring and Scully 1995; Randall and Svasand 2002. For studies particular to Russia, see Brader and Tucker 2001; Colton 2000; Colton and Hale 2004; Hale, forthcoming; McFaul 2001; Miller and Klobucar 2000; Moser 2001; Smyth, forthcoming.

The answer to this question is long and complex. There is an extensive theoretic and empirical base on which to build expectations about the types of parties that foster democracy. Samuel Huntington (1968) launched an important stream of research exploring the relationship between political party institutionalization and democratization, arguing that parties play an essential role in incorporating political masses and political elites into the new democratic regime. The analysis here takes a different approach, exploring the propensity of elites to choose strategies that build electoral infrastructure: their allegiance to party organizations and the effects of their actions on the structure of parties.

A related literature explores the implications of elites' strategies on mass incorporation and participation. Within this strand, some analysts focus on the role of parties in producing reliable information for voters and politicians (Cox 1997; Downs 1957; Hinich and Munger 1994; Popkin 1991). Others focus on the nature of mass–elite ties or the currency of electoral politics – collective goods versus particularized benefits – and their implications for governance (Kitschelt 2000; Piattoni 2001; Samuels and Shugart 2002). A distinct literature examines the role of parties in governance by exploring their impact on solving the social choice problems that plague majoritarian institutions (Aldrich 1995; Cox and McCubbins 1993; Kitschelt 2000).

A less well-studied element of parties as infrastructure is the critical role that parties play as safe havens for opposition politicians to weather the storms of electoral defeat. In preserving the capacity of ambitious politicians to live to fight another day, party institutions preserve the potential for opposition in the future and provide an impetus for sustaining the contingent consent bargains that shore up the regime. This function cannot be fulfilled solely through coordination.

The complex roles of parties in democratic consolidation demand a clearer picture of the types of parties that fulfill these functions by examining the relationship between parties and their core actors. A good deal of work has been done on the relationship between parties and voters. The analysis presented in later chapters focuses on the relationships between candidates and parties. The approach is consistent with theories of party formation describing the process in terms of cooperation among individuals, most notably in the work of Aldrich:

My basic argument is that the major political party is the creature of the politicians, the ambitious office seeker and officeholder. They have created and maintained, used or abuse(d), reformed or ignored the political party when doing so has furthered their goals and ambitions. The political party is thus an "endogenous" institution – an institution shaped by these political actors (1995: 4).

Similarly, writing about Spain, Richard Gunther (1989) notes the critical role of candidates in determining electoral outcomes including information and party organizations. Stressing the importance of the relationship between candidates and parties in Brazil, Scott Mainwaring writes, "The Brazilian case is an extreme example of electoral rules that encourage individualism among politicians and loose linkages between parties and politicians" (1991: 26). Building on this theme, Barry Ames (2001: 77–84) underscores and develops the importance of candidate behaviors in order to understand the national-level outcome: the deadlock of democracy in Brazil.

Cooperation within party organizations can be examined in a number of ways, but the most elemental is candidates' willingness to join political parties. The institutional variation across countries that provide significant opportunities for candidates to remain free of partisan attachments reveals much about the relationship between coordination and democratic development. For example, in Russia and Armenia, where democratic development has been stunted, the number of independent candidates has been extremely high. Elections in Ukraine have also featured greater numbers of independents, although it remains to be seen whether the recent moves to democracy will change this pattern. In contrast, more successful democratizers such as Lithuania, Hungary, and even Albania experienced rapid incorporation of elites into parties. Surprisingly, by the fourth round of elections in the early United States, nearly all candidates on the ballot affiliated with political parties. This difference marks a clear distinction between the Russian and early American examples, which are often loosely compared as cases in which democratic deepening occurred over a longer period of time and suggests that different outcomes are likely in the two cases. It also points to the need to better understand the role of elite commitment and interest aggregation in the larger process of political development following the introduction of competitive elections.

Looking Ahead: A Model of Candidates' Choices

The quantitative analysis presented in this chapter reveals that Russia is one of a few postcommunist cases that fails to progress toward democracy under the impulse of competitive elections. In the wider global context, however, Russia is less anomalous. As recent discussions of the "illusion" of consolidation reveal, competitive elections failed to produce healthy democracies across Africa, Asia, and Latin America. These cases reveal a gap in the consolidation literature and raise a serious set of questions about when elections are likely to derail democratic consolidation and how democracy assistance resources are best able to forestall this possibility.

Considered together, the three-pronged concept of electoral infrastructure provides a mechanism to explore the effects of repeated competition on democratic consolidation. Without infrastructure, elections do not provide direct links between voters and representatives, nor do they create the conditions for efficient or effective governance. Clearly, different countries start with very different types of and levels of infrastructure. Some transitional countries introduce electoral competition with strong bases, while others, such as Russia, begin with almost no foundation. Although we often expect repeated elections to produce infrastructure in time, the growing number of countries that have stalled on the path to consolidation suggests that this progression is not inevitable.

The infrastructure measures point to concrete tools to assess the capacities of new regimes in order to understand the trajectory of political development. The variation across states in terms of electoral volatility, the number of candidates who run in each district, and the number of independents who participate alongside partisans raises the additional question of how to explain this variation on the candidate level. The next chapter provides a framework to examine the individual choices of candidates during the election cycle. In aggregate, these decisions provide insight into the conditions under which candidates' actions within the context of repeated elections provoke the accumulation of electoral infrastructure essential to ensure democratic governance and stability.

3

The Microfoundations of Democratic Responsiveness

CANDIDATE STRATEGIES AND ELECTORAL INFRASTRUCTURE

The empirical findings in the previous chapter present a challenge to the current understanding of when competitive elections yield successful democratic consolidation and when they do not. The evidence shows that it is not just national institutions, economics, or attitudes that condition a successful endgame to democratic transitions. Political leaders' participation in electoral competition, and the subsequent molding of opportunities for voter participation, also matter for larger political outcomes. The second finding is that while political parties are often the most important vehicles for prompting elites to work together and invest in strategies that further democratic development, the types of parties that ensure this behavior are not the inevitable outcome of electoral competition, particularly in the early going. In these cases, it is necessary both to look beyond political parties to consider the effects of independent candidates and to scrutinize the internal operation of parties in order to understand the types of parties that contribute to democratic development.

Both of these findings point to the need to study the conditions that lead individual politicians, and in particular candidates and party leaders, to invest in electoral strategies that support the nascent democratic regime. The three components of electoral infrastructure – information, coordination, and cooperation – provide a road map to define democracy supporting strategies. For example, some political leaders forego electoral competition altogether and seek power through appointment or indirect pressure. Some candidates join political parties, while others do not. Some partisans campaign on the party platform, while others promote their own experiences, attributes, or agendas. To explain these differences, this chapter turns to four key decisions that are the focus of later analysis:

- Potential candidates' decisions to run for office
- Candidates' decisions to affiliate with a political party or to run as an independent
- Affiliators' decisions to run only in a single-member district, only on a party list, or in both venues
- The decision about what factors to emphasize during the campaign: personal characteristics, personal policy preferences, or the party platform

These decisions can be viewed as both dependent and independent variables. In other words, it is important to explain what factors shape candidates' strategic decisions – why, for example, some candidates affiliate with a party while others decide to run as independents. It is also essential to understand how the sum of these choices influences the accumulation of electoral infrastructure over time and ultimately citizens' capacities to demand representation, accountability or effectiveness from government.

The argument presented here is not that candidates altruistically make choices that build electoral infrastructure and engender responsiveness, or that they selfishly refuse to do so. While both behaviors are seen in Russia and other emerging democracies, a focus on normative judgments masks a deeper truth. While the participation and election of "true" democrats are sometimes touted as the key to effective democracy, this book reveals that even candidates who profess to value democratic governance often make decisions that undermine electoral infrastructure, and thereby work against the creation of an effective democracy. More generally, while the argument in this chapter and the empirical analysis in subsequent chapters are focused on Russia, the aim is to use this theory to illuminate the relationship between elections and democratic transitions suggested in the findings presented in the chapter.

The discussion proceeds as follows. The first section describes the research strategy that I employ to reason from individual candidates' choices to national-level outcomes. This discussion provides a foundation for the microlevel model that is tested in the next four chapters. The next section identifies the dependent variables: the strategic choices at the heart of the empirical analysis. The subsequent section describes the key independent variables that explain the variation in candidates' strategies at each of these points. Models of candidate choices in the West inform this discussion, but

The Microfoundations of Democratic Responsiveness

these models are modified with an eye toward the critical starting conditions in transitional electoral regimes such as Russia.

A Research Design for Testing the Micro Model

Testing hypotheses about candidate behavior, the accumulation of electoral infrastructure, and democratic consolidation requires individual-level data on candidates' perceptions of the electorate, their access to resources, and their goals. To collect these data, I conducted two rounds of survey research targeted at candidates for national parliamentary office. The survey instrument emerged from early fieldwork I did in 1993, where I had a chance to conduct open-ended interviews with candidates in the Saratov region of Russia. This experience pointed to critical areas of candidate activity and the potential causes of candidate behavior and allowed me to look at candidate surveys from other contexts, with an eye toward questions that might translate well into the Russian context. A translation of the survey instrument is included in Appendix B.

The survey encompassed all of the candidates who ran for office in two elections (1995 and 1999) in four Russian regions, or oblasts. In 1999, an additional five ethnic Republic regions were added to the sample in order to create a second point of comparison. The sample allows for comparison of candidates' behavior over time and within very different cultural contexts. The choice to forego a random national sample followed from the fundamental premise of the work: that every candidate in the race, even those who get 2 or 3 percent of the vote, affects the accumulation of electoral infrastructure. As a result, I wanted to ensure that the sample included the variation in candidates' demographic and political characteristics as well as their capacity to win votes. While this last characteristic that is hard to control for in a national sample, it is critical in a transitional state, where winning vote margins are very small and the number of candidates who compete is very large. This saturation design also fits with the goal of understanding the interactions among different candidates in the same district: partisans and independents, politicians and political outsiders, winners and losers.

The regions used in the analysis were selected to maximize variation in indicators such as urban and rural populations, economic structure, and size. Within the Russian regions, two have significant ethnic divisions while the other two are relatively homogeneous. To develop a valid comparison, I chose the additional republics to approximate the regions in the Russian sample in a paired comparison design.

45

Candidate Strategies and Electoral Competition

Although the surveys were the primary sources of data, I also conducted a wide variety of open-ended interviews with candidates, party leaders, activists, journalists, Duma deputies, and political observers in each of the case study regions and in Moscow between 1993 and 1999. Mindful of the vagaries of interview data, I use these interviews as illustrations and as contrast to the survey results. Additional supplements to survey information included newspaper reports, tapes of television ads and speeches, party platforms, and campaign materials from each region. Perhaps most importantly, the two points of survey data are embedded in aggregate-level data from elections held between 1993 and 2003. Together, this evidence provides rigorous tests of the propositions defined by the microlevel theory presented in the remainder of the chapter.

Candidate Strategies as the Dependent Variable

The institutions that govern electoral competition in Russia define the dependent variables in each chapter, and because of the vagaries of the Russian rules, they are different from the decisions that candidates face in other contexts. The fundamental assumption in this analysis is that the decisions that candidates make during a campaign are arranged in a sequence or hierarchy. These assumptions are depicted in Figure 3.1, which describes the decision path of Russian candidates.

First, the would-be candidate must decide whether or not to run for national parliamentary office. Second, candidates who decide to run must then decide whether to affiliate with a political party or to run as an independent. Third, all candidates must choose a district. Independents are limited to nominal (single-member) districts, but may choose among the 225 districts across the Federation. Partisans face a more complex decision: whether to run only in a single-member district, only on a party list, or in both venues. Finally, both partisans and independents must decide how to run their campaigns: whether they will stress their personal characteristics, their policy preferences, or, if they affiliate, their party's platform. The left-hand side of the figure shows the chapters that address each of these decisions.

Figure 3.1 is intended as a guide to the data analysis in subsequent chapters. Even so, it captures the essence of candidacy and campaigning in a transitional democracy such as Russia. It describes these decisions as fundamentally independent, and occurring in a specific sequence. Intuitively, it seems clear that these decisions are interrelated. For example, a would-be

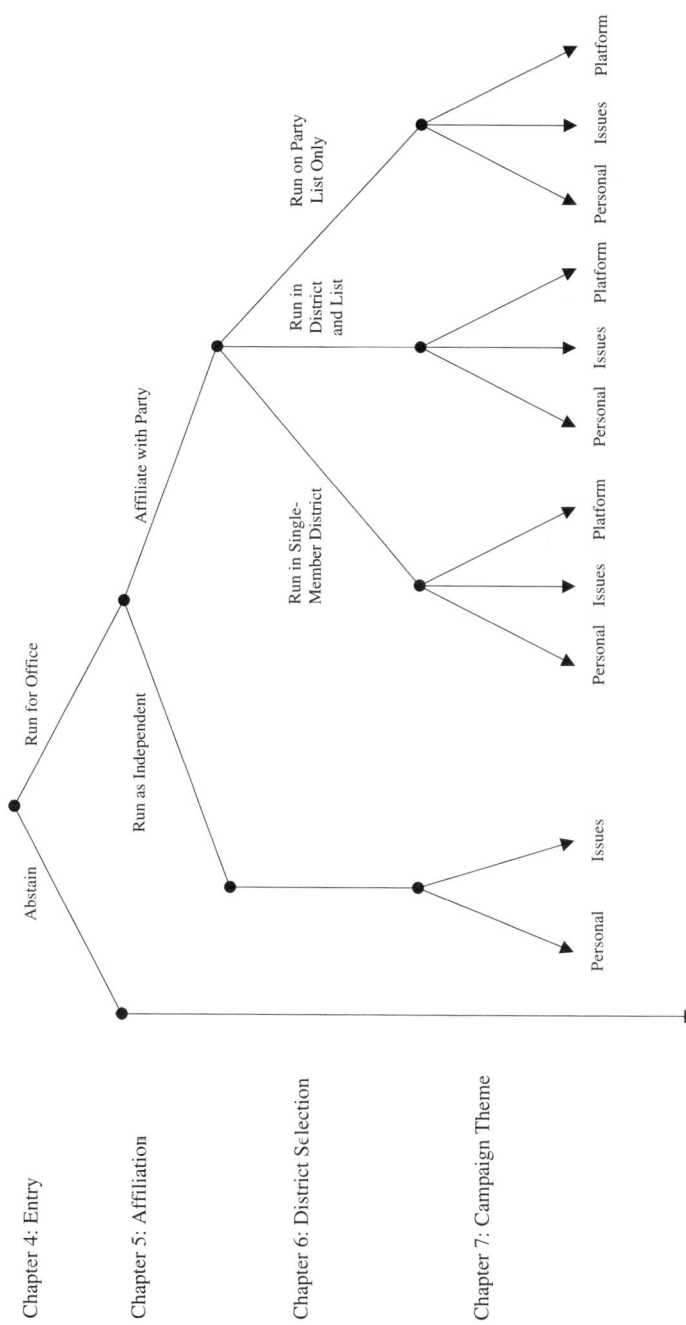

Figure 3.1. Candidates' Decisions

candidate's decision to run might depend on an offer from a party to run on its list. Affiliation decisions might be affected in similar ways. However, the transitory nature of organizations and alliances in Russia – and many other new democracies – makes these calculations problematic. At the point that a Russian candidate decides to run, perhaps six months or a year before the election, he or she may be unsure which parties will still exist at election time, let alone what sorts of issues a party will emphasize in the campaign. Especially at the regional or local level, parties may be unable to guarantee their candidates campaign resources or a winnable district. Under these conditions, it is reasonable to assume that candidates will be unwilling or unable to make simultaneous choices, as much as they might like to do so.

This sequential description of candidates' decisions does not imply that the decisions are completely independent. On the contrary, it underscores that decisions made early in the election cycle (candidacy, affiliation) have consequences for a candidate's later decisions (district selection, campaign emphasis). Yet, given both the political context and the fact that not all candidates face the same choices, it makes sense to analyze each decision separately. For example, a candidate who runs as an independent cannot appear on a party list. An independent candidate also cannot run on a party platform, except as an expression of his or her personal policy preferences. While this list of decisions is not exhaustive (for example, it only encompasses the campaign period), it reflects my focus on the coordination and cooperation dilemmas that have the greatest impact on immediate electoral outcomes and on the accumulation of electoral infrastructure.

Explaining Candidate Decisions: The Independent Variables

A wealth of literature in both the American and comparative subfields provides insight into candidates' strategic choices. In general, these works explain behavior relying on factors such as candidates' goals, resources, information about voter preferences, and the incentives created by electoral institutions. The models and frameworks developed in these studies cannot be applied wholesale to Russia and other new democracies. Some rely on variable measurements that are beyond the reach of data available in new systems. Many rest on problematic assumptions, such as the existence of strong party organizations, that do not fit the reality of transitional regimes. Nevertheless, this literature provides insight into the categories of variables that might be relevant in the Russian case, alternative

The Microfoundations of Democratic Responsiveness

measurement strategies, and the points where these variables interact to produce unexpected results.

The argument here is not that Russian candidates will always behave in the same way as their counterparts in established democracies. In fact, the argument is precisely the opposite: The factors that provoke one kind of behavior in established democracies can have very different effects in transitional democracies such as Russia. What the two types of democracies have in common is that candidates' decisions flow predictably from a core set of variables: their goals, resources, information, and structural incentives. The next sections review the literature on each of these variable categories from the perspective of the analysis of new systems.

Electoral Institutions

There is an extensive literature on the effects of electoral institutions – particularly electoral laws – on party behavior.[1] This literature focuses not only on the formal structures of institutions, but how these structures alter the behaviors of organizations that operate within them. With a few notable exceptions, the focus of this work is on institutional incentives to form political parties and the impact of these incentives on the structure and stability of party systems.[2] This book extends the focus of institutional studies to understand how electoral systems also influence individuals' decisions from entry to investment in the party's message during the campaign period, since these decisions have far-reaching implications for the accumulation of electoral infrastructure.

Russia's electoral system is commonly referred to as an example of a parallel system, side-by-side system, or mixed-member system. This category actually encompasses a very wide variety of institutional structures that create varying incentives for coordination and cooperation among different types of candidates. The common characteristic among mixed-member

---

[1] For an overview of these debates, see Cox 1997; Lijphart 1995; Rae 1967; Taagepera and Shugart 1989. For work that focuses on the Russian context, see Ferrara and Herron 2003; Herron 2002; Moser 2001.

[2] Much of this literature focuses on mechanisms that underpin Duverger's Law. For example William Riker (1982) examines the nature of elite and mass coordination engendered by different institutional structures. John Carey and Matthew Shugart (1995) investigate the incentives that electoral structures present to candidates to coordinate behavior or build personal votes. Most importantly, Gary Cox (1997) studies mass and elite responses to different electoral systems, including the interaction between parliamentary and presidential elections.

systems is that they fill parliamentary seats based on two simultaneous but procedurally distinct elections. Representatives elected in geographically defined districts fill a proportion of seats, while deputies elected through party list proportional representation fill the remainder. Beyond this basic feature, mixed systems vary on a series of parameters that influence the proportional representation part of the competition, the single-member district competition, or the interaction between the two.[3]

To define the incentives presented to Russian candidates and voters participating in elections under these rules, Table 3.1 focuses on the key elements of electoral systems: ballot structure, district magnitude, and seat allocation formulas. Ballot structure defines the nature of choices presented to voters. In Russia, voters cast one vote in each race (list and district), so it is possible for them to split their tickets and support two different parties, a party and an independent candidate, or to abstain in either race.[4] This structure also shapes strategic opportunities for some candidates. Ballot access provisions interact with ballot structure to define when and where candidates run. For example, partisan candidates can run in a list race, in a single-member district, or in both, while independent candidates can run only in district races.

The third factor, district magnitude, is the number of candidates elected from each district. Rein Taagapera and Matthew Shugart (1989) identified district magnitude as the most important institutional determinant of coordination and cooperation in the electoral arena.[5] This observation is at the root of the debate of the mechanisms that drive the outcomes posited by Duverger's Law – the mechanical effect and the psychological effects produced by coordination among voters (strategic voting) and candidates (strategic entry). Absent interaction between the two races in a mixed system, this argument would lead us to expect high district magnitude in the PR race to encourage a large number of parties to compete for office, while

---

[3] For an exhaustive typology of mixed systems, see Shugart and Wattenberg 2001: 9–24.
[4] In fact, White and McAllister (1997) report that just around 40 percent of Russian voters were planning to split their votes in the period leading up to the 1993 and 1995 elections; in 1995, another 40 percent were likely to split their vote. Similar data collected in a post-election survey in early 2000 report that 32 percent of voters reported voting for the same party, 32 percent did not, and the rest could not remember. Source: htttp://www.russiavotes.org/slide128.htm, accessed August 2002.
[5] In mixed systems, this conclusion may not hold since other factors, such as the distribution of seats across the two races or candidates' decisions to enter district races as independents, may have strong influences on patterns of coordination and cooperation in the campaign period.

Table 3.1. *Russian Electoral Institutions*

Electoral System Factor	National (List) Race	District Races	Effects
Ballot Structure	Parties listed on ballot Voters cast one vote	Candidates listed on ballot Voters cast one vote	Some overlap in registration requirements Structure allows for split ticket voting
Ballot Access	200,000 signatures, party affiliation necessary	Voter signatures, no party affiliation necessary	
District Magnitude	1 national district District magnitude = 225	225 districts District magnitude = 1	The large district magnitude in the proportional representation (PR) race encourages a multiparty system that recruits candidates for competition in the single-member district (SMD) race, increasing the number of candidates in each district
Seat Allocation Formula	D'Hondt electoral threshold = 5%	Plurality Turnout requirement = 50%	The total seats awarded to a party are the sum of the seats won in SMD and PR races, generating incentives for parties to maximize their chances in both races

Table 3.2. *The Effect of the Electoral Threshold on Election Outcomes, 1999–2003*

	1993	1995	1999	2003
Number of Parties Competing	13	43	26	23
Number of Parties That Surpassed the Electoral Threshold	8	4	6	4
Percentage of Votes "Against All Parties"	4.2	2.8	3.3	4.7
Percentage of Wasted Votes (Votes for Parties That Did Not Surpass Threshold)	8.7	44.8	13.4	25.1

Source: Project on Political Transformation and the Electoral Process in Post-Communist Europe and official statistics (2003).

a district magnitude of one in the district races should encourage a winnowing of candidates to just two.

The final factor in Table 3.1 is the seat allocation formula. These are the rules governing how votes determine election outcomes. In many mixed systems, the formula links the two systems by tying the seats awarded in the district races to a party's success in the list race. In Russia, the races remain unlinked. The total number of seats a party wins is equal to the number of seats it wins in PR plus the number of seats it wins across the 225 nominal districts. In the PR race, seats are awarded in proportion to votes cast.

However, stringent electoral thresholds can introduce disproportionality into PR systems. The threshold defines the minimum percentage of votes a party must receive in order to win seats in the list race. Electoral engineers implement thresholds to encourage cooperation among smaller parties in order to preclude party system fragmentation. Thresholds range from 1–2 percent in some West European democracies to 10 percent in Turkey. Until 2005, Russia's electoral threshold was 5 percent, and it created significant potential for disproportionality, since the winning parties receive substantial seat bonuses if voters support a large number of parties that failed to surpass the threshold. The effects of the threshold are reported in Table 3.2, which summarizes the success of parties in the PR races between 1993 and 2003.

The table demonstrates that through 2003, the relatively high threshold did keep the majority of electoral blocs from winning seats in the Duma. For example, in the 2003 election, twenty-three parties competed, but only four parties won seats in the list race. While the high electoral threshold is designed to mitigate party system fragmentation, it clearly does not work at the entry stage, suggesting that a purely institutional argument cannot adequately explain the behavior of partisan entrepreneurs and candidates in the Russian context.

In the district races, seats are allocated by a plurality rule. In established democracies, this procedure generally leads to a district race where two candidates converge around the preferences held by the median voter. As we will see in the next chapter, the average number of candidates in Russian district-level elections remains quite high even after Putin's first term in office. Thus, in both sides of Russian elections, candidate behavior has not matched expectations generated by Duverger's Law – an interesting anomaly that is addressed in the next chapter.

Information and Uncertainty

The information available to candidates, particularly information about their chances of winning office and the viability of other candidates, is a critical influence on their behavior. To some degree, these perceptions are shaped by the nature of electoral institutions and, specifically, by the electoral threshold or the expected number of votes needed to win. But institutional considerations alone can be misleading. The problem is not only a dearth of accurate information but also an abundance of disparate types of information and signals since available information about candidate preferences is rooted in past experience as well as the present regime structures and in informal norms and practices as well as formal rules. As John Kingdon writes:

> A full account of representation, therefore, must include representatives' perception of their constituents as a variable intervening between the constituents and the behavior of the elected policy-maker. These perceptions may or may not be accurate, but it is necessary to take them into account in order to explain the behavior of the politician (Kingdon 1962: 7).

As Kingdon suggests, many theories of candidate behavior, particularly those developed to explain established democracies, assume that these informational complexities are worked out, so that candidates converge on common expectations.

This assumption is relatively safe in countries where stable political party systems structure electoral competition. Yet in transitional systems such as Russia, the lack of shared information about constituents' preferences is

Table 3.3. *Information About Candidates: Types and Sources*

Information About Candidates	Source of Information		
	Candidates	Electorate and Society	Other Sources
Behavior in Office	Past actions in office		
	Campaign platforms		
	Partisan affiliation		
	Professional experience		
Electoral Viability	Electoral resources	Social cleavages	Electoral laws
	Media access	Support from organized groups	Party system
	Partisan affiliation	Voters' party identification	Public opinion polls
	Number of candidates	Previous election returns	State intervention in elections
	Campaign platforms		
	Electoral experience		
Credibility	Incumbency	Trust	Dominant national political figure
	Party affiliation	Social capital	Resources outside parties
	Campaign platforms	Support from organized groups	State capacity
	Endorsements by politicians		Legislative-constitutional structure
			National economic conditions

significant. To make effective decisions, a candidate must be able to assess the underlying political support for different electoral platforms in the context of the platforms that other candidates are likely to choose. To make this assessment, a candidate must know the distribution of voter preferences over candidates and parties as well as the criteria they would use to assess the candidates running for office. The problem of assessing electoral viability becomes even more complicated if a candidate considers affiliating with a political party. The candidate needs to assess the relative value of the party label, both in the current election and in the future. Table 3.3 lists the sources of information that are typically available to candidates and voters in established democracies.

The Microfoundations of Democratic Responsiveness

The table divides information into three categories: information about candidates' likely behavior in office, information about their viability (chances of winning), and information about their credibility (the likelihood that they will implement their promises). It also identifies potential information sources. Candidate-related sources include the candidate's own platform and partisan affiliation, the candidate's electoral experience and access to electoral resources, and the number of candidates running in the race (recall that the last factor lowers the electoral threshold). Sources in the electorate and society include the presence or absence of social cleavages, support from parties or other political groups, voters' party identification, and previous election returns. Other sources of information include the nature of electoral laws, the party system, poll data, and, finally, whether the state intervenes in elections.

The table underscores that candidates and voters have many potential sources of information. This abundance of sources increases the chances that all participants have access to at least some information on which to base their campaign decisions. However, many of these information sources may not be available in new democracies, or they may be available only to some candidates or voters. Existing party organizations may be so volatile or so weak that they do not provide clear information. Voters may not be willing or able to assess blame for transitional economic woes. Societal organizations and cleavage structures may be ill defined or illusory. Moreover, available sources of information may contradict each other. As a result, situations may arise where candidates running for the same seat hold very different conclusions about the viability of different platforms, or about the value of a party label.

Russian candidates' assessment of their fit with their districts – how well their policy preferences match with the preferences of their voters – reflects these complexities. Table 3.4 reports candidates' evaluation of the match between their electoral appeals and voters' demands in their districts. The table collapses two types of data. The top two rows of the table contain results from the 1995 survey, where candidates were asked whether their campaign targeted groups within their district. Targeting is a reasonable proxy for the availability of information, as a candidate must know something about voter preferences to know which groups to pursue.

While the rate of targeting in the 1995 sample is relatively high (greater than a majority), the results indicate considerable uncertainty. For 1999 candidates, the table reports responses in three categories: those who were

Candidate Strategies and Electoral Competition

Table 3.4. *Candidate Beliefs About Voters, 1995 and 1999*

Year	Region	Information About Voters	Percent (N)
1995	Russian	Informed	67.5% (56)
		Uncertain	32.5% (27)
1999	Russian	Good fit	46.7% (116)
		Uncertain	42.1% (104)
		Bad fit	11.0% (27)
	Non-Russian	Good fit	44.0% (33)
		Uncertain	52.0% (39)
		Bad fit	4.0% (3)

Source: Candidate survey conducted by the author.

confident that they were a good fit with their district, those who were confident they were a bad fit, and those who were uncertain. The data are further divided into candidates in Russian and non-Russian regions. As Table 3.4 shows, a little less than a majority of candidates in 1999 believed they were a good fit to their districts, with about 10 percent believing they were a bad fit. However, nearly 40 percent were unsure. The comparison of candidates in ethnic republics and Russian regions reveals higher rates of uncertainty for candidates in ethnic republics. This finding is consistent with other work on voting behavior and national identity in Russia's ethnic republics, suggesting that the cultural identities remain divided as a result of Soviet-era practices. More generally, this comparison argues against a simplistic assumption that ethnic divisions will define voting behavior in transition.

The pattern revealed in the data can be viewed as a case of half-empty versus half-full. After all, a substantial fraction of the sample know enough about voter demands (or thought they did) to believe their fit was good. Even so, roughly the same percentage were unable to assess their fit. Such a finding would be extremely surprising in an established democracy, where there are many sources of good information about voter demands. While these data provide information on only a fraction of Russian candidates, they suggest that a relatively large percentage of Russian candidates lack good information about voter preferences, and therefore have a hard time assessing their electoral viability or that of other candidates.

The dearth of information in the electoral arena has two important implications for candidates' strategies and for electoral infrastructure. First, without an accounting for uncertainty, candidates' choices in transitional democracies may appear unexpected or odd in comparison with behavior

The Microfoundations of Democratic Responsiveness

in established democracies. For example, the decision to run as an independent may be driven by uncertainty about the content of party brand names, or uncertainty as to which label will attract support from voters. In contrast, in an established democracy, eschewing the party label is more likely to be a response to good information – information that voters are highly dissatisfied with existing parties. Second, absent clear information to guide a candidate's decisions, factors that don't usually appear in analyses of candidate behaviors in established systems may rise to the forefront of the explanation for behavior in transition. For example, as candidates become less and less sure of what voters want, the size of a candidate's personal vote – a small group of strong supporters – becomes more and more important in determining whether the candidate enters and how he or she campaigns.

Candidate Goals

Political goals define what candidates ultimately want to derive from their participation in politics. In established democracies, most analyses assume that candidates enter because they want to win and establish a long-term political career. In this context, policy considerations are instrumental tools toward the larger goal of winning office. As David Mayhew argues in his seminal work on the U.S. Congress, "...saints aside, the electoral goal has an attractive universality to it. It has to be the proximate goal of everyone, the goal that must be achieved over and over if other ends are to be entertained" (1974: 16).

Assuming that most candidates in established systems place career goals over other motivations is a pretty safe bet, since these systems have mechanisms that undermine the efforts of amateur politicians or activists. As Barbara Geddes writes, "This is not to deny that for some politicians, ideological considerations outweigh the desire to be elected. The electoral process, however, weeds out such individuals; they are elected less frequently than those who consider winning of paramount importance" (1991: 378).

Yet even in America, where the party system and well-developed career ladders influence candidate behavior, a number of scholars have shown that candidates often face trade-offs between policy and electorally expedient decisions. Moreover, recent literature on the role of political amateurs focuses on the importance of policy goals in shaping the political behavior of U.S. elites (Canon 1990). Put another way, it is just as wrong to say that candidates in established democracies are single-minded seekers of reelection as it is to say that they care only about enacting good public policy or

Candidate Strategies and Electoral Competition

are driven by some other motivation. Different candidates have different goals, and the intensity of these goals also varies among candidates.

The potential significance of policy goals is even more obvious in West European parliamentary democracies, where proportional representation creates room for multiple parties across the political space. Thus, candidates and parties with strong reputations for policy could attract votes because of, not in spite of, their reputations as policy-driven activists. By this logic, the PR portion of the Russian electoral system should also encourage candidates with policy goals to participate in the electoral process and to run on the party list. The high cost of policy change during transition as well as the high benefits from early capture of office may also encourage policy-minded individuals to enter electoral competition even if they have only a small chance of winning.

Candidates in transitional democracies such as Russia may have an even wider range of motivations than their counterparts in established democracies. For example, candidates might enter a political race without hope of winning office because they seek to introduce their concerns into the public debate. Candidates may also run as spoilers, participating as a way to defeat other candidates. It also is possible for individuals to enter the electoral arena specifically to extract rents and bribes, to broker deals with Moscow bureaucrats, or to obtain a residence permit and job in the capital.[6] While all of these behaviors are rare in established democracies, the unique conditions of transitional politics (uncertainty and a wide-open political system with weak parties and tenuous career ladders) suggest that they will occur more frequently in new regimes.

Table 3.5 shows the distribution of candidate goals in the 1995 and 1999 surveys. Data are reported on three goals: building a political career, enacting preferred policies, and building a political party.[7] The columns report the percentage of candidates who said a particular goal was very important or important.[8] The 1999 data distinguishes candidates in Russian and non-Russian regions.

---

[6] A politician's goals may change over time, thereby affecting his or her subsequent behavior in the legislature (Kitschelt 1989; Michels 1978). The relationship between political goals and organizational structure will be discussed in subsequent sections.

[7] For a discussion of the survey instrument, see Appendix A. See Appendix C for a definition of these variables. Additional goals questions were asked in the survey, but are not reported here or used in the analysis because they are highly correlated with one of the three goals listed in Table 3.5. Factor analysis confirmed this relationship.

[8] Other possible responses in the survey were "not important" or "don't know."

The Microfoundations of Democratic Responsiveness

Table 3.5. *Candidate Goals, 1995 and 1999*

Region	Goal	Candidate Responses 1995	Candidate Responses 1999
Russian	Have a political career	29.3% (24)	35.2% (87)
	Enact good public policy	97.6% (80)	91.1% (225)
	Help build a political party	37.8% (31)	43.7% (108)
Non-Russian	Have a political career	–	30.7% (23)
	Enact good public policy	–	96.0% (73)
	Help build a political party	–	66.7% (50)

Source: Candidate survey conducted by the author.

At least for the candidates surveyed for this book, these data show that careerism is something of an exception to the rule. While virtually all of the candidates profess to hold policy goals, relatively few say they are interested in a political career. Open-ended interviews suggest that this finding is not a product of normative bias against careerism. Candidates who had significant political ambition did not seem reluctant to boast about their goals. Rather, this evidence highlights the fact that at least in 1995 and 1999, many Russian candidates entered political competition without any expectation of winning office. While accounts of the 2003 election show that these hopeless candidates continued to run, there was also a change in the tactics of careerist candidates, who joined Putin's United Russia Party in droves.

Somewhat more candidates say that they are interested in building a political party (the numbers are also higher in the non-Russian regions in 1999), but insofar as party organizations are one way to build electoral infrastructure, these results suggest that relatively few candidates are interested in implementing this solution, either directly or as a vehicle for their political ambitions.

Electoral Resources

In his work on elite coordination, Gary Cox (1997) asks how is it that a political party becomes the monopoly supplier of electoral resources – all of the things necessary to run an effective campaign, ranging from money and activists to office supplies and transportation, as well as endorsements or brand names that will attract voter support. Clearly, insofar as parties control these resources, candidates have strong incentives to affiliate with political parties and to campaign as party members, for if they do not, they will not receive the resources needed to contest the election and will surely be defeated. Even when other sources of resources exist, such as in the United States, parties remain an important if not critical supplier, one whose support is a practical necessity.

While the expectation of a party monopoly or practical monopoly on resources is a central fixture in many studies of candidate behavior in established democracies, it is not an accurate depiction of Russia and similar cases of transition, where the coexistence of old and new structures can create many competing sources of campaign resources. Social organizations and economic interest groups compete to provide a wide range of assets, from money and stable constituencies to the capacity to print posters, provide activists, or even fix the vote. Incumbent candidates' reputations may be crucial in the campaign. Cox's query about the origins of partisan monopolies raises a second important question: What happens before parties have a monopoly over electoral resources? Or, to put it in the terms used here, how does the availability of resources outside of the party system shape candidates' investments in electoral infrastructure, including party building?

Electoral resources are difficult to measure in any political system and at any level of analysis. Even if candidates are willing to talk candidly about the resources they control, the value of those resources can depend on many other factors. Still, alternative sources of support were quite obvious in interviews. While candidates who controlled government offices and relied on bribes and side payments to finance their campaigns rarely discussed those resources, their opponents were extremely forthcoming in charging violations of the election rules. Executives who paid bribes or printed posters in exchange for signatures on official documents were also forthcoming about their experiences. Likewise, candidates backed by regional governors almost never identified the governor as a source of support beyond a personal endorsement, and yet their campaigns were housed in regional government offices and relied on regional staff to get the work done. Still, in transitional situations where both candidates' resources and the contexts in which they are deployed are variable, it is likely to take some time for the relative values of different resources to become clear.

The analysis here focuses on resources that are likely to be useful regardless of context, such as leadership of social, political, and economic groups; incumbency, business ownership or management; a past position in

The Microfoundations of Democratic Responsiveness

the Soviet-era government; or a reputation as a political activist, political appointee, or manager. Taken together, these factors shape whether candidates are in charge of their electoral fate – whether they can campaign effectively on their own, or whether they are forced to affiliate with a party – any party – to have a shot at getting elected.

This section begins by assessing party control over electoral resources in contemporary Russia and shows that even after the 2003 elections, parties are not perceived to be the near-monopoly providers of resources observed in many established democracies. The discussion then turns to resources controlled by candidates and others outside the party system, and to data on the distribution of these resources within the candidate samples that form the basis of the analysis in later chapters.

Electoral Resources: The Limited Extent of Party Control. The Russian Federation vaulted very quickly from a single-party system to a rapidly evolving multiparty system and back to a nascent predominant party system. Until President Putin's victory in 2003, some analysts concluded that party organizations are developing brand names as well as roles as providers of other resources, while others view the party system as inchoate.[9] To some degree, these vastly different conclusions derive from different levels of analysis, but overall they reflect rapid changes from election to election and organization to organization. As discussed earlier, many party organizations have little to provide their candidates. Even parties such as Fatherland–All Russia (FAR), Yabloko, and the Communist Party of the Russian Federation (KPRF) that have had relatively high levels of success in one or more elections remain vulnerable to sudden shocks that upend the party system, dramatically altering their electoral support and ability to provide candidates with electoral resources.

Against this backdrop of relatively low availability of partisan resources, two sets of parties stand out in terms of candidates' perceptions. The first distinct set of organizations is the parties of power, a group that culminated in Putin's United Russia (UR). The second stand-out is a single

---

[9] For arguments in favor of the development of nascent party identification see Brader and Tucker 2001; Colton 2000a; Miller, Erb, and Hesli 2000; Miller and Klobucar 2000. For the alternative perspective, see Colton and Hale 2004; Rose and Munro 2003; Smyth forthcoming; White, Rose, and McAllister 1997.

organization: the successor party to the Communist Party of the Soviet Union (CPSU), the KPRF.

The parties of power are organizations manufactured by the Kremlin in each election. They rely solely on state resources and state access to media to mount their campaigns. They also depend heavily on charismatic appeals of their leaders in order to win support.[10] Table 3.6 summarizes the parties of power that have formed in Russia since 1993.

These parties have two distinctive advantages over all other parties. The first is that they can offer candidates significant material and human resources. The expansive state structure provides opportunities to channel resources such as computers, media equipment, and phones to candidates.[11] In some regions, campaign headquarters were located in universities, while in others the organizations were housed in regional administrative offices.[12] Between 1999 and 2003, the most successful party of power, UR, relied heavily on the manipulation of state resources to generate elite coordination and create a perception for voters that its success was inevitable. With help of the Kremlin, UR orchestrated a legislative coup that unseated all of its KPRF rivals from leadership positions on key pork-barrel committees (Smyth 2002). The parties of power also had a distinct advantage over all other parties in their access to media, in particular to television. For example, in the 1999 and 2003 elections, Unity and its successor, UR, relied heavily on state resources, including increasing control of coverage on national television (Oates forthcoming). By 2003, UR also borrowed heavily on the unprecedented reputation of its de facto leader, President Putin, at the polls.

The successor party to the Communist Party of the Soviet Union (CPSU), the KPRF, controlled a different set of resources. In the late Soviet period, the KPRF materialized as a regional backlash against the reform movement within the CPSU. After the 1991 coup, the conservative KPRF inherited the remaining resources of the banned CPSU, including a

---

[10] In this sense, Russia's parties of power share common characteristics with other governmental parties (Panebianco 1988: 113). For accounts of Russia's parties of power, see Colton and McFaul 2001; Fish 1995; Rose and Munro 2003; Smyth 2002.

[11] A 1995 memo written by the governor of Chelyabinsk and obtained through field research detailed the resources that should be made available to the regional Our Home Is Russia organization, including access to cars, meeting space, office support, and television time.

[12] In 1999 the leader of the Unity slate in Chelyabinsk described the support of the Governor Petr' Sumin in constructing and supporting the Unity organization. The fact that the interview was held in his office inside the regional government building confirmed this support.

Table 3.6. *Russian Parties of Power, 1993–2004*

	Russia's Choice (RC)	Our Home Is Russia (OHR)	Fatherland–All Russia (FAR)	Unity	United Russia (UR)
Origins	Kremlin	Kremlin	Regional Powers	Kremlin	Merger of Unity and FAR
Date Formed	Summer 1993	Spring 1995	Fall 1998	Fall 1999	2001
Leaders (Position at Founding)	Yegor Gaidar (first deputy minister)	Victor Chernomyrdin (prime minister)	Yury Luzhkov (Moscow mayor), Evegeny Primakov (former prime minister)	Sergei Shoigu (emergencies minister)	Boris Gryzlov (interior minister)
Current Status	Merged with Union of Right Forces (SPS)	Merged with Unity in United Russia	Merged with Unity in United Russia	Merged with FAR in United Russia	Active

national structure that included a core of loyal voters, a regionally organized network of leaders, and a sizable following of party activists. The KPRF was able to parlay these resources into a strong reputation for being the only viable opposition to the government – a reputation that Putin undermined by ending the party's parliamentary influence. By 2003, the party lost almost half of its electoral support and was increasingly fraught with internal conflict and leadership challenges.

Even these two sets of parties did not have monopoly control over electoral resources between 1993 and 2003. Many successful Duma candidates ran as independents or as incumbents who shifted from the list to district races in different elections, or even changed their party affiliation between elections. Moreover, even with the strong presence of UR candidates in districts in 2003, the number of candidates who competed for office in districts and on the list was remarkably high. At least prior to the election, UR was not perceived as a monopolist. As Table 3.6 illustrates, despite their many advantages, Russian parties of power have proved transitory. Their resources have not been enough to ensure their survival or their ability to attract candidates over the long term. While UR had remarkable success at the polls in 2003, the durability of the organization remains in doubt. Much of its success is linked to Putin's popularity, yet Putin is still not an official member of the organization. Moreover, his status is ambiguous due to constitutional term limits. Increasingly, the Kremlin relies on coercion and institutional manipulation to maintain the party structure and position. The overall effect is not a contribution to electoral infrastructure but a shift to the construction of authoritarian infrastructure – a theme I return to throughout the work.

Other Russian parties vary in their control over resources. In 1995, regional organizations of the Liberal Democratic Party of the Russian Federation (LDPR) each had an office with a three-person staff including a chauffer and car for the regional party head. In addition, the offices were outfitted with rare equipment – computers, faxes, copiers, and video technology – as well as a large amount of party literature. Officials told stories of Zhirinovsky himself traveling to deliver a car to regional leaders or meet the rank-and-file members. These resources ensured the loyalty of regional party officials but did not attract effective candidates beyond the national list. Nor did these resources secure voter support, which has been extremely volatile and unpredictable.

In contrast to the LDPR, the Women of Russia bloc never developed a significant presence in any of the case study regions, despite claims on

The Microfoundations of Democratic Responsiveness

its web site of a nationwide organization. Following its surprisingly strong showing in 1993, rather than building regional and local party organizations, the organization used its control of Duma seats to garner financial contributions. Thus, candidates in legislative districts were very much on their own in their pursuit of office. The bloc split after failing to surpass the 5 percent barrier in the 1995 list race, with none of the surviving organizations winning seats in 1999 or 2003.

Most party organizations in Russia fall between these extremes. Some have significant resources to convey on their candidates, some have very little to give out, while others hoard their resources at the center. The vulnerability of the right party organizations was evident throughout 1993–2003. The natural constituency for these organizations was quite small and the number of organizations was relatively large. Leadership battles were notorious and extremely acerbic. Until 1999, the parties relied heavily on the state, oligarchs, and international nongovernmental organizations (NGOs) for support. None of these alliances won any of the parties much love from voters. As the oligarchs were jailed or exiled, this funding dried up, as did the credibility of the organizations.

Surveying the electoral landscape as of early 2005, United Russia remains the only organization with any consistent access to resources. For the most part, however, these resources were not used to generate a viable party organization but rather to eliminate the opposition. There is no denying that a great deal of UR's appeal to candidates stems from the fact that it is currently the only game in town for ambitious politicians and the only viable choice for voters.

Resources Outside Parties: Personal Votes. Bruce Cain, John Ferejohn, and Morris Fiorina describe personal vote as "the proportion of a candidate's vote that originates in his or her personal qualities, qualifications, activities and record" (1984: 111). Similarly, Steven Ansolobehere, James Snyder, and Charles Stewart argue that personal vote resources are a product of "the ways in which incumbents serve their constituents – providing help to voters via casework and bringing home federal spending, acquiring a detailed knowledge of voters' tastes, building a local base of volunteer election workers, and so on" (2000: 18). In terms of the argument here, a candidate's personal vote is composed of electorally relevant resources accrued independently of a party organization, although partisan candidates can also deploy such resources. Personal votes are characterized by relatively unconditional voter loyalty that is unlikely to vary with the other candidates running for office. Environmentalists' support for the Green candidates in Chelyabinsk, Volga Germans' support for the single ethnic German candidate in the race, and workers' support for their successful enterprise managers are all good examples of personal votes. These resources not only help candidates to campaign effectively and guarantee a core of support, they also provide an alternative measure of viability.

While the concept of personal votes has been used to explain outcomes in Western legislative elections, its explanatory power is equally large for studies of transitional democracies, particularly when parties do not hold a monopoly on electoral resources. The analysis here uses a number of factors to describe a candidate's personal vote:

- Whether the candidate held a leadership position in a social or political group
- Whether the candidate held a local, regional, or national elected office
- Whether the candidate owned a business
- Whether the candidate held a senior position in the Soviet (pretransition) Communist Party or in the state apparatus

The rationale for focusing on these factors is as follows. Social organizations – ranging from political organizations to environmental movements to local associations – can give their leaders a headquarters, campaign workers, money, and, more importantly, name recognition and support from organization members and like-minded voters. This mechanism is important in transitional Russia, as the suppression of social activity during the Soviet period led to a mushrooming of organized groups in the perestroika era. These groups spanned a wide range of concerns from ethnic organizations to labor unions as well as the early people's front organizations that pushed for further democratization in the late 1980s and early 1990s.

Social organizations provided candidates with a potential new source of networks and resources. In particular, these organizations mobilized activists to invest time and labor in election campaigns. Some clusters of voters organized around issue positions, such as the antinuclear groups in Chelyabinsk. Still others, such as nationalist groups in Saratov, relied on long-standing issues from the Soviet period to prompt voters' investments in political campaigns. Moreover, when partisan attachments do not structure the electorate, such ties may provide the best information about viability. In other words, a candidate may say, "I don't know what voters in my district want, but I know that my organization has many members in the district, as well as many nonmembers who are sympathetic to our goals. Therefore, I think I have a fairly good chance of attracting enough support to win office."

Along the same lines, elected officials can use their position as a source of office space, workers, and money, as well as a mechanism for gaining name recognition and favorable evaluations from the electorate. Ownership of a business can provide name recognition and a reputation among voters, as well as access to the mundane necessities of electioneering. In both cases, the recognition and reputation-based benefits of these positions may also give candidates confidence that voters will support them.

The final resource listed previously accounts for factors that candidates control by virtue of their position prior to the democratic transition. In a sense, this variable captures an important aspect of the legacy of the Soviet past and its impact on candidate behavior and election outcomes. This conception invokes Juan Linz and Alfred Stepan's (1996) typology of regime legacies by focusing on aspects of the communist and early transition experiences that shape the expectations, skills, and resources available to postcommunist elites as they contest elections. According to this rubric, these factors include nascent forms of civil society (precommunist mobilization), political society (the structure of the former party system), and the usable state (the nature of the civil service) (1996: 284–53). Following Kenneth Jowitt (1996) and Stephen Hanson (1995), I focus on how these factors shape elites' expectations and patterns of behavior. This approach maps closely to Anna Grzymala-Busse's (2002) notion of "portable skills" and "usable pasts" that drive elites' decisions to support or abandon communist successor parties in the postcommunist era.

For example, the Soviet use of large-scale enterprises provided significant reputation-based resources for enterprise managers. These enterprises acted as local governments, providing social services from hospitals and clinics to daycare and housing, so it is not surprising that a director's effectiveness in delivering these services in times of resource scarcity was an important signal for voters. Along the same lines, by the mid-1990s, a series of regional financial industrial groups (FIGs) sprang up around old Soviet enterprise networks. Henry Hale (2005) provides convincing evidence that the FIGs pose a serious challenge to organized parties by recruiting and funding candidates for national office to secure support for pro-business policies. Data on these components of personal vote are shown in Table 3.7.

Candidate Strategies and Electoral Competition

Table 3.7. *Personal Vote Resources, 1995 and 1999*

Type of Resource	Year	
	1995	1999
Social Movement or Organization	Leader: 16.9% (14)	Leader: 23.9% (77)
	Head: 22.9% (19)	Head: 18.9% (61)
Elected Office	21.1% (17)	8.1% (26)
Own Business	–	25.2% (81)
Soviet-Era Position	Mid-level: 25.3% (21)	Mid-level: 10.9% (35)
	High-level: 26.5% (22)	High-level: 1.9% (6)

The data on resources are not broken out for Russian and non-Russian regions because there is little variation across this factor.
Source: Candidate survey conducted by the author.

The first row provides data on the candidates' role as leaders in social organizations. For example, in the 1999 sample, just under 20 percent of the candidates surveyed headed such organizations, while nearly 25 percent held a leadership position such as a board member. The second and third rows are simple yes/no indicators of whether candidates held elected office or owned a business. The final row gives data on the distribution of candidates who held positions in the Soviet-era party or state structure. This variable is the only one that shows real variation across the two samples, with the percentage of candidates holding any sort of Soviet-era position declining sharply between 1995 and 1999, signaling a potential turnover in cadres.[13]

In addition to these measurable indicators of personal votes, the survey also asked candidates about their reputation – as a businessperson, political activist, elected official, or holder of appointed office. Responses to this question are presented in Table 3.8.

Only a small percentage of candidates (less than 5 percent) said they had no reputation. Conversely, less than 10 percent of the sample cited more than one reputation-based factor. As the table indicates, a large percentage of candidates cited their reputation in business or other economic activities, with relatively few mentions of reputations arising from elected office. Mentions of appointed office and political activists' reputations fell in between.

---

[13] For details on the construction of these variables, see Appendix C.

Table 3.8. *Reputational Measures of Personal Votes, 1999*

Content of Candidate Reputation	% Yes (N)
Business/Economic Activity	69.8% (225)
Elected Office	6.5% (21)
Appointed Position in Government	30.7% (99)
Political Activist	44.4% (144)

The table only presents data from the 1999 sample, as the 1995 survey did not include the reputation-based questions.
Source: Candidate survey conducted by the author.

Conclusion: Candidate Behavior and Electoral Infrastructure

For the most part, candidates around the world face a similar set of choices: to run for office, choose a party, select a district, and identify a successful appeal to potential voters. Yet, their reactions to these choices, the strategies that they pursue to win office, are very different in established and transitional systems. A critical factor in candidates' decisions is the degree to which the party organizations and party system structure these choices. In established systems, party organizations level the playing field among candidates. Parties control the majority of resources necessary for reelection, and provide critical information about voters' demands and the viability of competing appeals. Established parties and party systems also play a gatekeeping role, weeding out inexperienced or ill-prepared candidates.

In transitional systems, new parties are less likely to fulfill these functions. Absent stable, institutionalized party organizations, candidates rely on a wider set of factors to govern their choices. In transition, electoral resources can be drawn from organizations and experiences that potential candidates had under the old regime, in the transition period, or in the new regime. Resources can be concentrated within new parties or outside of the party system. They can be dominated by the state or come from the private sector. Given the lack of information about voters' policy preferences and the followings of potential rivals, resources can often provide a less than ideal information proxy for viability.

The interaction between the actual resource distributions and the structure of constituencies determines the value of different resource endowments. A proliferation of local- or regional-level resources prompts different strategies under proportional representation and single-member district rules. Because these resources are not well suited to winning national-level office, candidates are more likely to invest them in party building than candidates running under plurality rules. Still, in a new democracy with a wide range of resources, available to different candidates, it may take significant time to sort out the relative values of resource endowments as well as the relationships between individuals and parties and among party organizations.

In short, the range of factors defined in this chapter – from the strength of parties at the point of founding elections to candidates' goals – is extremely wide in Russia. These distinctions lead candidates to make very different strategic choices in terms of the investments in electoral infrastructure. As the analysis in the subsequent chapters will show, the interaction between individual candidates' attributes and the political context in Russia undermined the accumulation of all three components of electoral infrastructure at every stage of the electoral process.

Viewed as a whole, the strategic choices of Russian candidates generated little consistent information and extremely anemic patterns of coordination and cooperation. In other words, their choices did not yield electoral infrastructure. As a result, President Putin's efforts to transform elections into noncompetitive mechanisms to shore up central power faced very little organized opposition. The product of the Kremlin's effort was the antithesis of electoral infrastructure – a set of institutions and behaviors that can be identified only as authoritarian infrastructure: a dominant state party that wins allegiance and support through coercion and the manipulation of state resources.

4

Many Candidates, Few Choices

We are about to enter a new millennium. The world will be celebrating. But nobody will bring us any joy. I tell you, there is nobody to vote for in Russia.
                                    Irina, unemployed mechanical engineer[1]

The hallmark of any democratic election is a ballot that presents voters with distinct choices over candidates and parties and, presumably, policies. Candidates shape these choices through their electoral strategies – whether they run for office, whether they join a party, which district they contest, and how they campaign. Thus, candidates and their decisions shape election outcomes, ranging from national results – winners and losers, legislative factions and governments – to electoral infrastructure – information about voters' preferences and the viability of candidate or party strategies, coordination among voters and candidates, and cooperation in political parties. This chapter focuses on the first of these decisions: the decision to contest a seat in the State Duma.

As noted in Chapter 2, Russia's experience with competitive elections highlights an important paradox: Offering voters choices between different candidates does not always produce a consolidated democracy. The analysis of candidate entry provides the first illustration of this phenomenon. While the number of candidates contesting each seat in Russia has declined over time, it remains high. Many hopeless candidates vie for each national legislative mandate. Some races are decided by a small plurality of votes. Many candidates run as independents. In each contest, the fact that elites presented voters with a range of choice was not entirely positive, since

---

[1] From http://users.aimnet.com/~ksyrah/ekskurs/elect.html, accessed December 22, 1999. No longer available.

it signaled an important failure of coordination and cooperation among elites and muddled the information available to voters. None of these factors encouraged the evolution of electoral infrastructure, responsiveness, or accountability.

This chapter relies on aggregate candidate data, survey evidence, and a case study of a single district, Saratov's central district number 156, to explain why so many Russian candidates continue to contest elections that they have very little chance of winning. The persistence of a large number of contestants in both the party list and district races in Russia defies a core expectation in the democratization literature and in the literature on the effects of electoral institutions on political behavior. In their classic work on transition, Guillermo O'Donnell and Philippe Schmitter write, "Founding elections seem to have a sort of freezing effect upon subsequent political developments. Where they are followed by successive iteration of the electoral process, few new parties get into the game, and many minor ones are likely to drop out" (1986: 62). The large number of candidates competing in the district races also defies Maurice Duverger's (1966) Law that plurality rules should yield just two parties or two contestants.

The analysis draws on three theories originated to explain candidate behavior in developed democracies. The first approach is a purely institutional explanation of political behavior exploring ballot access requirements. The second approach, rooted in rational choice institutionalism, focuses on the mechanisms that underlie Duverger's Law and provoke coordination and cooperation among candidates. Finally, ambition theory focuses on the evolution of career ladders to predict candidates' entry. All of these theories highlight the impact of candidates' goals, information and resources on candidates' decisions to run for office. Moreover, they all support the same conclusion, that the plethora of candidates in Russian elections is no surprise.

Defining the Dependent Variable: Coordination and Cooperation in Candidate Entry Decisions

The dependent variable in this chapter is not who runs for office in Russia but why so many candidates enter. This question hones in on the theoretic concerns previously raised and also addresses a very practical problem inherent in the study of candidate entry. Studying who runs for office demands an accounting of potential politicians who consider running but ultimately

Many Candidates, Few Choices

Table 4.1. *Patterns of Candidate Entry in Russian Duma Elections, 1993–2003*

	1993	1995	1999	2003
Candidates	3,253	8,351	5,746	5,173
Candidate/Seat Ratio	7.2	18.6	12.8	11.5
List Race Candidates	2,474	6,764	4,097	3,280
Candidate/Seat Ratio	11.0	30.1	18.2	14.6
Parties	13	43	26	23
SMD Race Candidates	2,249	3,699	2,755	2,457
Partisans	1,434	2,613	1,661	1,781
Independents	825	1,056	1,144	676
Candidate/Seat Ratio	10.0	16.4	12.2	10.9
Partisans	6.4	11.6	7.4	7.9
Independents	3.6	4.8	4.8	3.0

Sources: Project on Political Transformation and the Electoral Process in Post-Communist Europe (2003) and official statistics. Note that the number of candidates in district and list races exceeds the total number of candidates because some candidates ran in both races.

decide against it. These "dogs that don't bark" present a perennial and almost intractable problem for analyses of candidacy decisions. The problem is particularly acute in new democracies, where trajectories of political careers and pathways to office are not established and behavior is harder to predict.

My interviews with candidates between 1993 and 2000 underscored how difficult it would be to identify the set of potential candidates in Russia. Many potential candidates never made it onto the ballot. In Saratov in 1993, thieves who stole registration petitions knocked out a leading contender for the Communist nomination, Valery Rashkin. Rashkin, who served as secretary of the regional KPRF organization, later became a leader in the regional Duma, and ultimately won a seat in the State Duma in 1999. In 2003, he ran as the district incumbent and lost to the national hockey star Vladislav Tretyak, but won a mandate on the KPRF party list. Likewise, in Chelyabinsk, prominent leaders of the pro-democracy movement in 1991 were denied positions on party rosters.

To form a clearer picture of the candidate pool and its changes over time, Table 4.1 summarizes the patterns of candidate entry between 1993 and 2003. The discussion of entry is complicated by Russia's mixed electoral system. As indicated in Chapter 3, Russian contestants are candidates and parties, partisans and independents, contestants on the national list and in single-member districts (SMDs). In addition, some candidates run both on the list and in a district.

The table shows that there has been an overall decline in the number of candidates per seat since 1995. However, the decline between 1999 and 2003 is quite modest, despite the increasing strength of President Putin's Kremlin-backed party of power, United Russia. Overall, the size of the candidate pool remained quite large.

The table also underscores that the proliferation of candidates has occurred in both list and district races. As with the SMD races, the number of political parties in each race remains very high even by postcommunist standards. In 1993, thirteen political organizations managed to overcome the registration hurdles in time to get on the ballot in the snap elections. This number rose to a remarkable forty-three parties in 1995 and fell to twenty-six and twenty-three parties in subsequent elections. The large number of candidates who make themselves available to these parties is also striking. At the height of party entry in 1995, more than thirty candidates contested every seat in the national list race. This ratio dropped to eighteen contestants per seat in 1999 and fifteen candidates per seat in 2003. While the trend is lower, the number of candidates who compete for every seat remains higher than theories of candidate behavior would predict.

The pattern is similar in district races. The total number of candidates competing in each district has declined over time although it remains substantial. In 1995, over sixteen candidates contested each district seat, dropping to just over twelve candidates in 1999 and eleven in 2003. Importantly, the rate of partisan candidates remained remarkably stable and even increased slightly between 1999 and 2003, while the number of independents declined significantly between 1999 and 2003. These trends suggest that to the degree mechanisms that deter entry are working they had different effects on different candidates. The table also begins to shed light on the impact of political parties on candidate entry. The rise in partisan candidates running in nominal districts suggests that some parties, notably UR, played a greater role in entry decisions.

It is important to note that some other postcommunist countries have experienced similar rates of candidate entry. In 2000, Lithuania had a candidate-to-seat ratio of just under nine. Croatia had a remarkable ratio of twenty-seven candidates for each seat. Both of these countries have experienced high levels of political scandal, unstable party systems, and volatile election results, although their Freedom House scores suggest high levels of

Many Candidates, Few Choices

Table 4.2. *Success Rates in Russian Duma Elections, 1993–2003*

	1993	1995	1999	2003
Candidates	6.9%	2.7%	3.9%	4.3%
List Race Candidates	9.1%	3.3%	5.5%	6.9%
Parties (% Winning List Seats)	61.5%	9.3%	23.1%	17.4%
SMD Race Candidates	10.0%	6.1%	8.2%	9.2%
Partisans	6.6%	3.4%	7.3%	8.7%
Independents	15.8%	7.3%	9.2%	10.1%

Sources: Project on Political Transformation and the Electoral Process in Post-Communist Europe (2003) and official statistics.

elite commitment to democratic processes. These cases demonstrate that while coordination dilemmas surrounding candidate entry can generate important problems for democratic systems, they do not always condemn the system to failure. However, as the subsequent analysis of the Russian case will reveal, coordination failures in the beginning of the campaign increase the likelihood that these failures will be magnified throughout the electoral process.

Table 4.2 sharpens this analysis by reporting the success rates among different types of candidates. These numbers underscore that the probability of winning office is very low for any candidate regardless of how he or she runs.

The first finding reported in the table is that very few parties that compete for list seats actually make it into the Duma. This high failure rate among party organizations is a result of the 5 percent electoral threshold as well as the large number of parties running in the list race. The success rates of individual candidates who run on party lists remain quite low, even among Duma incumbents. This value is driven by the number of parties as well as the large number of candidates included on each party's list. Likewise, by sheer force of the numbers of candidates competing for office, success rates among district candidates are also low.

Valery Rashkin's home district, Saratov district number 156, starkly illustrates candidates' lack of success and the volatility in vote totals over time. In 1999, Rashkin carried the district with 32 percent of the vote. Only two of his rivals won support from more than 10 percent of the electorate. Seven got less than 2.5 percent. In 2003, Rashkin lost the district to the

Candidate Strategies and Electoral Competition

Moscow-based Tretyak by 4 percentage points, 25 to 21 percent. Nine of their rivals failed to garner more than 2.5 percent of the vote. The results in this district underscore that most candidates are truly hopeless, in the sense that they have very little chance of winning office.

It is easy to dismiss these hopeless candidates as irrelevant to an explanation of Russian election outcomes or Russia's transition to democracy. However, inasmuch as many of these candidates are affiliated with a political party, they demonstrate the weakness of many party organizations in contemporary Russia and the marginal value of their party labels. Moreover, given that candidates are winning Duma seats with relatively small pluralities, the entry of a candidate who attracts even a few percentage points of the vote can change the outcome. Finally, the fact that so many candidates contest the typical Duma seat complicates the choice facing voters – and complicates the choices that candidates face, such as whether to affiliate with a party, where to run, and how to campaign.

Who Are the Candidates?

While repeated electoral competition did not "freeze" the individual actors or organizations in Russia, it has frozen the composition of the candidate pool. The social and economic characteristics of Russian candidates are increasingly predictable. The Soviet-era patterns of legislative delegations that mirrored the composition of the general population have given way to a deputy corps that is largely male, well educated, and drawn from the ranks of state officials. Table 4.3 summarizes the patterns of entry by demographic characteristics.

As the table shows, the Russian candidate pool is remarkably homogenous and remarkably stable. Women run for office at far lower rates than their counterparts in Western Europe but at about the same rates as in the United States and higher than their counterparts in Asia and Latin America (Moser 2001; Norris 1996). As in other countries, the upper strata of society, defined in terms of education and not purely class characteristics, dominates the candidate pool. As the average age indicates, the system is biased toward those with established careers and past political experience, a finding that resonates with the discussion of resources in Chapter 3.[2]

---

[2] There is some variation in the demographics of candidates by party. Historically, Yabloko nominates more women than other organizations except for Women of Russia. The KPRF has the highest median age of candidates, hovering around fifty-one as opposed to an average

Many Candidates, Few Choices

Table 4.3. *Demographics of Russian Duma Candidates, 1993–2003*

		\multicolumn{5}{c}{Election}			
		1993	1995	1999	2003 PR	2003 SMD
Gender	Male	91.5%	86.6%	85.3%	87.0%	88.3%
	Female	8.5%	13.4%	14.7%	13.0%	11.7%
Age	Average	44.6%	45.4%	46.8%	46.6%	46.2%
Education	Higher			92.7%	90.5%	92.6%
	Incomplete higher			2.0%	2.6%	1.6%
	Secondary general			1.9%	2.5%	2.1%
	Secondary vocational			3.5%	4.4%	3.7%
Occupation	State officials	19.1%	23.1%	19.7%	23.1%	36.6%
	Business	26.1%	25.5%	28.1%	27.2%	22.2%
	Military				0.3%	0.8%
	Professionals	31.4%	25.4%	22.6%	27.2%	22.1%
	Party officials				3.4%	2.9%
	Nongovernmental	18.2%	14.4%	11.4%	7.0%	6.6%
	Semi- or low-skilled	2.0%	2.4%	2.6%	1.6%	1.8%
	Pensioners	0.3%	1.3%	4.2%	5.6%	3.4%
	Students	NA	0.6%	0.4%	1.5%	0.6%
	Not employed	1.9%	1.1%	3.5%	3.8%	3.9%

Source: Data compiled by the author from official sources.

Again, Saratov's central district illustrates these patterns. Only one woman candidate – Svetlana Oleinik, an activist in Motherland and the wife of a candidate who contested another seat in the region – has ever run for the seat. In 1999 and 2003, all of the candidates had some higher education. With the exception of Vladimir Yuzhakov, a student whose father was a Russia's Choice deputy from 1993–5 and ran in 2003 in the contiguous district, all of the candidates were middle-aged. Many had some political and campaign experience. Others had significant managerial experience in industry or retail business.

The biggest change in the type of candidates on the ballot in 2003 is the growing numbers of regional-level officials particularly in single-member districts. In large part, this increase reflects UR's strategy of nominating regional officials to support its electoral efforts. The party recruited

in the low to mid-forties for reform and state parties. The LDPR is the outlier on education, where a scant 9.1 percent of its candidates had higher education on its initial 1999 candidates' list.

twenty-seven governors at the top of regional lists and included sixty-one Duma incumbents and sixty-one regional officials (mostly regional Duma incumbents) in single-member districts. In addition, United Russia nominated a number of businesspeople in nominal districts, demonstrating an impressive merger of state, economic, and political elites on the parties' candidate roster. While this show of force represents significant cooperation under the auspices of United Russia, the Kremlin's reliance on nondemocratic means to affect this change does not constitute growth in the electoral infrastructure.

Despite the Kremlin's increasing intervention in the electoral process, as of 2003 a large number of candidates continued to compete for every seat in the parliament. Phrased in terms of the central concerns of this book, these candidates illustrate the lack of all three components of electoral infrastructure in contemporary Russia: reliable information about voters' preferences and the value of parties' labels and candidate viability, coordination in the form of strategic entry, and cooperation in building strong, stable party organizations.

Explaining Candidate Entry Decisions in Transition

To explain the variation across the Russian candidate pool, the next section relies on institutional, rational choice, and ambition theories developed to explain candidate entry in the Western context. These theoretic frameworks highlight the variables outlined in the previous chapter: resources, goals, information, and institutions. Considered together, they provide important insights into why so many candidates seek office in Russia and the effects of those decisions on long-term political developments. Ironically, the discussion reveals that the same mechanisms that reduce the number of parties and candidates in established democracies have had either no effect or the opposite effect in contemporary Russia because of the differences across political contexts.

The Impact of Rules: Defining the Costs of Entry

The starting premise for this analysis is that candidate entry reflects a benefit/cost decision, where a would-be candidate compares the discounted benefits of running for office (the probability of winning multiplied by the benefits) minus the costs (fixed costs of obtaining ballot access, resignation of an existing elected office, time, money, the consequences for future campaigns). The discussion is organized in terms of defining these costs and benefits and the factors that might distort or skew candidates' perceptions of this cost/benefit calculation.

Comparative research demonstrates that institutions and, in particular, electoral laws influence candidate entry patterns in two ways. Electoral regulations (for example, ballot access requirements) establish the fixed costs of candidate entry. They also have important indirect effects on candidates' decisions because they provide information about a candidate's probability of winning office. As most discussions of institutional effects demonstrate, the devil is in the details. Minor changes in the rules governing elections can have profound effects on potential candidates' cost/benefit calculations and dramatically alter patterns of candidate entry. In particular, Russia's relatively complex electoral rules demand significant attention to understand their impact on behavior at each phase of the electoral cycle.

The First Step: Ballot Access. The regulations governing ballot access are the first hurdle facing all contestants. These rules can be roughly divided into two categories: rules that define clear tasks for candidates to obtain ballot access, and rules that establish gatekeepers or intermediaries who exert some control over individuals' abilities to get their name on the ballot.

Most democracies place limits on citizens who are eligible for office, and the postcommunist cases are no exception. The Russian electoral law mandates that all candidates must be a citizen of the Federation and at least twenty-one years old on voting day. Many countries, including Hungary, also add residency requirements to this initial screen. Russia, Ukraine, and Lithuania do not. Potential candidates who make it through these filters then face a second layer of regulation that sets the requirements or threshold for nomination.

In Russia, until 1999 all candidates running in a single-member district, regardless of whether or not they affiliated with a political party, needed to collect signatures from 1 percent of the voters in the district. Using force or bribery to obtain signatures was strictly prohibited but also extremely common. College students frequently were paid to collect signatures, often offering small bribes to signatories. In 1993, the going rate for a signature in Saratov was about $1.00. For new voters, the price was lower. The son of a local historian reported that his classmate brought candy and cigarettes into his classes to collect signatures on behalf of his father, a prominent candidate for the Democratic Russia organization.

Since Russia's electoral law did not mandate party membership for candidates to run in a nominal district, party organizations did not have a formal role in controlling entry for those races. Even so, the signature regulations presented an advantage to party organizations and partisan candidates. Party-sponsored candidates who collected signatures to run in a single-member district could count those signatures toward the fulfillment of the requirement for the national list. Likewise, the party could allocate signatures collected in support of the list to individual candidates. For candidates who lacked resources to collect signatures, this provision provided an opportunity to piggyback onto signatures collected on behalf of the party. A Moscow-based party, even one without a stable local following, became an important tool for regional candidates who lacked the resources to obtain ballot access on their own. The ability of party organizations to allocate signatures across their candidate slates is one of the very few formal links between the district and list races in Russia. More importantly for the study of entry decisions, this rule provides the first clue about how the electoral system promotes entry in district races. In effect, some would-be partisan candidates did not have to worry about (or pay for) collecting signatures for their candidacy in a district race, removing a significant roadblock to their candidacy.

In contrast to the district races, the list race did give parties a potential gatekeeping role, since only party-sanctioned candidates could run on the list. The rules governing access to the national list race were not onerous. Parties needed to collect two hundred thousand signatures in no less than fifteen oblasts of the Russian Federation, with no more than 7 percent of the signatures collected in the same region.[3] These requirements made it virtually impossible for regional parties to run candidates in the national list race. In 1999, the law was altered to allow parties to pay a refundable deposit to gain ballot access. The deposit was forfeited if the party failed to garner 3 percent of the list vote. About half of the parties that registered in 1999 did so by paying the fee, and even more did so in 2003. These new regulations were designed to enhance the formal barriers to the party ballot and to diminish the number of contestants while still retaining the advantage for governing parties. As the earlier data suggest, these efforts were only partly successful. In 1999, the Ministry of Justice registered approximately two

---

[3] This requirement changed over time. In 1993, parties could collect no more than 15 percent of all signatures from a single region.

hundred organizations. Of these, twenty-six made it on to the ballot.[4] In the lead-up to the 2003 elections, a new law on political parties established even more stringent controls over party registration but failed to reduce the number of competing parties significantly.

On the whole, while the formal barriers to entry have discouraged some contestants, most candidates and parties find them to be a nuisance but not a deterrent. The formal barriers to entry in Russia do not seem to raise the cost of competition significantly; in fact, in some ways they actually reduce these costs. For example, the barriers make it easier for parties to transfer signatures. Still, a full explanation of the proliferation of candidates in Russian elections requires a move beyond the basic legal requirements.

The Effects of Electoral Rules: Russia's Unlinked Mixed System. Russia's mixed electoral system multiplies the number of candidates who run for office in a number of different ways. While there is little formal linkage between the district and list races, there are many potential informal ties, generating interactive or contamination effects across the races. Parties interested in maximizing their representation in the Duma have a strong incentive to recruit candidates for as many district races as possible. If even a fraction of the parties that gain ballot access in the PR race recruit candidates in single-member districts, the result will be a multiplicity of candidates in these races. Moreover, parties faced strong incentives to stand candidates in districts where there was already stiff competition. John Ishiyama observed, "Parties nominated candidates not in more populous districts, but in districts where the electoral threshold was lowered by the presence of a large number of candidates" (2001: 406). The mechanism driving this counterintuitive behavior is simple. Each additional candidate who enters a district race will receive some proportion of the vote, driving down the electoral threshold and increasing the incentive for other candidates to enter. Moreover, the declining threshold acts as a catalyst for entry by other independent candidates with some personal vote, since they may believe that they will attract enough support to secure office.

---

[4] The trend in shaping the law to restrict party participation in elections continued in the 2001 revisions, which required parties to have organizations and a significant number of members in more than half of the regions in Russia (that is, more than forty-five of the regions).

In addition, the national list race provides strong incentives for parties to spread out across the ideological space in order to define their constituencies and win support. Insofar as these parties place candidates who share their platforms, they generate inducements for other candidates to enter and spread themselves across the ideological spectrum. Again, this mechanism generates incentives for entry far beyond Duverger's predictions. This finding is not unique to Russia. Large numbers of candidates continue to compete in other mixed systems, including Lithuania, Ukraine, Hungary, Kazakhstan, and Armenia.[5]

These effects are magnified by the lack of a replacement mechanism in Russia's electoral law. While many mixed electoral systems allocate seats based on the proportion of votes received in the PR race, in Russia the total number of seats awarded to a particular electoral coalition is additive – seats won in SMD plus seats won in PR. This mechanism provides incentives for party leaders to recruit local candidates in order to put a local face on parties emanating from Moscow and to maximize their electoral gains. Many of these candidates run in both the PR and plurality races despite their poor chances of winning office in either race. The entry of new candidates decreases the electoral threshold, further stimulating entry.

Party Organizations and Candidate Recruitment. Russia's mixed system defines parties as the path to ballot access in the party list race. In established democracies, political parties function as gatekeepers, decreasing the number of candidates running for each parliamentary seat. However, if the party system is fragmented, volatile, or underinstitutionalized, as in Russia, the opposite situation can occur. Party organizations may increase the number of contestants by playing a strong role in recruiting contestants. There is some evidence that Russian parties influence candidacy decisions in this way, as shown in Table 4.4.

Candidates report that party leaders actively recruit contestants and that the party organizations provide enticements to some candidates in the form of party resources. Not all parties are created equal in this regard. A relatively small number of candidates stated that they joined the party because of the value of the party's label or material resources. Slightly more claim to

---

[5] For an excellent detailed discussion of the interaction between district and national list races in the Hungarian case, see Kenneth Benoit, "Evaluating Hungary's Mixed Member Electoral System," unpublished manuscript, 1998, http://www.politics.tcd.ie/kbenoit/papers.html, accessed September 15, 2004. For a comparative discussion, see Ferrara and Herron 2003.

Many Candidates, Few Choices

Table 4.4. *Why Did Candidates Join Parties, 1999*

Reason	Pct. Mentioned
Party leaders recruited	42.7% (91)
Wanted to run on party list	21.1% (45)
Wanted party support in SMD race	17.8% (38)
Party was popular in my district	19.2% (41)
Party could give material and financial support	17.8% (38)

Source: Candidate survey conducted by the author. Percentages reflect partisans only (N = 213).

Table 4.5. *Party Recruitment of SMD Candidates in the 1999 and 2003 Election*

	1999		2003	
Party	Total Candidates	Pct. Seats Contested	Total Candidates	Pct. Seats Contested
FAR	91	41	–	–
KPRF	67	30	171	76
LDPR	94	32	173	77
Motherland	–	–	49	22
SPS	66	29	90	40
Unity/United Russia	31	13	135	60
Yabloko	113	50	89	40

Source: Compiled from Central Electoral Commission data at www.fci.ru/gd99/spiski/spiski.htm and http://gd2003.cikrf.ru.

have wanted the party support to get on the ballot, either on the list or in a district. Often Russian candidates shop around and even compete for party mandates based on the party's resources. In sum, while it is true that parties shaped some entry decisions, it is clear that they have not played a decisive or even primary role in many cases. Table 4.5 provides some confirming evidence for this assertion. The table shows the total number of candidates recruited by each political party that won seats in the Duma in the 1999 and 2003 elections.

No party competed in all 225 districts, with percentages typically in the 30–50 percent range. In other words, for all the recruiting parties do, their efforts or enticements are not sufficient to produce a complete nationwide slate. In some cases, multiple candidates ran in district races under the same party banner. Michael McFaul (1998) reports that in 1993, conflicts between the national and regional organization of Democratic Choice of Russia produced two party-sponsored candidates in one district. The majority of independent candidates surveyed report being supported by a party, even when these organizations had their own candidate running in the district. Almost 30 percent reported being aided by two or more party organizations. These data suggest that uncertainty about candidate viability prompted regional party leaders to hedge their bets rather than commit to a single contestant. This description of problematic coordination was accurate in the case of a prominent national politician who ran as a Yabloko candidate. During my interview with the head of the Democratic Choice of Russia regional office, the candidate's campaign manager came in to pick up a thick envelope that the party leaders said was "help for a friend." This type of covert support encouraged multiple entries in each district.

Ishiyama (1999, 2000, and 2001) shows that Russian parties clearly have very different abilities to recruit and back candidates. The evidence in Tables 4.4 and 4.5 confirms this finding, showing that even the established parties' capacities to recruit candidates can rise and fall over time. With the exception of Yabloko, an organization that was beset with a poor performance in 1999 and the loss of its patron, Yukos CEO Mikhail Khordorkovsky, on corruption charges, all other organizations that won seats in 1999 increased their capacity to field nominal district candidates in the 2003 election.

While parties do seem to be playing an increasing role in candidate recruitment, the large number of parties competing in Russia cannot fully account for the excess of candidates willing to compete for each parliamentary seat. For one thing, independent candidates clearly fall outside of party influence. In addition, it is not clear that candidates who compete in party lists are enticed by parties; likewise, if the causality runs in the other direction, it is unclear that parties function as vehicles for ambitious candidates. Finally, it is important to note that these parties themselves rely on the willingness of a very large number of candidates even though they have little chance of being elected. The challenge, then, is to identify when parties do influence entry, but also to account for the other factors that influence entry decisions.

The Role of Alternative Gatekeepers. Non-partisan gatekeepers – social organizations, individuals, and politicized groups – also play important roles in candidates' entry decisions. A number of gatekeepers emerged in the post-Soviet environment, from financial industrial groups to powerful political actors.[6] These gatekeepers often pit regional and national political forces against each other for control of national policy.

This section offers an analysis of the role that two competing sets of regional gatekeepers play in Russian elections. The first is an analysis of the power of rural elites. It is widely believed that a legacy of the Soviet system was that rural elites had disproportionate influence in shaping vote choices. Consistent with this belief, rural regions would be more likely to have fewer candidates than urban regions. This impulse can be measured by looking at the relationship between rural population and the candidate pool. The second set of propositions center on the role of the regional governor. The expectation is that the more powerful the regional governor, the greater his or her ability to constrain candidate entry.

A full test of these propositions demands district-level data, including information on socioeconomic conditions, the reach of regional networks, and the nature of political competition. Such data are not available. However, preliminary tests can be conducted using oblast or regional-level data, and examining the average number of candidates in each district in the oblast as a dependent variable. The urban–rural cleavage can be measured with the percent of rural population. A measure of gubernatorial strength is the percent of votes he or she received in the first round of the most recent election. Other variables (the average number of candidates in the last election across districts in the region, and the average winning candidates' victory margins) are included as controls. The results are reported in Table 4.6.

The parameters highlight the importance of strong governors in reducing candidate entry in 1999. However, the rural nature of an oblast has little impact on candidate entry. The control variables also provide insight into entry decisions. The results indicate that the closer the previous races, the greater the number of candidates who will contest the next election. The same relationship holds for the average number of candidates in the last election. These findings underscore the potentially powerful role that regional elites can exert on national politics, supporting the strands of the recruitment literature that look beyond political parties to other

---

[6] For an alternative discussion of party substitutes, see Hale forthcoming.

Table 4.6. *The Effects of Alternative Resources on Candidate Entry, 1999*

Variables	Parameter
Constant	9.9*
	(1.2)
N of Candidates in the Last Election	.244*
	(.048)
Vote Margin	−.60*
	(.016)
Strength of Governor	−.047*
	(.011)
Percent of Rural Population	−.005
	(.016)
Russian Region	.766
	(.634)
N	89
R^2	.313

* = $p < .10$, ** = $p < 05$, *** = $p < .01$.
Source: Candidate survey conducted by the author.

gatekeepers in order to understand candidate participation in national legislative elections.

Again, Saratov's district 156 illustrates the political struggles between regional and central powers that go on around candidate entry. In 1999, the governor, Dmitry Ayatskov, was a lightening rod for candidates. Vyacheslav Mal'tsev, a regional Duma deputy and former State Duma candidate, ran as the leader of the local electoral bloc "Foundation for the Struggle Against Ayatskov." His campaign slogan, "Down with Ayatskov," won him a pair of human ears delivered to his doorstep with a threatening note. In 2000, the Communist Rashkin mounted an unsuccessful challenge against Ayatskov, and later brought a case against the governor charging him with improper involvement in business. The case failed. Ayatskov's former protégé and deputy governor, Aleksander Paradiz, lost the governor's support during the campaign. Still other candidates had close ties to the governor. Yury Usynin, an Our Home Is Russia candidate, was a leader in the regional organization of the retired officers union that had been key to Ayatskov's success in 1993. Spartak Tonakanyan had been Ayatskov's insurance candidate in the 2000 election. His presence as a nominal opponent in the election was required to ensure the election would be validated even if all other candidates withdrew from the race.

Many Candidates, Few Choices

Between 1999 and 2003, President Putin's Kremlin waged a struggle to undermine the role of alternative gatekeepers at the national and regional levels. He exiled or jailed oligarchs who dared to enter the political fray. He stripped regional governors of their roles in the upper house of parliament, installed presidential representatives in the regions to monitor governors, and coerced them into joining the party of power, United Russia. This power transfer intensified after the 2003 elections as Putin proposed to abolish gubernatorial elections. All of these efforts shifted power away from regional governors and back to the central state. As the governors' powers decreased, their role as gatekeepers also decreased. This argument is consistent with the fall in the number of district candidates, and in particular the number of independent candidates in the nominal districts over time.

In sum, while the formal barriers to entry have discouraged some contestants, by and large candidates and parties find them to be a nuisance but not a deterrent. These barriers do not seem to raise the cost of competition significantly; in fact, in some ways they may actually reduce these costs. For example the barriers may make it easier for parties to transfer signatures and recruit candidates. Other institutional features, such as political parties and alternative gatekeepers, actually increase, rather than deter, candidate entry. Still, a full explanation of the proliferation of candidates in Russian elections requires a move beyond the basic institutional requirements to consider the incentives facing individual candidates to cooperate and coordinate their behavior. The next section examines the factors that influence candidates' perceptions of their capacity to win office or, more correctly, the factors that distort their perceptions of their chances of winning office and alter the cost/benefit analysis.

Assessing the Likelihood of Success: Institutions and Context

A second element in candidates' decisions to run for office is their capacity to assess the probability of success. In the Western context, we expect that hopeless candidates are unwilling to incur the considerable costs of running in the face of dismal prospects of winning. In Russia, we see large numbers of seemingly hopeless candidates competing for office. Many of these candidates enter the race with very few resources and little political reputation. A significant number get painfully few votes. Clearly, the relatively low cost of running for national parliamentary office offsets the low probability of obtaining benefits for many candidates, but this explanation is not complete or satisfactory. Indeed, a number of features of the Russian context interact with the institutional structure to lead potential candidates to imprecise assessments of their electoral potential. This section explores the impact of a key factor, information, on entry decisions.

Assessments about the viability of candidates and the resulting cost/benefit calculations are much easier in America and other established democracies, where political elites have a good sense of what sorts of characteristics and issue positions translate into voter support in different states or districts. In contrast, in transitional systems such as Russia, there is considerable uncertainty over what constitutes a viable candidate or platform. The effect is to make candidates who are very electable doubt their chances of winning, and make unelectable candidates inflate their own vote-getting capacities. To explore these processes, this section focuses on the sources of candidate information such as election rules, parties, and incumbency, and explores how they encourage entry.

Electoral Systems and the Probability of Success

Electoral rules provide candidates and parties with important information about the numbers of votes they need to win office. The rules define the electoral threshold or the numbers of votes that each contestant must obtain to win a seat in parliament. The effects of electoral systems are codified under Duverger's Law. Not surprisingly, much of the subsequent work in this area examined cases where the number of contestants violates this empirical regularity. To explain these deviant cases, scholars focused on the two mechanisms specified by Duverger (Cox 1997; Lijphart 1995; Rae 1967; Riker 1982; Taagepera 1998; Taagapera and Shugart 1989):

- A *mechanical effect*, where the incentive of parties or candidates to enter electoral competition decreases as a function of the electoral threshold. The threshold decreases as the number of seats at stake increases (one in a single-member district race, more than one in a multimember district or list race), and decreases as the number of candidates who enter the race increases.
- A *psychological effect*, where the probability of a candidate winning an election influences the willingness of supporters to vote for the candidate. As the probability of success decreases, voters are likely to engage in strategic voting – switch to a candidate who they like less, but who has a better chance of winning.

While the proliferation of political parties in Russia's list race does not strictly defy expectations derived from Duverger's observations, it seems clear that these effects did not operate as expected. Even in the party list, the relatively high 5 percent electoral threshold did not deter party entry or encourage mergers. As Table 4.1 indicates, many parties contested each election even though few were able to surpass the threshold. The levels of wasted votes – votes cast for parties that did not win seats in the list race – were extremely high. In 1995, 50 percent of voters supported parties that did not win seats in the list race. In 1999, even with the Kremlin-backed party, United Russia, in the race, 36 percent of voters supported a party that did not make it over the threshold. In the district races, candidate behavior also defied Duverger's expectations, since the average number of candidates in each district never fell below eleven contestants.[7]

Why did the mechanical and psychological effects fail to operate in Russia? As noted earlier, the mixed system provides incentives to parties and candidates that increase the numbers of contestants in each race. The lack of a stable party system also decreased the availability of reliable information and generated overly optimistic expectations of success in both races, thereby stimulating entry. The powerful presidential system and the timing of parliamentary and presidential elections encouraged party leaders to try to build organizations in order to capture executive office. Olga Shvetsova (2004) characterized the Duma race as a presidential primary in which ambitious candidates form parties to demonstrate their voter support, precluding cooperation among party leaders. These incentives, combined with the incentives inherent in the mixed system, contributed to entry of many parties in each contest.

The Lack of a Stable Party System. Duverger's initial analysis, as well as work that builds on his prediction, are united in their expectation that politicians operate in the context of a stable party system, where the value of a party's endorsement and electoral resources is both substantial and well-known to all, and where an independent candidacy or affiliation with a new organization carries significant risks, as it forces a candidate to forego the benefits of a party's brand name and a position within the organization.

---

[7] The large number of parties competing in Russia's national district does not strictly violate Duverger's Law; as Gary Cox (1997) points out, the mechanisms that underlie the law do not create an upper limit on the number of organizations in proportional representation party systems. Even so, it is important to note that the presence of districted seats in Russia has not counteracted the tendency of proportional systems to yield a multiparty system.

The absence of a stable party system in Russia and other transitional systems has two implications for candidacy decisions. The first is that the presence of an endorsed candidate in a district race generally does not deter entry by other candidates, since the value of the endorsement is unclear. Moreover, without stable parties, no actor in the political process can play the role of guarantor to enable bargains among contestants to limit entry. Similarly, the absence of strong parties means that candidates are free to choose their campaign strategies, which in turn encourages entry, as candidates can match district preferences rather than being forced to campaign on their party's platform as they typically do in established systems. Without these incentives, it is no surprise that many candidates enter electoral competition. In general, theories of information and politics predict that uncertainty will preclude actors from taking action. However, in the Russian electoral arena, the lack of good information about candidate viability has the opposite effect – it increases the number of candidates who compete for every seat in the Duma.

Saratov's central district again illustrates the point that voter support for candidates was highly contingent on the composition of the candidate pool and not party loyalties. No incumbent managed to hold the district for more than one term. In 1995, General Boris Gromov ousted the KPRF representative Anatoly Gordeev. In 1999, Gromov did not stand for reelection and the seat reverted back to a local KPRF leader, Rashkin. By 2003, Tretyak traded on his hockey fame to wrest the seat from Rashkin.

However, it is important to note that the 2003 contest brought about a critical new development. Since 1993, Russian elections have been influenced to some extent by the presence of a party of power, an organization backed by the Kremlin and dependent almost entirely on state resources to mount a campaign. In the first three elections, the parties of power had little effect on candidate entry patterns beyond adding their own candidates to the mix. This trend shifted in 2003, when between 1999 and 2003 President Putin used state resources, institutional changes, and his own reputation to shore up the United Russia organization and diminish the role of the opposition. The overwhelming show of force of the party of power prior to the 2003 campaign period appears to have decreased the number of independent candidates in nominal districts, although it did not have the same effect on partisan candidates. Since 2003, the growing Kremlin control over resources and ballot access, along with dramatically diminished opposition, should greatly increase the future power of the United Russia organization to control ballot access. In particular, new regulations limiting party formation, registration, and entry will enhance the Kremlin's ability to limit electoral competition.

Voter Uncertainty. Duverger's psychological effect, or strategic voting, describes voters' responses to the probability that a candidate or party will win office. The expectation is that rather than waste their votes on a sympathetic but hopeless contestant, voters will choose the candidate who is closest to their own positions and who has a good chance of winning office. Anticipating this behavior, candidates whose chances of winning are relatively poor will either withdraw from the race or not enter in the first place. The result is a winnowing of candidates in a district race to exactly two contestants under plurality rules.

When applied to Russian elections and other cases of transition, a critical problem emerges: to motivate strategic voting, candidates and voters need to have shared beliefs about both the positions and viability of different candidates. Otherwise, voters cannot be sure how to cast their strategic votes, and candidates have little incentive to withdraw in anticipation of voters' decisions. As discussed in Chapter 3, uncertainty is a fact of life for the participants in transitional elections and especially in Russia. In a situation where candidates have difficulty assessing voter demands, where voters know little about candidates' viability or expected behavior in office, it seems unrealistic to assume widespread strategic voting.

Absent a strong party system, voters must find alternative signals about the viability of different contestants in order to engage in strategic voting. Elite strategies (endorsements, allocations of campaign funds) play an important role in activating strategic behavior. However, as later chapters will show, parties and other political organizations in Russia do not always engage in these activities, further complicating the task facing the electorate. On the whole, the lack of a stable, institutionalized party system that provides voters with clear signals about candidate viability makes it extremely difficult for Duverger's mechanisms to operate.

In sum, Russia's electoral laws, combined with uncertainty about voters' preferences and weak party organizations, encourage candidate entry above the effects of pure proportional representation and plurality systems. Parties have strong incentives to recruit candidates to participate in single-member district races as a way of promoting the party with a local face, developing local organizations, and increasing the size of a parliamentary delegation. Entry requirements that double-count signatures collected for candidates and parties give would-be partisan candidates a strong incentive to enter. At the same time, these candidates are then included in the national and regional party lists, changing the face of the party in the proportional representation race. The dual-market nature of mixed systems underscores the interdependence of the two races and undermines the mechanisms that might produce outcomes consistent with Duverger's hypotheses. The effects of these mechanisms are reinforced by the pervasive uncertainty that exists in all transitional democracies, Russia included. The result is an electoral system that does not deter, and to a large extent encourages, candidate entry.

Stocking the Pool: Defining the Benefits of Candidacy

All theories of candidate entry decisions center on two broad factors: the incentives or constraints present in the political system and the candidate's own response to those incentives. In the institutional theories previously outlined, electoral institutions define the incentives and candidates' or parties' responses are largely driven by their desire to win office or to maximize the number of party seats in parliament. Following this logic, the literature on political ambition attacks the broad question of why some candidates run at specific times and for specific offices (Black 1972; Canon 1990; Fowler 1989; Rohde 1979; Schlesinger 1966).

Ambition theories generally focus on candidates' desires to move up the ladder of political office. As discussed in Chapter 3, the goals held by Russian politicians are considerably more variegated. Many candidates ran for office in pursuit of perks – access to cars, offices, apartments in Moscow, or a government job. The potential benefits of office also extended beyond the Duma. Since the mid-1990s, Yeltsin and Putin have recruited professionalized representatives from legislative bodies into appointed positions in their ministries. An excellent example on the federal level is the career of Alexander Pochinok, a State Duma deputy elected from Chelyabinsk, then plucked from the legislature to serve as a deputy prime minister under Yeltsin, next as head of the tax collection agency, and finally as the equivalent of secretary of labor under Putin. In all, the Central Election Commission web site reported in 1999 that about 5 percent of Duma deputies were recruited into the executive branch. Other deputies secured permanent positions within the Duma apparatus. These examples hint at a second, bureaucratic career track that is available to some ambitious officials, removing them from electoral competition and complicating any definition of career ladders.

Many Candidates, Few Choices

Still, not all Russian candidates are motivated by their quest for office. The survey responses shown in Chapter 3 demonstrate that Russian candidates hold a wide range of policy goals, from pro- and anti-reform goals to pursuit of regional policies and, for some, the building of political parties. This wide range of goals explains why some candidates run even if they are sure that they will not win the seat. For example, in 1993, a number of candidates ran in Saratov, to prevent the Russia's Choice candidate from winning office, arguing that the race was not about policy but about power. An environmental candidate in Chelyabinsk ran to call attention to the lingering effects of nuclear accidents in the oblast. A successful regional official in Perm ran because she believed her expertise in the pension system could further benefit pension reform. Others ran because their bosses ordered them to do so.

A second element of the ambition literature is the assumption of a predictable career track through increasingly powerful offices. In Russia, the career track reverses the pattern observed in the United States. Throughout interviews in 1993, 1995, and 1999, candidates spoke of using the national elections to position themselves for upcoming regional elections. A quick comparison of lists of candidates who ran in 1993 and the current composition of regional legislatures in the case study regions today suggests that this strategy was effective, as many of these individuals do hold office in the regional legislature.

Again, Saratov's central district illustrates this trend. In 1993, a number of candidates ran for office in order to build constituency bases for the upcoming regional legislative elections. By 2003, the region's overbearing governor, Dmitry Ayatksov, was exiting office having lost the favor of the Putin regime. As a result, a number of candidates competed in Duma elections to build their campaign organizations and reputations for the gubernatorial race. This strategy did not always work. Dmitry Udalov's scant 4 percent of the vote demolished his status as gubernatorial front-runner. The LDPR candidate, Alexei Chernyshev, a close confidant of Vladimir Zhirinovsky, also stated his intent to run for governor. He won less than 2 percent of the vote in the Duma race but received a seat via the LDPR party list.

David Canon's (1990) work on political amateurs in the United States speaks to the large numbers of hopeless candidates who run in every race. Amateurs are candidates who have no previous political experience. Such amateurs frequently run for seats in the U.S. House of Representatives even though the chances of winning are quite low, such as in a contest against an entrenched, popular, and well-financed incumbent. Canon argues that these decisions are in no way irrational, but in fact reflect a keen appreciation of the circumstances faced by the typical amateur. Since these candidates do not hold an elected office and typically do not spend much of their own money on a campaign, they have little to lose by running against an incumbent. And while their chances of winning are small, they are not zero.

Many candidates in Russia look a lot like Canon's amateurs. In district 156, amateurs ranged from the hockey standout, Tretyak, to the head of the region's dog lovers' organization. The chances of these candidates winning office varied widely depending on their personal qualifications but also on the characteristics of their race, such as how many other candidates entered. In Tretyak's case, for example, the odds of winning were quite good but by no means certain. Even for candidates who thought they had little chance of winning, the reality of Russia's democratic transition gave them an additional reason to run. If they waited and ran in a future election – when parties are stronger or candidates have a better idea of which appeals work best in different districts – they would likely be denied ballot access or lose to a well-financed professional politician. Their chances of winning in an early election might not be good, but they are as good as they will ever get.

At the opposite end of the spectrum, the late Soviet period produced myriad incumbents from defunct legislatures. In his election-led reforms, Mikhail Gorbachev initiated three levels of legislative structures: two Congresses of Peoples Deputies, at the All-Union and Russian Federation levels as well as regional-level soviets. The All-Union Congress died with the Soviet Union, and Yeltsin abolished the latter two levels of legislative structures after the legislative standoff in late summer 1993. These changes left innumerable unemployed incumbents, all of whom had some political experience and a claim to a constituency. These candidates added to the ranks of the candidate pool in the early years of Russian democracy. Rashkin, the KPRF candidate previously mentioned, is a good example of a Duma candidate whose career began in the 1990 regional legislature. A number of candidates in Rashkin's district had run unsuccessfully for State Duma seats. Still others had lost races for seats in the regional Duma. In all, the political career ladder in Russia remains unclear. The increasing role of the party of power, United Russia, is likely to be a stabilizing force, and few credible candidates will be willing to challenge the party.

Many Candidates, Few Choices

		Candidate 2	
		Run	Withdraw
Candidate 1	Withdraw	Candidate 2 Wins (2,2)	Candidate 3 Wins (0,0)
	Run	Candidate 3 Wins (0,0)	Candidate 1 Wins (2,2)

Figure 4.1. Strategic Withdrawal as a Simple Coordination Game

The Last Chance for Coordination: Strategic Withdrawal

Until this point, the analysis has shown that both the institutions and circumstances of Russian elections operate to drive would-be candidates toward entry into the political process. Put another way, the findings imply that any restraint on candidate entry would come from the candidates themselves or the institutions that govern candidate entry. It is also possible that the candidate pool could be shaped by interactions between different candidates or party organizations. For example, strategic withdrawal or the exit of one candidate in favor of another may occur through coordination after candidates acquire new information about their viability either because the full roster of opponents is revealed or voters' preferences become clear as a result of campaigning. Strategic withdrawal might also occur if two candidates have similar policy goals that would be equally well served by the election of either candidate. Intuitively, this argument suggests that some candidates would be driven to strategic withdrawal, dropping out of the campaign in order to aid in the election of a colleague from the same party, or a candidate with similar policy concerns.

Much of the evidence already presented, ranging from high rates of entry and the presence of multiple candidates from the same party in district races, suggests that there is very little strategic withdrawal in Russia. Why? This section offers a series of simple game-theoretic models to illustrate how information and its alter ego, uncertainty, influence the propensity of candidates to coordinate their candidacy decisions.

The conventional wisdom about strategic withdrawal is captured by a coordination game that describes the effect of interaction between three candidates for the same legislative seat. Candidates one and two hold similar policy goals, goals that are different from those held by candidate three. This game is depicted in Figure 4.1.

Candidate Strategies and Electoral Competition

This situation presents candidates one and two with the following choice: If only one of them runs, that candidate will win, but if they both run, candidate three will win. (The payoffs in each cell reflect this situation, with the first giving candidate one's payoff, and the second giving candidate two's payoff.) Put another way, the candidates have a strong incentive to coordinate their behavior, making a deal that requires one of them to withdraw from the race, or not run in the first place. For example, if players one and two represent Yabloko and the Union of Right Forces (SPS) – both right-leaning parties – one of the candidates might agree to withdraw in order to ensure that they don't split the right vote and cause a left candidate, a representative of the KPRF, player three, to win office.

Using this simple game to explain coordination in Russian politics raises two problems. First of all, the game's predictions do not match reality – strategic withdrawal was not widespread in Russian elections even in 2003. While stories of coordination among candidates and parties abound, there is little systematic evidence of coordination. Very few candidates withdraw from competition during the course of the campaign and most of the withdrawals come on the party list side of the race.

Second and more fundamentally, the structure of the game fails to capture two important factors highlighted in the previous discussion. One is that candidates in Russia and other transitional systems may lack the information necessary for coordination. Even late in the election cycle, candidates may be unsure of their own support and their opponent's support. They may not know if their withdrawal would shift enough support to guarantee victory to a like-minded colleague. These uncertainties could easily lead candidates to ignore the possibility of coordination, even if their actions throw the election to a candidate whose election they oppose.

The evidence presented earlier in this chapter suggests that strategic withdrawal is rare because candidates hold very different views of their own viability. They interpret any new information through those lenses, often reasoning to conclusions very different from those of their competitors in the same district. An extremely dramatic illustration of this effect occurred in the Engles district of Saratov in the 1993 contest. Late in the campaign, a poll administered by the independent candidate on the democratic side showed that Nikolai Lysenko, the nationalist candidate, would most likely win the election, the option least preferred by all other candidates. The Yabloko organization led a campaign to have all candidates withdraw in order to nullify the race. The KPRF candidate, Oleg Mironov, refused, both because he did not believe the poll data but also because he felt his

Many Candidates, Few Choices

		SPS Candidate	
		Run	Withdraw
Yabloko Candidate	Withdraw	SPS Candidate Wins (1,2)	KPRF Candidate Wins (0,0)
	Run	KPRF Candidate Wins (0,0)	Yabloko Candidate Wins (2,1)

Figure 4.2. Strategic Withdrawal as a Costly Coordination Game

own career and party-building efforts, as well as the democratic process, would be undermined by mass withdrawal.[8] Mironov may have been right. He lost the nominal race to Lysenko but won a seat in the Duma on the KPRF list and subsequently captured the district seat in 1995.

The second factor omitted from the game depicted in Figure 4.1 is that even if two candidates agree on the desirability of strategic withdrawal in the abstract, they may disagree about which of them should drop out. In substantive terms, while the Yabloko and SPS candidate agree that it would be good to ensure the defeat of the KPRF candidate, each may prefer that the other drops out, even if their policy goals are similar or even the same. Why? Each candidate may want to be elected in order to further his or her political career, to help build his or her party organization, or to gain the material benefits of office. While these complications do not make coordination impossible, they create a new strategic situation, as depicted in Figure 4.2.

In this game, candidates have preferences both for what type of candidate wins and also for which candidate wins – in effect, each is rooting for himself or herself. In this kind of costly coordination game, full information is not sufficient for coordination because the players disagree on which mode of coordination is preferable. There are two outcomes where coordination occurs, but clearly the SPS candidate prefers the top-left outcome while the Yabloko candidate prefers the bottom-right.

Figure 4.2 shows that a failure to account for political ambition or other political goals can easily lead analysts to overstate the potential for coordination among candidates and voters. Elections are not just about the selection of policy bundles; they are also about the identity of the victors. Candidates typically have strong preferences over both factors. In established democracies, where electoral infrastructure – party organizations and brand labels,

---
[8] Interview with Mironov in his Duma office, January 1996.

candidates' reputations, and viability assessments – exists, this coordination problem is much less likely to arise. One candidate's advantage based on any of these factors is likely to discourage like-minded opponents from running in the first place. In transitional systems such as Russia, these signals do not generally exist. As a result, candidates face the problem of costly coordination with the very real potential that their failure to coordinate will lead to their mutual defeat and the election of a candidate whose goals are antithetical to their own.

These examples indicate the dilemmas facing Russia's candidates and party leaders. Given uncertainty and weak parties, strategic withdrawal or, indeed, any other form of coordination is extremely unlikely. Besides the impact on election outcomes, the failure to coordinate has long-term implications, as it works against the production of other forms of electoral infrastructure. For example, strategic withdrawals that reveal the relative vote-getting power of the right versus left can lead to pre-election coalitions or party mergers in the next round. In contrast, when coordination does not occur and the field of candidates remains crowded, the information about the relative vote-getting power of any policy platform is limited, and does not promote joint efforts by like-minded candidates or party organizations.

This formal depiction of the strategic withdrawal decision could easily be applied to initial entry decisions. As the evidence shows, not all political parties have equal capacity to broker deals to limit competition in the districts. On the left, there is some evidence of agreements between the KPRF and other left parties such as the Agrarians (APR) not to run like-minded candidates against each other in nominal districts, as well as to plan joint campaign activities. Similarly, candidates of the Agrarian Party of Russia (APR) were included in the Fatherland–All Russia list in regions where there was significant support for APR candidates. In exchange, Fatherland received the support of the APR administrative and financial resources in those regions.

Right and centrist parties have been less successful in pursuing common interests than the left, where the monolithic KPRF imposed bargains on weaker organizations. In interview after interview, regional officials reported that right-leaning organizations attempted to coordinate their strategies but complained about Yabloko's unwillingness to join with them. This lack of cooperation is also seen at the national level, with prominent national consultations among these candidates breaking down before each election. After the 1999 election, Yabloko and SPS signed an agreement uniting the two organizations. The deal included the pledge to nominate a single party list and to unify the regional party branches. In reality, regional branches refused to unite, and attempts by national-level actors to encourage cooperation in the lead-up to the 2003 elections also failed.

Again, Saratov's central district illustrates the difficulty in provoking coordination in the Russian context. In 2003, the Communist incumbent, Rashkin, was challenged by a fellow Communist, Anatoly Volkov, a supermarket entrepreneur who ran as an independent. On the center-left, the gubernatorial aspirant, Dmitry Udalov, proposed a primary of sorts under the organizational banner, "United Candidate." In August 2004, Udalov's supporters organized a vote between himself, Yuzhakov, and his centrist opponent, Poleschikov. The outcome was not surprising. Udalov won and the two other candidates refused to withdraw from the race. The regional press also reported that Ayatskov pressured Udalov and Mikhail Poleschikov to withdraw in favor of Tretyak in order to ensure Rashkin's defeat. Both candidates resisted these efforts as well.

The games and the example from the district illustrate that uncertainty and strong policy or career goals can lead candidates to select strategies that maximize their own chances of winning but produce a winner who holds policy goals that are orthogonal to their own. These coordination failures speak to the ways in which the nature of the candidate pool distorts the inferences that can be drawn from election outcomes and impedes the formation of stable political parties and party coalitions as well as the representation of voters' interests.

Conclusion: Candidate Entry, Democrats, and Democracy

The argument in this chapter shows that factors that deter candidate entry in established democracies are likely to have the opposite effect in Russia and in many other cases of postcommunist transition. A simple cost/benefit calculation demonstrates that many candidates in transition have little to lose and much to gain by running for office. The cost/benefit framework also focuses attention on the factors that influence candidates' perceptions of those costs and benefits: information, electoral institutions, existing parties, alternative sources of campaign resources, and candidates' goals. These effects are magnified by the pervasive political uncertainty that is endemic to transitional democracies in general and to Russia in particular.

These findings foreshadow a result that will be repeated in subsequent chapters: Although institutional arguments provide important insights into the process of transition, they must be supplemented by contextual factors such as the Soviet legacy, the pervasive uncertainty, or the goals that motivate candidates to run for office, in order to explain candidates' choices. In the case of candidate entry, a number of factors highlighted by different approaches conspire together to perpetuate individual decisions to run for office even when there is little hope of winning.

More generally, entry decisions have a fundamental impact on electoral infrastructure. The proliferation of candidates raises the number of bargains that need to be struck to generate electoral coalitions. Organizations and candidates may see the current election as their one hope of launching into a significant role in the political arena. Further, the volatility in support of parties over the transition period makes it problematic to cut deals with parties that look strong in the election period. Any number of organizations that secured significant votes failed to survive their terms in parliament.

The large number of contestants in Russian elections also has important implications for the voters. The proliferation of messages creates a cacophony in the election period that undermines the ability of voters to assess contestants' messages. In addition, the proliferation of contestants yields an explosion of different messages and groups in government, undermining voters' abilities to assign blame for policies or for stalemate. As Cox (1997) shows, the proliferation of candidates in single-member district races makes it impossible for voters to coordinate around particular candidates. Such elections can also result in the victory of candidates with very little electoral support. Similarly, the large number of party organizations, coupled with the large number of candidates looking to run in single-member districts, creates a tendency toward party switching as candidates search for the best possible electoral vehicle.

Entry decisions also have implications for the amount of information generated by elections. Given that the typical Russian election has ten or so candidates competing for one seat, the results may say more about the vote-getting abilities of specific candidates than broad generalizations about voter preferences. As a result, contestants in the next round are on very shaky ground as they seek to strike bargains with like-minded opponents. The lack of clear information also undermines coordination and cooperation, creating a cycle in which the information about candidate viability, or even information about what candidates would do in office, is not revealed in the campaign period, leading to uncertainty being perpetuated in future rounds. This dynamic explains some of the instability in the national party system as well as why the party system has not become a focal point or impulse toward coordination for all candidates.

Many Candidates, Few Choices

This chapter also points to factors that might limit the proliferation of candidates and parties. Institutional changes that strengthen the role of parties as gatekeepers and simultaneously decrease the capacity of alternative gatekeepers should decrease the number of contestants. President Putin's proposals to replace the current electoral system with a proportional representation system are also likely to decrease the number of contestants. United Russia's growing monopoly over electoral resources is likely to preclude competition in the next rounds of elections. A political or economic crisis might also provide critical information about the efficacy of a set of actors or the probability that they can garner support in the next election. These events would have both the direct effect of influencing candidates' assessment of future vote choice and also altering candidates' strategies vis-à-vis parties by increasing the value of party brand names.

Diminishing the amount of non-party resources available to potential candidates would also decrease the number of contestants. The Putin government has taken a number of steps toward this end, most notably in its efforts to limit the power of regional governors. The decline in the availability of alternative resources also directly alters candidates' cost/benefit calculation with regard to entry. Such a decline would change the relative value of party resources for some candidates and change their relationships with the party organizations. Finally, settling the struggle over the regime or direction of reform and focusing attention on specific policy goals would also decrease the incentives for many candidates to enter.

The proliferation of candidates in Russian elections is the first step in fragmenting national and regional constituencies and thwarting electoral mechanisms of representation and accountability. Although these patterns are not fatal to successful democratic consolidation, they raise the possibility that subsequent behavior will continue to undermine the accumulation of infrastructure. The next chapter begins to explore this possibility by examining the factors that lead candidates to join political parties. The lack of investment in party organizations magnifies effects of candidate proliferation, generating a great deal of instability across electoral outcomes.

5

To Join or Not to Join

CANDIDATE AFFILIATION IN TRANSITIONAL RUSSIA

> ... As rational individuals, office seekers will put forth only as much effort [in creating party organizations] as they believe is essential to realizing their own ambitions. They will only join in creating, shaping and maintaining political organizations best suited to their purpose.
>
> Schlesinger (1994: 33)

The growing influence of President Putin's United Russia (UR) party organization marks a critical junction in post-Soviet political development. Between 1999 and 2004, UR emerged suddenly and with no structure and established itself as a dominant party organization. Increasingly, the party, orchestrated by Kremlin-based puppeteers, relies on coercion and out-of-system behavior to ensure electoral success and legislative discipline, thereby increasing the power of the executive and diminishing or eliminating political opposition. The meteoric rise of UR was impossible without the more general instability and disarray within the party system that was rooted in the very weak ties between party elites and voters, and elites and the organization, as well as the large numbers of independent candidates and incumbents who participated in elections.

Consistent with the general argument, this chapter explains the weakness of Russian political parties and the rise of UR in terms of individual candidates' strategies. The Russian electoral system presents candidates for the national legislature with an interesting and substantively important choice: Run for office under a party banner, or campaign as an independent. Candidates who choose to affiliate are faced with the additional decision of which party to join. This chapter explains candidates' affiliation decisions – whether they join, and which party they choose.

To Join or Not to Join

Why study affiliation? Given the relatively large number of Russian candidates who run and win as independents, including the majority of presidential candidates, it is important to understand the factors driving independence, and the implications of these decisions for Russia's transition. Affiliation decisions also clearly influence the accumulations of electoral infrastructure or democratic capacity as they shape the information available to voters and other candidates in elections; stabilize ties among candidates, representatives, and voters; establish venues for making policy bargains after the election; and provide safe havens for unsuccessful opposition candidates.

In terms of theory building, the fact that Russian candidates face decisions generally not faced by candidates in other countries also creates the opportunity to test fundamental assumptions about the evolution of political parties. Relaxing the assumption that candidates will inevitably join political parties raises a series of important questions. What happens in elections when affiliation is a real choice? Who affiliates, and who remains independent? Which parties do different types of candidates join? And what are the consequences of affiliation decisions for campaigns, party organizations, election outcomes, and governing?

The argument of this chapter is that the Russian electoral system acts as a sorting mechanism, pushing some candidates to affiliate and others toward independence. Consistent with the framework presented in earlier chapters, I argue that the critical factors that shape candidates' responses to the electoral structure are their goals, the availability of alternative resources, and their preexisting connections to a party or political organization. Using an expanded set of policy goals, the analysis also shows how these factors shape a candidate's decision of which party to join.

The next two sections define the dependent variable, clarifying the choices available to Russian candidates and showing their response to those choices over the course of four elections. The third section identifies factors that drive affiliation decisions and develops hypotheses for later analysis. The model is tested using logistic regression. The picture of Russian party development that emerges from the analysis is one of a fragmentary system that influences but does not control candidates' actions. This finding stands in sharp contrast to some of the voter-level analyses that conclude that party development is proceeding rapidly in Russia. The difference in these perspectives, I argue, portends very different implications for the collapse of Russia's democratic regime as it is playing out in the front pages of the *New York Times*.

Defining the Dependent Variable: Partisan or Independent Candidates

For the most part, theories of candidate affiliation with political parties describe this decision as automatic and all but inevitable. This expectation is driven by the perceived value of affiliation for achieving the candidates' goals in light of the institutional structures that govern electoral competition. Much like models of strategic voting, candidates are assumed to affiliate with the party closest to their own policy ideals that can also help them to pursue their political goals (Aldrich 1995; Kitschelt 1999). In proportional systems, where voters support party lists rather than individual candidates, candidates who want to enter electoral competition must find a party vehicle to gain ballot access. In plurality systems where candidates are not forced to affiliate, the expectation is that parties supply critical electoral resources to their candidates – a brand name to attract voter support, and material resources (money, workers, and so on) to help candidates campaign and govern effectively. Thus, either as a matter of law or practical necessity, affiliation is viewed as a non-decision.

Russia's electoral structure creates the opportunity for candidates to join a party or remain independent. Moreover, the relative weakness of Russian party organizations – in terms of their brand names, their control of electoral resources, and their lack of influence over policy making in government – means that the affiliation decision is a real choice. Some candidates may see their interests best served by joining a party, while others may be better off (in terms of winning office, protecting local interests, and so on) running as independents.

The parallel structure of Russia's law adds a layer of complexity to candidates' decisions. Because ballot access in the proportional representation race demands affiliation, candidates have an added element in their decision calculus: If they join a party, they must decide where to run (in a nominal district, on the party list, or in both races). This sequence of decisions is depicted in Figure 5.1. District selection is analyzed in the next chapter. For now, note that in addition to all of the factors already mentioned, affiliation decisions are significant in that they shape a candidate's future choice of where to run.

Do Russian candidates take advantage of their ability to run as independents? Table 5.1 reports affiliation decisions of partisans and independents in Russian elections since 1993.

To Join or Not to Join

Table 5.1. *Affiliation and Electoral Success in Russian Elections, 1993–2003 (Nominal Districts)*

Year	Number of Candidates in Nominal Districts	Percent of Independents Running
1993	2,331	37.4% (873)
1995	3,653	28.9% (1,055)
1999	2,227	50.6% (1,126)
2003	1893	35.7% (676)

Source: Official statistics.

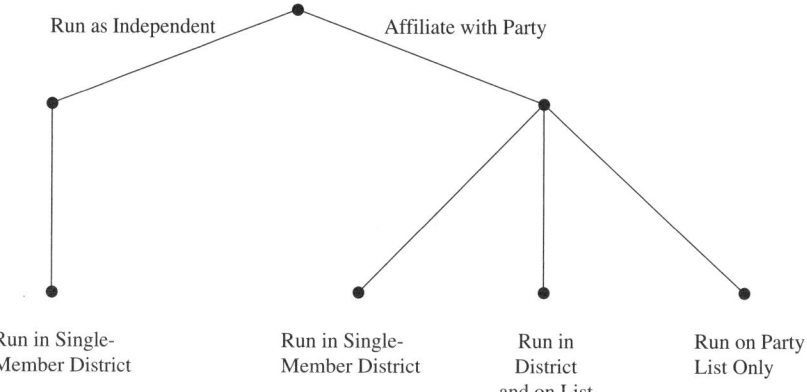

Figure 5.1. Affiliation and Its Consequences

As the table indicates, a substantial number of Russian candidates have chosen to run as independents in Duma elections, although the number of independents declined between 1999 and 2003. While the decline in the absolute number of independents is very large, the effect of this decline may have been much less significant. The success rates of independent candidates remained relatively constant, while the relative increase in success rates of partisans was quite small. These data suggest that lesser qualified independents have dropped out of competition. The evidence presents mixed messages about the counterclaim that parties are becoming more integral to the political process. On the one hand, elites are more likely to

105

join parties; on the other hand, voters still give significant support to independent candidates. Moreover, it appears that the trend is not that parties or the party system are growing in power, but rather that a single party, UR, has become essential to the political process.

As the discussion indicates, to understand the effects of affiliation decisions on the larger questions of partisan development and democratic consolidation, we must understand who these independents are and what motivates their decision to forego affiliation. For instance, if independents tend to be inexperienced candidates without significant resources, then their decisions do not deprive parties of the resources they need to contest elections. However, if candidates who run as independents possess significant resources and reputations, then the opportunity cost of these decisions for party organizations and infrastructure accumulation is quite high.

An analysis of affiliation decisions in Russia will also clarify the impact of the mixed system on the early stages of partisan development so that we can examine general theoretic predictions regarding the effects of these systems. Given the structure of the Russian electoral system, party organizations are the key coordination mechanisms across the two races. An analysis of affiliation patterns will show whether electoral competition is laying the foundation for a two-tiered, linked system of representation of constituents' interests, or whether it is producing two distinct types of candidates who behave differently in office and embody fundamentally different linkages to constituent interests.

Characterizing the Affiliation Decision

In light of the uncertainty that is endemic to transition, the affiliation choice is best viewed as a lottery. Essentially, party affiliation is a trade between the candidate and an organization. If a candidate affiliates with a party, he or she gets voter support conveyed by the party's brand name and, potentially, some material resources to support his or her campaign. In return, the candidate gives up some of his or her own resources that are invested in the collective effort of party building. These resources can be concrete – workers, office equipment, or money – or less tangible, such as a candidate's reputation, which some voters will transfer to the candidates' party. The candidate also accepts the potential of future constraint if the party is able to invoke discipline in the legislature. The threat of such discipline may limit a candidate's ability to appease constituents who oppose the party's positions or to pursue his or her career or policy goals (for a similar argument, see Ishiyama 2000).

The particulars of this lottery will vary across candidates and parties. William Bianco and John Aldrich (1992) argue that party brand names and the support – and public expectations – that they engender are critical to understanding decisions to affiliate with a party when entering politics, or to switch from one party to another.[1] Similarly, Gary Cox stresses the value of partisan endorsements as a mechanism for coordination of appeals and platforms across candidates:

> How party endorsements come to be preeminent, eclipsing endorsement by newspapers, prominent businesspersons, and so forth, is a fascinating question. My own hunch, based on a reading of the historical literature of the development of nomination procedures in the U.S., is that party nominations are constructed to be more persuasive about underlying strength in the electorate than are the endorsements that an interest group can issue (Cox 1997: 160n).

Here again, affiliation is characterized as a signal or indication to voters of what a candidate might do in office, and also how likely it is that he or she will be able to fulfill those campaign promises.[2] As a result, the willingness of candidates to affiliate with a party, as well as willingness of voters to draw inferences about candidates based on these labels, stand as important components of electoral infrastructure. In this light, the high percentage of independent candidates in Russia stands as an important indicator of low levels of electoral infrastructure.

Yet, it is clear that brand names are not the only resources that parties supply to candidates. Aldrich (1995) argues that in an era of

---

[1] While the Aldrich-Bianco (1991) model focuses on the American case, there is no reason to believe that the authors' intuition about reputations and brand names only holds when elite competition is resolved by primaries. In fact, it is even more likely that potential candidates will venue shop when closed-door meetings between national leaders are the cornerstones of nomination procedures.

[2] It is important not to overstate the significance of the party brand names. Particularly in transitional democracies, some parties may not have a coherent reputation. Moreover, a party may present clear signals about intent but an ambiguous signal about its capacity to pursue these policies in government. The value of a party's brand name will also vary across districts – a party label that attracts support in urban Moscow may have the opposite effect in a rural agricultural district. Candidates may also be unsure or mistaken about the value of a party's brand name (Gunther 1989). Finally, the idea that brand names matter does not imply that all voters view candidates exclusively through a partisan lens. As we will see later, voter evaluations can be shaped by a candidate's subsequent decisions, such as district selection or the nature of the candidate's campaign appeals.

candidate-centered elections, partisan affiliation decisions are based in the ability of the party to provide material resources and services to the candidate, both in government and in the campaign period. These services range from the assurance of effective followings going into the campaign period, to expertise, to funds to access television and other media outlets. For Russian candidates, key services may include access to television time, funds to pay workers, the printing of leaflets and posters, transportation costs, and other elements that increase name recognition.[3] As the Russian case illustrates, these resources may also be derived from coercive or extralegal action, such as the use of courts to remove viable opposition candidates, or from rent-seeking behaviors that siphon off state resources into candidates' campaign coffers.

These two types of party-based benefits suggest an important distinction among party organizations that influence candidates' affiliation decisions. The electoral value of a party's brand name is effectively a collective good: A party provides this benefit to all their candidates. Moreover, a party that attracts candidates on the basis of its brand name is then dependent on those adherents' willingness to reinvest in maintaining that label – in saying and doing things that generate and reinforce favorable perceptions of the party and its candidates. In other words, affiliation with a party that has a coherent brand name gives candidates a way to signal their preferences, campaign promises, and future behavior, and makes candidates participants in the maintenance of the label itself.

In contrast, material resources are private goods, in that a party can give different amounts to different candidates. However, it is rare that a single party has a monopoly on material resources – other parties can provide them, as well as non-party organizations and some candidates themselves.

---

[3] No doubt organizations other than parties exist in Russia and other transitional democracies that can provide these resources. The focus here on party organizations follows from the goal of explaining affiliation, and from the important role that party organizations are thought to play in the development of effective democracy. Even so, it deserves emphasis that party endorsements, whether in the form of a brand name or material resources, have qualities that are not shared by other sources. While endorsement by a newspaper or a financial industrial group can convey a sense of the candidate's priorities and capacity to act on some policy initiatives, such resources do not offer much insight into how effective the candidate might be in the national parliament – whether the candidate can carry out his or her promises. Relative to party organizations, the reputation-based resources of these organizations can be even more ambiguous, in that they can convey what a candidate wants to do, but very little about his or her capacity to fulfill these expectations if elected.

To Join or Not to Join

For example, if a candidate needs money to pay campaign workers, he or she can potentially get funds from a number of parties, from local organizations or businesses, from friends or family, or even from their own pocket.[4] With brand names, the situation is different; for example, if a candidate wants a brand label that signals his or her opposition to wholesale market reforms and the candidate's support of state management of the economy, he or she has only one good option: to affiliate with the KPRF.

More generally, the distinction between reputation-based and material resources has important implications for the kinds of candidates who will join a particular party and for the degree of discipline that a party can impose on its candidates, both during the campaign and thereafter. These implications turn the usual predictions about collective and private goods on their head. Typically, it is assumed that providers of private goods will find it easier to constrain the recipients of these benefits than providers of collective goods. After all, providers can withhold private goods from one recipient without denying them to others, while withholding collective goods from one recipient requires that all recipients be made worse off. However, this expectation does not hold for the sorts of benefits discussed here. A party that controls ballot access can deny a candidate the benefits of its brand name by refusing to allow the candidate to run on the party ticket. Put another way, while reputation-based benefits are collective, they are also excludable.

Material resources have very different properties. True, it is easy to exclude a candidate from receiving these benefits; all a party has to do is refuse to write the check or deliver the car or office equipment to the candidate's headquarters. However, a party does not have a monopoly on these resources. Regional officials, financial industry groups, personal business ties, and other interest organizations all compete with parties to support candidates. Faced with a threat of withholding resources, candidates can simply search elsewhere for an alternative supplier, whether

---

[4] One of the ways to describe the difference in Russian electoral politics before and after the 2003 elections is the near monopoly that the dominant state party, UR, has over material electoral resources. In fall 2003, opposition organizations mustered the reputation-based and tangible resources to mount campaigns, but voters swung in behind the president, providing UR with a two-thirds majority in the legislature – enough to alter the constitution. Putin has used this majority to strengthen further the position of the executive branch and the UR and to weaken all remaining opposition. Given this growing control, we would expect radically different patterns of competition in the next election cycle.

Candidate Strategies and Electoral Competition

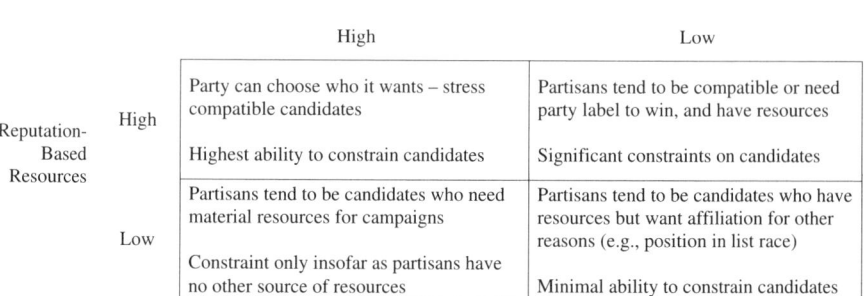

Figure 5.2. The Impact of Resources on Affiliation and Coherence

inside or outside politics. And insofar as candidates succeed, or expect that they can if necessary, the threats will have little value. The only situation where resource-based threats will be useful is with candidates who have no resources of their own and no way to get them. This discussion suggests an important distinction between party organizations in transitional democracies based on the amount and content of resources that they provide to their candidates. This distinction is codified in Figure 5.2.

As the table indicates, parties that can supply both kinds of resources are in an extremely strong position in relation to their candidates. Because of their brand name, they will attract candidates who see this reputation as electorally advantageous or who agree with the party platform. Moreover, the material resources available to these parties will attract other candidates who need these resources for their campaign. Faced with this situation, the party has the ability to pick good candidates – candidates who will help to build the brand name or who have other valuable resources. Our expectation is that parties of this sort will tend to be established organizations, who have a brand name by virtue of their past behavior and material resources or by virtue of their control of some government offices or other pieces of the state apparatus.

The combination of resources enables the party to impose constraints on its candidates, forcing them to emphasize certain issues in their campaign or to take certain actions in the legislature. Because of its strong brand name, the party tends to attract like-minded candidates, or at least candidates who tow the party line. And the supply of material resources means that the party can consider ideological purity when constructing its slate, rejecting resource-rich candidates who differ with key positions. Finally, when disagreements arise, the party can uses its resources to reward loyalty.

The KPRF is the only party that controlled high reputation-based resources and also high material resources in early Russian elections, mostly in the form of a core of activists and an extensive set of elite networks (Colton and Hough 1998; Haspel, Romington, and Smith 1998; Kitschelt and Smyth 2002). However, both types of resources are prone to sudden shifts. For example, the Kremlin's recent efforts to marginalize the KPRF Duma faction influenced voters' perceptions about the capacity of the party to fulfill campaign promises, and the value of the party's reputation fell accordingly. Subsequently, the schisms that had been evident within the organization for some time widened, and open conflict erupted among factions as the more moderate party members held a parallel party conference. Although the KPRF leadership managed to hold on to its position, it is clear that the pressures to move the party toward the center of the political space are growing stronger.

In contrast, a party that has little material resources but a well-developed reputation will tend to attract like-minded candidates, as well as candidates with personal vote resources of their own. On the one hand, these candidates have an incentive to help build the party brand name, for this is how they signal their intentions to the electorate. Moreover, given that they are like-minded, they will not often find themselves crosswise with the party platform. The problem is, given its lack of material resources, the party may have to accept resource-rich candidates who do not agree with the party platform as a way of filling out its slate across the nation. Such candidates will likely ignore attempts to constrain their behavior. The party can threaten to drop these candidates from the ticket, but only at the cost of losing resources and a good chance of winning a seat. These factors complicate the party's attempts to constrain its candidates.

While the absence of material resources may deter affiliation with these parties, it is important to note that the brand name itself will be a considerable attraction to some candidates – those who agree with the party's platform, or who believe that a substantial number of voters where they expect to run will agree as well. In this sense, Figure 5.2 provides a rationale for why some candidates affiliate with an organization that can provide little material support for their campaign. While material support is important, it is not the only resource that a party can provide, particularly in the long term.

The center-right party Yabloko is a good example of an organization with a strong brand name but a relatively small supply of material resources. The party depended almost entirely on the oligarchs for funding, and as Putin arrested or forced them into exile, those resources dried up. This party also points to the relative fragility of brand names: A party that attracts support because of its policy aims may lose support over time if it is increasingly seen as unable to influence policy outcomes. An example of this situation is the rapid decline of Fatherland–All Russia in 1999, as it became clear that neither of the party's leaders were likely to control the presidency or its vast resources. The party's vote totals fell far short of popular expectations and its remnants were quickly absorbed into the UR organization.

A party with no brand name but substantial material resources (the top-right cell in Figure 5.2) is attractive to candidates for obvious reasons: They gain resources for their campaigns without any reputational baggage. However, such a party may have only limited control over its candidates, since this control exists only as long as these candidates cannot find another way to get these resources. Thus, resource-poor candidates with weak policy goals will dominate such a party's pool. Such candidates see affiliation with the party as their only hope of waging an effective campaign. Good examples of this sort of organization are the various state parties of power, which have no strong ideology other than favoring their own control of state power, a goal that allows them to deliver material benefits to districts where the party is powerful. Insofar as these parties have any brand name at all, they are defined in terms of their leaders. For example, Democratic Choice of Russia was pro-market and pro-West as exemplified by its leader, the reform economist Yegor Gaidar, while Our Home Is Russia reflected the more moderate positions of its leader, then Prime Minister Viktor Chernomirdin. These signals were muddied by a lack of state commitment to the parties' programs. Until the rise of Unity in 1999, the lack of presidential endorsement of any particular party also cast doubt on the capacity of the organization to fulfill its promises.

Finally, parties that have neither kind of resources have little to offer candidates to accept their nomination. Perversely, candidates from these parties are likely to be either hapless amateurs with no chance of winning office or well-endowed, resource-rich candidates who can organize and fund their own campaign, and who affiliate for other reasons, such as the desire to gain power within the organization or build a national reputation by running on the party's list.

To Join or Not to Join

Predicting Affiliation: Goals, Resources, and Reputations

The argument here is that affiliation decisions – whether to affiliate, which party to affiliate with – are driven by a combination of three factors: a candidate's goals, his or her personal vote resources, and his or her reputation. These factors determine whether a candidate has any intrinsic interest in joining a party, and what sort of party he or she would want to affiliate with, insofar as the candidate is interested in affiliation at all.

Goals and Affiliation. The discussion here and in earlier chapters about the benefits and costs of affiliation suggests that each of the goals described in Chapter 3 – career, policy, and party building – will have a separate and distinct impact on affiliation decisions. With regard to party building, the prediction is easy: A strong interest in building a party organization will make affiliation more likely, and drive a candidate to affiliate with an established political party. Established parties are a better bet in terms of the success of the party-building effort, especially in contrast to new, smaller organizations that are likely to have relatively small, regionally concentrated support, minimal resources, and no brand name following.

Predictions about career goals are similarly easy to specify. In general, at the margin of other factors, candidates with strong career goals are likely to run as independents – they will forego affiliation with organizations that may not exist at the time of the next election. This prediction is completely crosswise with the literature on established democracies, where careerist candidates are typically assumed to affiliate in order to pursue a political career within a party organization. The situation is completely different in a new democracy such as Russia, where parties cannot credibly promise candidates either the potential for advancement or a safety net. Thus, insofar as candidates want a political career, they should opt against affiliation.

Insofar as careerists affiliate with any party at all, they will affiliate with established parties – parties that had previous parliamentary representation or were sponsored by a state apparatus, such as the parties of power, especially UR. The expectation here is that these organizations are the most likely to persist over time and, because they have already elected candidates to the legislature, have some organizational foundation and support in the electorate. Such parties provide a good venue for the pursuit of a political career. Moreover, we would expect careerists to gravitate toward the centrist parties to generate the maximum flexibility in appeals to voters and the maximum capacity to evade the future constraint of party discipline.

The UR case deserves special mention in this context. By 2003, the Putin administration initiated institutional reforms designed to reassert significant central control over regional officials. As the previous chapter illustrates, this control was used to force the affiliation of a number of governors and other high-ranking regional officials across the Federation. Clearly, these career-minded politicians understood that their careers hinged on supporting the party with their own reputations and base. Not only was UR the only game in town in terms of resource access, it also threatened to use its power to get rid of recalcitrant officials.

The relationship between policy goals and affiliation requires a specification of the content of these goals. In addition to the canonical measure of policy goals shown in Chapter 3, two additional measures of policy concerns were described, one tapping a candidate's interest in furthering democratic reforms, the other asking about a candidate's desire to change the direction of reform. We will use these variables in the analysis of the specific parties with which candidates affiliate. Our expectation is that an interest in democratic reforms will drive candidates to affiliate with established parties of the right (Democratic Russia, SPS) or center (FAR, Unity, Yabloko) or with new parties, whereas an interest in reversing the direction of reform will drive candidates to affiliate with established parties of the left, such as the KPRF and the LDPR.

To summarize, the predictions about the relationship between goals and affiliation are as follows:

- H1: Strong career goals will push candidates toward running as independents, or to affiliate with established parties.
- H2: Strong party building goals will lead candidates to affiliate, especially with established political parties.
- H3: An interest in furthering democratic reforms will lead candidates to affiliate with established center or right parties or with new parties, whereas an interest in reversing the direction of reform will drive candidates to affiliate with established left parties.

Resources. The impact of personal vote resources on affiliation depends on the candidate's preexisting connection to politics and political organizations. On the one hand, resources allow a candidate to campaign on his or her own. As a candidate's personal vote increases, the affiliation lottery becomes less and less attractive to the candidate. Thus, at first glance, we would expect that candidates with personal vote resources would be less likely to affiliate.

There are two critical exceptions. As discussed in Chapter 3, some candidates are unable or unwilling to exploit their personal votes because of their past association with a party organization. Examples would be a candidate who has been a longtime member of a party, who has helped to build a party organization, who won office on the party list, or who heads an organization that is closely tied to a preexisting party. These candidates are essentially branded with the party label, for better or worse. Moreover, resource-rich, politically experienced candidates are likely to be the focus of recruitment efforts by parties looking to field the best possible slate, both to win elections and to build the party name. Thus, we expect an interaction between resources and reputations: Although control over personal resources should make independence more likely, resources coupled with a political reputation should move candidates toward affiliation.[5]

This discussion also suggests that resource-rich, politically experienced candidates will likely affiliate with established parties. Established parties would also seek out candidates with political experience and personal votes, as these individuals give the party a good chance of winning a district, as well as helping to shape the party brand name. Conversely, consistent with the earlier discussion of resources, we expect that resource-rich candidates who lack past political experience will affiliate, if they affiliate at all, with new party organizations in order to avoid party control of their future behavior.

The second exception to our resource expectation accounts for candidates who held positions of power within the Soviet-era party or state structure. As discussed in Chapter 3, we specify some of the forces underlying Juan Linz and Alfred Stepan's (1996) typology of regime legacies by focusing on the components of the precommunist and communist experience that shape the expectations, skills, and resources available to postcommunist elites as they attempt to build durable ties to party-based constituencies. By this logic, candidates who are still drawing on Soviet-era resources, including Communist Party resources, should head left to the KPRF. Such candidates are already constrained by their reputations and have little to lose from the threat of future party discipline.

---

[5] Some of the equations in later analyses do not implement this interaction for two personal vote variables: holding elected office, and holding a position in the Soviet-era state. The problem is that all candidates in the sample who have these characteristics also had political reputations, hence the resource variable itself captures the interaction.

This discussion can be summarized by three propositions about the impact of resources and reputations on affiliation:

- H4: For candidates who lack preexisting ties to a political organization, the availability of personal vote resources will increase their chances of running as independents. For candidates who have such ties, personal votes will either make affiliation more likely or have no effect.
- H5: Insofar as affiliation occurs at all, candidates with preexisting political ties are more likely to affiliate with established parties, whereas candidates who lack these ties are more likely to affiliate with new political parties. These effects should increase insofar as the candidate has personal vote resources.
- H6: At the margin of other factors, candidates who held positions of power in the Soviet-era government or party should be more likely to affiliate, and specifically to affiliate with the KPRF.

The next step is to test these propositions using the survey data, which is the focus of the next section.

Explaining Affiliation

The hypotheses developed in the last section predict both the decision to affiliate and the direction of affiliation – who affiliates, and with which parties they are led to affiliate. Accordingly, the analysis first considers the affiliation decision, and then considers the direction of affiliation.[6] The following equation is used to test the hypotheses:

$$\begin{aligned}\text{Independent} = &\ \beta_1(\text{Constant}) + \beta_2(\text{Career}) + \beta_3(\text{Policy}) \\ &+ \beta_4(\text{Party Building}) + \beta_5(\text{Org. Res.}) \\ &+ \beta_6(\text{Org. Res.*Pol. Rep.}) + \beta_7(\text{Own Bus.}) \\ &+ \beta_8(\text{Own Bus.*Pol. Rep.}) + \beta_9(\text{Elected Office}) \\ &+ \beta_{10}(\text{Soviet Connection}) + \beta_{11}(\text{Russian Region}) + \upsilon_1\end{aligned}$$

---

[6] This distinction also makes sense from an empirical standpoint. Given the large number of parties that compete in Russian elections, it is not a stretch to say that if a Russian candidate wants to affiliate, he or she is most likely to be able to find a vehicle. By and large, these organizations emanate from Moscow, trickling down into the regions during the pre-election period. Elsewhere (Buckley and Smyth 2001), I argue that to the extent that there is a party system in Russia, it is a national system. However, this argument covers only the largest organizations. The level of party permeation into the regions is extremely uneven across the Federation (Gelman and Golosov 1998; Golosov 1999b: 14–15; Kovalev, Robinson 1998; Stoner-Weiss 2001).

To Join or Not to Join

Table 5.2. *Independent Variables in Affiliation Regression*

Variable		Description
Dependent Variables	Independent	Candidate ran as an independent in the 1999 Duma elections
	Left	Candidate affiliated with an established left party (KPRF) in 1999
	Center	Candidate affiliated with an established center party (FAR, NDR, Unity, Yabloko) in 1999
	Right	Candidate affiliated with an established right party (Democratic Russia, SPS) in 1999
	New	Candidate affiliated with a new political party in 1999
Independent Variables	Career	Candidate's interest in a political career
	Party Building	Candidate's interest in building a political party
	Policy	Candidate's interest in enacting good policy
	Pro-Reform	Candidate's interest in furthering democratic reforms
	Career	Candidate's interest in changing direction of reform
	Own Business	Candidate owned a business at the time of the 1999 elections
	Own Business Pol. Reputation	Business ownership interacted with candidate's political reputation
	Organizational Resources	Candidate headed or held a leadership position in a social organization
	Org. Res. Pol. Reputation	Organizational resources interacted with candidate's political reputation
	Elected Office	Candidate was in an elected position in the local or national government
	Soviet Connection	Candidate held a position in the Communist Party or the Soviet state

The variables specified in this equation and in the subsequent party-specific regressions are defined in Table 5.2.

The dependent variable in the first equation is a simple dichotomy: Did the candidate run as an independent or as a partisan? The independent variables break into three categories: candidates' goals, their personal

Table 5.3. *Explaining Independence*

	Variable	Logit Regression Parameter
Candidate Goals	Career Goal	.29*
		(.20)
	Policy Goal	.54***
		(.24)
	Party-Building Goal	−.87***
		(.19)
Candidate Background	Organizational Resources	.15
		(.25)
	(Org. Res.)* (Political Reputation)	−.51**
		(.32)
	Own Business	.45**
		(.21)
	(Own Business)* Political Reputation	−.59**
		(.28)
	Elected Office	.18
		(.27)
	Soviet Connection	−.61**
		(.37)
	Russian Region	.18
		(.34)
	Constant	−1.13
		(.48)
	Model Chi Square	63.4
	N	322

Note: *** = sig. at .01, ** = sig. at .05, * = sig. at .10, all one-tail.

vote resources, and their political reputations.[7] To capture the resource–reputation interaction, the resource variables are interacted with the political reputation variables. Each equation also includes a regional variable that distinguishes among candidates' running in Russian regions and ethnic republics. Table 5.3 reports the logit regression parameters for the analysis of independence.

For the most part, the signs are in the predicted direction, and all but the elected office resource parameter are significant. Consistent with the

---

[7] For more details on the specification of the variables, see Chapter 3 and Appendix C.

To Join or Not to Join

hypotheses, careerists run as independents, as do candidates with significant personal votes. However, candidates with political reputations tend to affiliate, even if they have resources of their own. Overall, the analysis suggests that large quantities of political resources are not being invested in party organizations, but are being channeled into the campaigns of independent candidates. Notably, the parameter for policy goals suggests that this motivation pushes candidates toward independence and not toward parties, strongly suggesting that parties are not seen as guarantors of effectiveness, particularly for policies targeted at specific constituencies. This result is a strong indictment of the reach of parties in the post-Soviet period.

The other interesting finding in Table 5.3 is the effect of the regional variable that captures the behavior of candidates in the ethnic republics. Although Russian candidates are slightly more likely to run as independents, this effect is not significant. The analysis confirms the finding noted earlier, that to the extent that a party system exists in Russia, it is a national party system.[8]

To illustrate how these parameters translate into predictions about real-world candidates, Figure 5.3 gives the predicted probability of affiliation for several hypothetical candidates:

- A candidate with strong policy goals, no political experience, and no personal vote
- The same candidate with a large personal vote
- A candidate with strong career goals, no political experience, and a large personal vote
- The same candidate with political experience
- A party loyalist (with a strong interest in party building) who has a political reputation, has a high personal vote, and holds elected office
- The same candidate with a Soviet-era position of power

Although these archetypes do not capture the full range of Russian candidates, they provide insight into what specific types of candidates are likely to do, and through these predictions capture the forces that drive affiliation

---

[8] This finding is also consistent with increased party activism in ethnic republics as measured by levels of candidate recruitment (Ishiyama 1999, 2001).

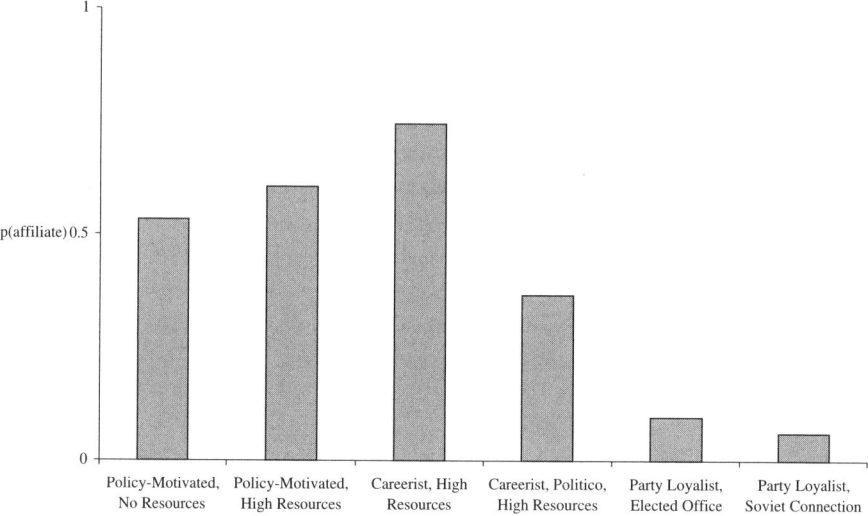

Figure 5.3. The Probability of Independence, 1999 Elections

decisions. Figure 5.3 uses the parameters from the regression analysis to calculate the probability of independence for each of these hypothetical candidates.

The predictions for these candidates are consistent with the hypotheses described earlier. Of these six canonical candidates, the one with strong career goals, a personal vote, and no political experience is the most likely to run as an independent. If a candidate lacks resources, has a reputation for political activity, holds elected office, has an interest in party building, or had a connection to the Soviet-era structure, the probability increases that he or she will affiliate with a party organization.

Explaining Which Party: How Candidates Choose Among Options

Just as the institutional structure sorts candidates into groups based on their goals and resources, so should candidates sort themselves across parties, based on their goals, resource endowments, and reputations. Moreover, as the earlier discussion suggests, party organizations may also exercise discrimination, favoring some candidates over others based on their motivations (that is, policy concerns) or the resources that they bring to the organization. The following equation is used to estimate a series of four unordered logistic regressions:

$$\begin{aligned}\text{Affiliate} = {}& \beta_1(\text{Constant}) + \beta_2(\text{Career}) + \beta_3(\text{Reform}) \\ & + \beta_4(\text{Change Direction}) + \beta_5(\text{Party Building}) \\ & + \beta_6(\text{Org. Res.}) + \beta_7(\text{Org. Res.}^*\text{Pol. Rep.}) \\ & + \beta_8(\text{Own. Bus.}) + \beta_9(\text{Own. Bus.}^*\text{Pol. Rep.}) \\ & + \beta_{10}(\text{Elected Office}) + \beta_{11}(\text{Soviet Connection}) \\ & + \beta_{12}(\text{Russian Region}) + \upsilon_1 \end{aligned}$$

This equation is estimated four times, each with a different dependent variable capturing affiliation with a particular party or parties. The categories reflect the distinction between established and new parties described earlier. The set of established parties is divided into three groups based on ideological concerns: right (SPS and Democratic Russia), left (KPRF), and centrist (NDR, Yabloko, Unity, and FAR), while all new parties are grouped together. The explanatory variables used in these regressions are the same as in the initial independence regression, with the addition of the two policy variables discussed earlier. The parameters for these regressions are given in Table 5.4.

The parameters for the goals variables are as predicted. Candidates with strong career goals tend to stay away from all parties, but the effect is strongest for new organizations. Candidates who hold anti-reform goals affiliate with left parties, while those who support reform tend to affiliate with center and right established parties and with new parties. Party-building goals drive candidates to the extremes – either left or right established parties – relative to centrist and new organizations.

With regard to resources, with the exception of candidates holding organizational resources, candidates with high personal votes gravitate toward the parties with lower capacity to constrain their candidates: the established centrist organizations. Candidates with existing political reputations are the most likely to affiliate with centrist parties. Surprisingly, candidates with Soviet-era resources are more likely to join state parties than the KPRF. Interestingly, the regional variable is not significant except in the case of affiliation with center parties. This finding supports the general notion that state parties dominate parliamentary electoral politics in these regions. In

Table 5.4. *Explaining the Decision to Join Particular Parties*

Variables		Affiliation with Established Party			Affiliate with New Party
		Left Party	Center Party	Right Party	
Candidate Goals	Career	−1.13*	−.30*	−.44	−1.45***
		(.71)	(.23)	(.46)	(.72)
	Reform	−2.2***	.36**	2.28***	.43*
		(.77)	(.19)	(.60)	(.33)
	Change	.87**	−.61***	−.28	.17
		(.47)	(.19)	(.36)	(.33)
	Party Building	1.08***	−.23	.45*	.11
		(.37)	(.20)	(.38)	(.37)
Candidate Background	Organizational Resources	−1.73***	−.48*	−.24	.93***
		(.64)	(.31)	(.48)	(.40)
	(Org. Res.)* (Political Reputation)	–	.55** (.36)	.39 (.57)	−.47 (.47)
	Own Business	−.58	.15	.14	−.35
		(.58)	(.23)	(.41)	(.46)
	(Own Business)* Political Reputation	–	.66*** (.28)	−.03 (.50)	−.20 (.70)
	Elected Office	.25	.03	.03	.20
		(.44)	(.26)	(.58)	(.42)
	Soviet Connection	.17	.55**	−.64	−.07
		(.61)	(.32)	(.98)	(.60)
	Russian Region	.07	−.51*	.43	.48
		(.59)	(.33)	(.68)	(.70)
	Constant	−3.17	−.47	−6.42	−3.93
		(1.07)	(.44)	(1.34)	(.97)
	Model Chi Square	79.6	47.6	31.3	17.4

Note: *** = sig. at .01, ** = sig. at .05, * = sig at .10, all one-tail. N = 322 for all regressions. Interactions are deleted from left regressions because of a lack of variation.

contrast, Russian candidates have greater incentives to spread out across the party spectrum or to run as independents.

These results suggest how the KPRF came to dominate the left side of the political spectrum, and why it will be difficult for some candidates to defect from the party even though it has failed to exert significant opposition to Putin in the Duma. Because of the party's strong brand name and material resources, candidates with strong anti-reform goals focus their

To Join or Not to Join

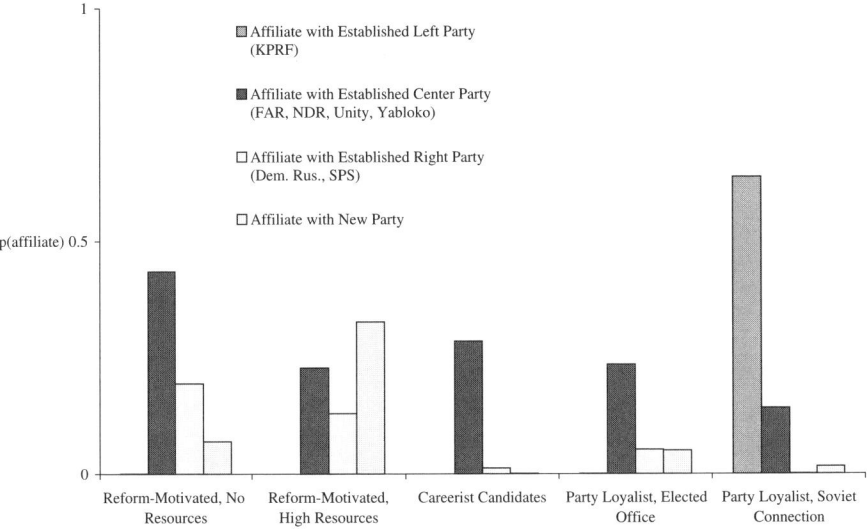

Figure 5.4. Affiliation with Specific Parties

attention on the KPRF rather than the new parties that might also espouse similar positions. In contrast, pro-reform candidates are spread across the compatible options, signaling that no party has secured its hold on the right as the KPRF did on the left.

To better interpret these parameters, Figure 5.4 generates predictions about affiliation for the various hypothetical candidates described earlier. (The figure combines predictions for the two kinds of careerist candidates, as they are virtually identical.)

The central finding in the figure is that although career goals push candidates toward independence, if these candidates do affiliate they are more likely to join centrist organizations, dominated by the parties of power. Careerists also have a substantial probability of joining new party organizations – organizations that allow the greatest flexibility for candidates to accommodate future political changes. This view of centrist candidates resonates with descriptions of them as pragmatists who will pursue whatever policies are necessary to retain office.[9]

---

[9] For a discussion of Russian pragmatists, see Remington 2001a. This finding resonates with Angelo Panebianco's (1988) assessment of candidate affiliation as an expression of common ideals or some sense of self-promotion or career goals.

123

In contrast, candidates who join the KPRF are largely those who have strong connections to the old regime and already hold elected office. While this is a relatively narrow segment of the sample, it is again an indication that to the extent that past electoral experience matters, it pushes candidates toward the most structured party in the system. This finding also supports the assertion that the KPRF is the most effective party at recruiting candidates with past political experience to run on its roster (Ishiyama 1999 and 2000). These candidates demand an organization that compels all its candidates to invest in preserving the key party resource, its reputation. In exchange, such candidates are prepared to accept party discipline directed at strengthening the brand name of the party. In contrast, the slates of established right parties seem to be split between candidates who have few resources and those who have high resources but no reputation. These candidates reflect acrimonious personality- and issue-based divisions within the organizations themselves.

In general, Figure 5.4 shows that the majority of existing resources within the electoral system are being merged with centrist organizations that tend to be state parties. Of these organizations, two were cannibalized by UR. Yabloko stands alone as the non–state-sponsored centrist party, but it failed to surpass the electoral threshold in 2003.

Together, these findings demonstrate some of the effects of the mixed electoral rules in a context where parties are extremely weak. Given the chance to remain independent, many candidates forego the benefits and the constraints of party sponsorship. Those candidates who do join parties tend to gravitate toward those organizations that provide little ideological constraint but offer significant potential for material resources in the campaign period and in the legislature. The concentration of state parties within the category is significant since they dominate both material resources and the expectation of future success.

Conclusion: Coordination, Cooperation, and Party Building

This chapter has focused on the decision to affiliate with a political party. The data demonstrate that in transitional Russia, affiliation is not an imperative. Some candidates affiliate because they want to help build a party organization. Others affiliate to gain resources for their campaign. Still others affiliate because of their preexisting ties with a party organization. Even so, there are just as many factors that move candidates toward running as independents. In particular, candidates with strong career goals or personal vote resources will likely as not forego party membership.

The analysis also reveals important regularities in the parties with which candidates affiliate. Insofar as careerist candidates join party organizations, they are likely to throw their hats in with organizations that have the lowest capacity to exert future discipline. In other words, these candidates seek to maintain the maximum independence possible. In contrast, candidates driven to help build party organizations tend to enter at the extremes, affiliating with the KPRF or one of the established parties on the right. The clear brand name of these parties clearly offers advantages to candidates who decide to affiliate. However, a reliance on reputation-based over material resources rooted in relatively extremist positions may constrain candidates who might want to push for moderation of the party's positions in an attempt to become viable at the national level.

Although these findings have been established only for contemporary Russia, they may also apply in other countries at times when affiliation is a variable of choice for candidates. The focus on career goals and resources may explain patterns of party switching in new democracies, as candidates abandon some types of parties and join others. The same factors may provide insights into why some minor parties succeed while others fail, or which parties are most likely to survive a period of extreme party system change, such as realignment or dealignment.

The final task in this chapter is to evaluate the impact of affiliation decisions on electoral infrastructure, including implications for cooperation within party organizations and the provision of information to voters and political elites. The aim here is to account for the trajectory of Russia's democratic transition, as well as to generate insights into the accumulation of electoral infrastructure in other transitional cases.

The Consequences for Party Organizations

This chapter's analysis of affiliation decisions in contemporary Russia highlights a critical and sometimes questionable assumption in the literature on state–society linkages in new democracies. For the most part, it is assumed that parties will be the central mechanism through which candidates forge ties to voters.[10] While some recent work reexamines the assumption that

---

[10] Even patronage structures are typically considered within the context of an existing party system, not as a root cause of the system (Kitschelt 2000; Piatonni 2001; Tarrow 1977).

partisan organizations will be based in agreement over policy, the focus on parties as the central state–society bond and candidates as creatures of their party organization remains intact (Kitschelt 2000; Kitschelt and Smyth 2002). Only in very rare cases have comparativists considered sources of candidate support outside party organization (Hale 2005).

The Russian experience with democracy, brief though it was, shows how this party-centered view of electoral competition can lead analysts astray. Russia's mixed electoral system operates as a sorting mechanism that pushes different types of candidates toward different electoral strategies. As the results in this chapter demonstrate, some candidates respond to these incentives by foregoing affiliation and running as independents. This decision is not based in a rejection of these candidates by existing organizations. Rather, the decision results from the candidates' calculation that their goals – including getting elected – are best served by independence. In other words, until 2003, Russian parties lacked monopoly control over electoral resources, as well as a monopoly over the most fundamental resource in political life: the power to determine who gets on the ballot and who gets elected.

This focus on candidates brings a new variable into the study of party development. Many studies of party development focus on the role of party leaders and notables in shaping a party's organization and vote appeals or on voters' election-to-election support for individual organizations. The analysis here supplements those studies by focusing on the complex interaction between the party structures offered by central leaders and the demands of candidates and would-be candidates. The message is that to focus on the actions of party leaders as an explanation for a party's electoral success or failure overlooks a critical variable: the candidates who choose to run under the party banner, the demands they place on the organization, and how they are perceived by the general public.

This view of party organizations through the lens of candidates and their decisions provides new insights into the political consequences of electoral institutions. If the rhetoric from both Russian and Western analysts is to be believed, the mixed electoral system was adopted to provide Russian citizens with national group representation through proportional representation together with a focus on narrower, local concerns in the district races (McFaul 2001; Moser 2001; Shugart and Wattenberg 2001). In theory, the party system ties together the two races and reconciles conflicts between these disparate sets of constituencies. Underlying this expectation is the assumption that the list race should quickly sort out voters' preferences across political parties, demonstrating their relative power as vote-getting mechanisms, both nationally and in specific districts, thereby motivating candidates to affiliate with party organizations. The description of this system as "the best of both worlds" has been used both as a justification of the selection of these institutions and as a predictor of their future performance.

The results show that the expectations embedded in the "best of both worlds" claim are problematic. For one thing, affiliation is driven by many factors, some of which have little to do with winning office. Candidates may opt against affiliation (or against affiliating with a particular party) because of their career goals, their policy concerns, their political reputation or the lack thereof, and the availability of personal vote resources. Thus, even if we set aside the very real problems of drawing inferences about the popularity of different parties based on their performance in the list race, the claims about the beneficial effects of mixed systems may not apply to Russia or elsewhere. Mixed systems may be the best of both worlds, but only under a narrow range of conditions that do not hold in contemporary Russia.

Affiliation and Information

Candidates' affiliation decisions have important implications for the informational component of electoral infrastructure. At best, the opportunity for candidates to run as independents increases the information burden on voters, since they must discern information about both the partisans and the independent candidates who compete for office. At worst, the possibility to run as an independent proliferates the number of candidates running in single-member district races, since the constraining logic of a purely spatial model breaks down as independents make appeals based on personal votes or other idiosyncratic factors. Precisely because independents lack access to partisan brand names, they must use other mechanisms to signal their qualifications and preferences to the electorate, such as endorsements by regional officials, personal characteristics such as ethnicity, or single-issue appeals. These strategies may help independents get elected, but they also undercut the value of party labels and complicate vote decisions. Moreover, the proliferation of appeals by independents complicates attempts to infer voter preferences or the value of party labels from election outcomes.

The possibility that candidates stress material over reputation-based resources in making their affiliation decisions also obscures the future value of a party's label. A candidate may choose a party precisely because it can help him or her get elected in a specific election but has little capacity to constrain the candidate's future behavior or their appeals during the campaign.

Such a candidate may not invest his or her own resources in the collective endeavor of party building, preferring to invest in building a personal vote organization under the party's umbrella.

Affiliation, Coordination, and Cooperation

The results clearly show that many Russian candidates do not see parties as essential for their pursuit of political goals. This finding holds even for candidates with strong policy goals. Ignoring the role of independent candidates or treating them as a single entity in analyses of party development generates misleading conclusions about party strength and the structure of organized opposition in the country. This finding has important implications for explaining behavior in the Russian legislature, and suggests that the current executive strategy of building a legislative coalition based on a party of power, coalition partners elected on the list, and the support of loyal independent deputies remains viable in the short term but poses obstacles to the consolidation of executive power in the longer run.[11]

The most significant direct effect of affiliation decisions on party development is the withholding of significant resources from the party system by independent candidates. The potential for alternative resources (for example, elite networks and financial industry groups) to back independent candidates compounds this problem. These resources are being used to elect individual candidates, not to build a national party system. The data show that the opportunity cost of these resources, including the resources affiliated with parties that have yet to secure representation in parliament, is potentially very high.

Moreover, the data show that to the extent that candidates join parties, they are widely dispersed across many organizations, some of which compete for the same pool of voters. Thus, uncertainty about the value of labels, coupled with the fact that Russian parties do not have monopoly control over electoral resources, leads to a proliferation of organizations that suit the needs of different types of candidates. In terms of party development, the analysis demonstrates that the number and structure of parties in early transition may depend on the motivations held by individuals who enter politics, and the range of resources available to these candidates and to party organizations.

---

[11] For a discussion of the role of independent deputies in supporting the president's reform program, see Remington 2001b; Smyth 2002. This situation is similar in some regards to the patterns of executive legislative relations in Brazil (Ames 2001).

This description of the relative weakness of Russian party organizations in shaping electoral competition stands in sharp contrast to the growing literature that argues for increasingly stable voter attachments to Russian parties (Brader and Tucker 2001; Colton 2000a; Miller, Erb, and Hesli 2000; Miller and Klobucar 2000). In part, this disagreement reflects different scholars looking at very different levels of analysis. Those who argue for nascent partisanship generally look at voters and voting behavior, often within a single election, or in terms of party families or ideological positions, a quasiparty system in which the individual organizations change from election to election but where the spatial relationship among key actors remains the same, and where preferences are defined in terms of support for the old system versus support for reform (Kitschelt and Smyth 2002; Myagkov, Ordeshook, and Sobyanin 1997).

A number of problems arise when one tries to interpret this pattern. First, the cast of parties has changed over time, so loyalties to individual organizations have not been stable. Moreover, the success of independent district representatives and high levels of ticket splitting suggests that voters do not necessarily see the political world in terms of a single policy dimension. Most recently, Timothy Colton and Henry Hale (2004) found that self-reported partisanship influences vote choice for only two parties: UR and the KPRF.

The prominent role for independents in elections and in the legislature weakened existing party organizations and generated unorganized opposition to the Kremlin. Putin and his advisors have been extraordinarily good at using this weakness against their opponents. The president used his influence in the Duma to steer resources and committee positions toward key independent incumbents, buying their support for crucial institutional and policy changes. In turn, these changes reduced the availability of alternative resources, and in particular the capacity of regional governors, to mount future independent candidacies. With the strength of UR increasing and all other parties in disarray, it is not surprising that Putin has proposed to eliminate the mixed electoral system in favor of a party-dominated proportional representation system where UR is guaranteed a role as the gatekeeper for all ambitious politicians. In this case, the internally centralized party organization that achieves cooperation through coercion and deployment of state resources is not an example of democratic electoral infrastructure but authoritarian infrastructure designed to subvert the democratic process.

Yet, even selective partisan affiliation does not explain the lack of durability and capacity of Russian parties, and opposition parties in particular.

Candidate Strategies and Electoral Competition

As crucial as the affiliation decision is for party development, it is only one of the first steps in the electoral process. This analysis suggests that a candidate's affiliation decision may not signal a commitment to invest resources in building the party organization, defining ties to constituents within the confines of a party organization, or submitting to future party discipline. As later chapters will show, not all partisan candidates fulfill their obligation to support the party in exchange for the party's endorsement. In terms of both their district choices and their decisions about campaign appeals, candidates can shirk their responsibility toward the party and maximize their own support over the party support.

6

Finding Fit: Candidates and Their Districts

> It was a major mistake running outside of the oblast capital. I didn't consider the local bosses. Of course, they would influence outcomes.
>
> Yabloko candidate, 1999[1]

Democratic governance is built on stable and reciprocal relationships between representatives and their constituents, typically mediated through political party organizations. To understand how candidates' decisions shape mass opportunities to press demands on government, insist on responsiveness, and provoke accountability, this chapter moves to the next step in a candidate's electoral calculus: where to run (which district) and, in the case of partisans, how to run (whether to run on a party list, only in a district, or in both races).

For Russian candidates, district selection is a real choice. Since 1993, the electoral law has codified two types of districts: 225 single-member ("nominal") districts, and a national (party list) district based on proportional representation. The national district race is characterized by a number of potential national constituencies rooted in common interests or identities. A number of institutional elements, including the relatively stringent 5 percent threshold and the regulations governing the registration of political parties, serve to dissuade regional interests from entering into the party list race. In contrast, the nominal or single-member districts capture geographically based constituencies that encapsulate different combinations of political, economic, ideological, or ethnic interests. As a result, Russian candidates face a broad and complex range of constituencies – potential electoral markets – in each election.

---

[1] Author's interview with the candidate on the day after the election, December 1999.

District selection is interesting and important precisely because affiliation does not determine where or how a candidate runs. Partisans may run in a district, on the list, or in both venues. Even non-partisans face significant district selection choices since the lack of a residency requirement frees them to run in whichever nominal district they wish. The question is, what factors drive these decisions? Are Russian candidates able to exploit the lack of residency requirements to run in constituencies where they have a good fit with voter preferences? To what degree are their choices constrained by party leaders? What are different kinds of candidates – careerists, party loyalists, elected officials, and other types – likely to do? And what are the consequences of all of these factors for electoral infrastructure?

This chapter addresses these questions using a combination of survey data, national election data, and candidate interviews. Due to data limitations, the bulk of the analysis focuses on the 1999 campaign. However, the collection of evidence shows that even in 2003, after a decade of competitive elections, there is strong evidence of a lack of electoral infrastructure to guide district choices and solidify the relationship between candidates and constituents and even between district and party candidates.

The chapter first defines the dependent variables for both partisans and non-partisans and describes actual choices facing candidates. The next section reports candidates' responses to survey questions about the pressures and influences that led them to their district choice. Surprisingly, until 2003, candidates reported that party leaders had minimal influence on district selection. Still, candidates' choices are not as wide open as we might expect. The localized nature of resources and reputations constrains many candidates in their search for a winnable district. These findings are confirmed and extended by a multivariate statistical analysis that characterizes the influences of key factors, including goals, resources, and information on district selection. Finally, the chapter shows how the lack of coordination among incumbents running in single-member districts undermines the capacity of representatives to build enduring ties to voters.

Defining District Selection

Once a candidate has decided to run for office, and decided whether to affiliate with a political party, he or she must decide where – in which district – he or she will try to win office. This question is not widely addressed in established Western systems, where strong institutional and partisan

Finding Fit

controls limit candidates' behavior. For example, in pure plurality systems, candidates can only run in a geographically defined district, typically with residency requirements that limit their candidacy to the district in which they live. In pure list systems, all candidates run in a national district. And in most established democracies, political parties have some say – sometimes a decisive say – in which candidates run under the party banner, or in which district they stand for office. In fact, to the extent that district selection is a focus of research in these cases, it is analyzed in terms of nomination contests within political parties, either primaries or leadership battles over list formation. Finally, most established democracies have strong career tracks that limit the agency of individual candidates. For example, in the United States, state legislators who want to run for the national House of Representatives will typically choose a seat whose congressional district contains their state legislative district.

The district selection choices open to Russian candidates result from an interaction between institutional features and the weak party system. Russian parties must form at least two lists: a central list and some combination of regional lists. This requirement is a limited constraint, since parties employ an extremely wide range of strategies in list construction. Some parties form two lists (a central list and a regional list), others form a list for each region, and some combine regions and republics to form a smaller number of regional lists. For the most part, the central list – limited to eighteen nominees in 1999 – is reserved for central leadership and prominent notables. Many parties choose to nominate the "faces" of the party, the top three leaders, on the central list. Others form a list for the Moscow region that includes party leaders. Regional party leaders typically run on regional lists, although these lists also contain a fair number of Moscow notables.

Figure 6.1 illustrates the concrete choices that face candidates at the point of district selection. How has the candidate pool proceeded down this decision tree? In some respects, candidates' responses to these decisions have been remarkably stable, as in the percent of candidates who run on national lists. There have also been some significant changes, such as a decline in independents running in district races. To begin to understand how this structure influences decisions, Table 6.1 provides data on district selection in four elections between 1993 and 2003.

There are several striking elements of this table. The first finding echoes the discussion in Chapter 4 concerning the plethora of candidates in Russian elections. Even in 2003, nearly as many candidates ran for office as in 1999,

Candidate Strategies and Electoral Competition

Table 6.1. *District Selection by Russian Duma Candidates, 1993–2003*

District Selection Choice	1993	1995	1999	2003
Independents in Nominal Districts (SMD)	25.4% (825)	12.7% (1056)	19.9% (1144)	13.1% (676)
Partisans in Nominal Districts (SMD-Only)	21.3% (694)	18.8% (1572)	18.8% (1083)	23.5% (1217)
Partisans in National District (List-Only)	30.56% (996)	56.1% (4682)	51.2% (2941)	52.5% (2716)
Partisans Running in Nominal and National District (SMD + List)	22.8% (740)	12.5% (1041)	10.1% (578)	10.9% (564)
Totals	3253	8351	5746	5173

Source: Project on Political Transformation and the Electoral Process in Post-Communist Europe (2003) and official statistics.

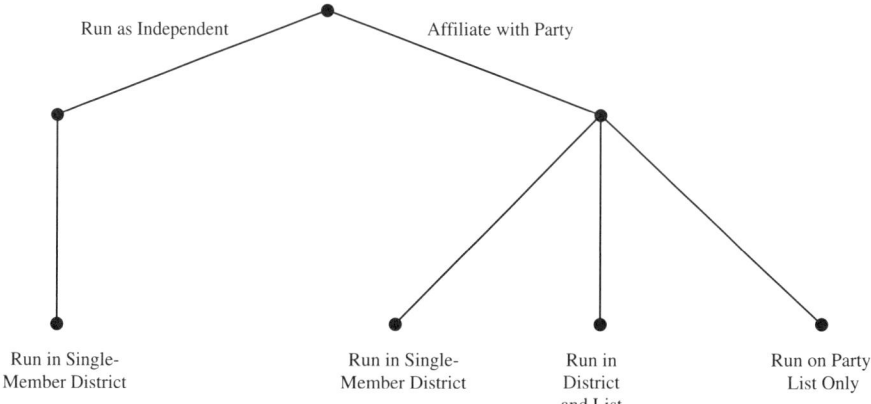

Figure 6.1. District Selection Decisions

and many more ran than in 1993. As the table indicates, since 1995, the majority of candidates ran for office only on party lists. Likewise, while total numbers of candidates running in single-member districts has declined – most notably among independents – the percentage of candidates running in the districts relative to candidates running on the list also has been relatively stable since 1995.

As noted in Chapter 4, despite the wide fluctuations in the number of parties competing, the average number of candidates nominated by each organization has been remarkably steady since 1993, holding at around

Finding Fit

eighty-four candidates per party. It is plausible that this finding of stability masks significant crossparty variation in capacity to steer candidates toward particular districts. Such differences would suggest that parties are following distinct electoral strategies, with some focusing on contesting nominal districts and others concentrating on the list race. Variation might also suggest that the leadership of these parties has significant control over the district selection choices made by candidates running under their banner. To explore this possibility, Table 6.2 presents data on district selection choices made by affiliated candidates in major party organizations in the 1995, 1999, and 2003 Duma elections.

The principal feature in Table 6.2 is the lack of crossparty variation. With some exceptions, by 2003, the percentages of candidates from each party who ran in a nominal district, on their party's list, or in both venues are roughly the same. The patterns of district selection for each party and across party organizations are also remarkably stable over time – in particular, between the Russia's Choice-SPS organizations and the Agrarian Party, despite their dramatically different sets of resources and electoral fates. In general, new parties put more emphasis on the list than in districts. More established organizations place more candidates in single-member districts.

The table does indicate an interesting shift in the nomination strategy of Putin's organization, United Russia (UR), between 1999 and 2003. In 1999, due to either lack of organization or intentional design, the party concentrated its efforts on the list and nominated very few district candidates. This strategy gave the party significant control over its legislative cadres. By 2003, the party's nomination patterns changed, in part due to the movement of incumbent list deputies to districts and the affiliation of non-partisan incumbents, and in part due to the increased capacity of the party in regional governments. The trade-off between vote getting and party discipline may have been less stark in 2003 because of the overwhelming strength of the party in the legislature and Putin's monopoly over state resources.

The reciprocal effects of partisan district candidates and the success of the list are difficult to measure, although they appear to be relatively minor for most parties. M. Yargomskaya (2002) shows that in 1999 there were very different relationships between the vote getting capacities of political parties and their district candidates. Almost all parties get more votes in districts where they nominate a candidate, but the party list vote and the vote for the candidate vary widely. On average, Unity's candidates secured

Table 6.2. *Variation in District Choice Across Major Parties, 1995–2003 Duma Elections*

Party	1995 Election			1999 Election			2003 Election		
	Dist-Only	List-Only	Both	Dist-Only	List-Only	Both	Dist-Only	List-Only	Both
KPRF	20.6% (68)	60.6% (200)	18.8% (62)	19.0% (61)	59.8% (192)	21.2% (68)	25.7% (89)	50.6% (175)	23.7% (82)
LDPR	24.2% (85)	47.6% (167)	28.2% (99)	54.6% (89)	45.4% (74)	–	24.9% (70)	38.4% (108)	36.7% (103)
Yabloko	4.6% (9)	64.8% (127)	30.6% (60)	20.8% (43)	44.9% (93)	34.3% (71)	25.6% (42)	45.7% (75)	28.7% (47)
NDR	24.9% (74)	65.3% (194)	9.8% (29)	20.1% (53)	65.9% (174)	14.0% (37)	–	–	–
Dem. Choice (RC/SPS)	7.2% (16)	67.7% (151)	25.1% (56)	15.8% (29)	64.1% (118)	20.1% (37)	12.6% (33)	65.5% (171)	21.8% (57)
Agrarian Party	10.7% (31)	70.0% (203)	19.3% (56)	–	–	–	9.8% (25)	77.0% (197)	13.3% (34)
Women of Russia	18.6% (16)	61.6% (53)	19.8% (17)	2.1% (2)	87.6% (85)	10.3% (10)	–	–	–
Lebed's Organizations	–	73.0% (181)	27.1% (67)	5.4% (10)	75.6% (140)	18.9% (35)	–	–	–
FAR	–	–	–	20.5% (61)	69.7% (207)	9.8% (29)	26.3% (95)	63.8% (228)	11.0% (40)
Unity/UR	–	–	–	8.9% (15)	81.7% (138)	9.5% (16)	–	–	–
Motherland	–	–	–	–	–	–	8.9% (18)	75.9% (154)	15.3% (31)

Source: Project on Political Transformation and the Electoral Process in Post-Communist Europe (2003) and official statistics. Blank cells indicate that the party did not field candidates.

Finding Fit

just over half of the votes received by the party in the same district. Similarly, KPRF candidates average 4 percentage points less than their organization, suggesting that the party label is more powerful than the candidates. In contrast, the Union of Right Forces (SPS), Yabloko, and Fatherland–Our Russia candidates do significantly better than their party organizations. In a similar analysis in 2003, most parties got a slight 2 percent boost in vote support in districts where they ran a candidate. In general, however, partisan district candidates do significantly better than their parties – suggesting the candidates help to pull up partisan support. The exception to the finding is LDPR candidates, who do notoriously poorly in district races, receiving an average of almost 8 percent fewer votes than the list. It is impossible to determine whether this result stems from the effect of a regional candidate working on behalf of the party or the party placing a candidate in districts where the party is relatively strong, but the data does suggest that any potential partisan effect was much less in 2003.

This discussion also underscores a potential effect of Russia's mixed system: party leaders' dilemmas in dealing with the trade-off between maximizing seats and maximizing the potential for party discipline. A party's legislative delegation will comprise deputies elected in the national list added to those elected in nominal districts. The problem is that there is no guarantee that district candidates will run on the same platforms or receive support from the same types of voters as those running on the list. Representatives elected from districts may also be more receptive than their list colleagues to a trade of support for the president's proposals in return for state resources invested in their districts. Given these problems, a party seeking to build internal discipline may focus on maximizing its seats in the list race, or only standing candidates in districts with constituencies that overlap with the party's national constituency. While this strategy minimizes the problem of reaching agreement within the party's legislative delegation, it also reduces the expected size of the delegation, making the party less of a national player.

The lack of over-time and cross-organization variation suggests that for the most part, party leaders have not been able to manage the trade-offs across constituencies or organizational goals. Rather, it seems plausible that candidates decide where to run mostly independent of party influence. These hypotheses foreshadow survey evidence that will be presented later in this chapter. Simply put, Russian candidates have significant freedom to make whichever district selection choices are consistent with their goals and individual constraints.

Variation in district selection has important implications for candidates, voters, and party organizations. By choosing where and how they run, affiliated candidates can decide the extent to which they wish to attach themselves to a party label. For example, by running only on the party list, a candidate in effect places his or her electoral fate in the hands of the party label and the party's attractiveness to a national constituency. At the other extreme, running only in a district allows a candidate to make an appeal based on his or her personal characteristics or record – their personal vote – in addition to the party label. Running in a district also allows a candidate to exploit local support for his or her party, if the extent of such support can be determined. However, insofar as party leaders have some influence over candidates running under their banner, affiliation may limit the range of districts in which a candidate can run due to internal competition among aspirants.

From the perspective of voters, however, these options introduce significant complications. Given the choices open to candidates, district races can include three very different kinds of candidates: affiliated candidates who are not on the party list, affiliated candidates running in the district and on a list, and independent candidates. These candidates may run very different kinds of campaigns in terms of their use of a party label, their support for the party platform, and their cultivation of a personal vote. The result is a relatively complicated task for voters attempting to choose their candidate given the proliferation of types and campaign appeals. Moreover, insofar as district selection influences campaign appeals, it can also affect the nature of the linkage between incumbents and the electorate. For example, an affiliated candidate who stays off his or her party's list in order to campaign on a personal vote will attract a different base of support than a candidate who runs in a district and on his or her party list and campaigns on the party platform. An example from a single region illustrates the variation in candidates' strategies and their results.

Yaroslavl: Two Candidates, Two Paths

Two case studies illustrate the implications of district selection for how incumbents campaign and govern. Both incumbents are from Yaroslavl Oblast. Both have been elected in all three legislative elections. Even so, there are profound differences in the ways in which these deputies have won and retained their seats.

The first candidate, Elena Mizulina, won office in three different districts and has switched party organizations three times. In 1993, as a member of

Russia's Choice, Mizulina won one of two seats to the Federation Council, the upper house of parliament. During her tenure, Mizulina actively opposed both the first Chechen war and the sweeping powers awarded to Russia's Constitutional Court. During this time, she also switched her party affiliation first to the movement Reforms–New Course and then to Yabloko.

After the decision to appoint rather than elect upper house members, Mizulina lost her seat and was forced to find a new constituency. In 1995, she contested and won nominal district 189 as a Yabloko candidate running against Duma incumbent Evgeniia Tishkovskaya, who had also emerged from the active women's organizations of the region. Once in the Duma, Mizulina continued to build a national profile as a member of the Committee on Legislation and Judicial-Legal Reform. Throughout this period, she was also active in trying to build reform-oriented regional organizations. She founded Equilibrium, an organization to support the candidacy of the incumbent governor and regional legislators. She also organized both the Interregional Congress of Reform Forces and the regional branch of Yabloko.

Mizulina's efforts to lead a consolidated reform movement in the region continued through 1999. She proposed fusing the Yabloko and SPS organizations within the region, an initiative that failed. This coordination failure was significant in the pre-election period. Mizulina's national profile did not deter significant opposition. In a field of seventeen candidates, she came in third. She garnered less than one-half of the votes received by the controversial winner, Sergei Zagidullin. Zagidullin, also a one-term deputy, was the president of a private security firm, Security Services, and capitalized on this background to become a leading figure in the safeguarding of nuclear material in Russia's regions. Despite her loss in the district, Mizulina won a Duma seat on the Yabloko list only to abandon her benefactors and shift her factional affiliation to SPS.

In 2003, she was nominated on the SPS list but the party failed to surpass the electoral threshold, interrupting Mizulina's legislative career. Despite this loss, she did not forfeit a career in politics. Her national reputation served her well and she was appointed the Duma's permanent representative to the Constitutional Court in February 2004. She remains active and visible in that position, drawing on the expertise she amassed in her Duma committee positions.

In contrast to Mizulina's constituency hopping, the second candidate, Anatoly Greshnevikov, is a three-time representative from Yaroslavl's second district, centering on the manufacturing city Rybinsk. Greshnevikov, an author and journalist who writes about ecological preservation, first won office in 1990 to the Congress of Peoples Deputies of the Russian Soviet Federation. In 1993, he was nominated by the nationalist organization Power to the People, won office, and was appointed to the Ecology Committee. He extended this interest to his district by working to preserve regional pine forests, install a new cleansing system in the region's reservoir, and prevent the import of nuclear waste. A close look at his actions in office show an effort at constituent service and efforts to deliver pork to the district in the form of libraries, hospitals, retirement homes, and the restoration of churches. By and large, this strategy has been effective. Over the course of three campaigns, Greshnevikov's opposition has been lower than average although not insignificant. He faced five opponents in 1995 and seven in 1999, including two candidates from competing nationalist organizations in each election, but has won both times. Remarkably, he held the seat again in 2003 as a member of the Motherland organization. In January 2005, Greshnevikov was one of seventeen Motherland delegates to sign an anti-Semitic manifesto, marking him as an extremist.

These candidates have very different electoral strategies. Mizulina focused her political energy on building ties to potential elite partners at both the national and regional levels, and on establishing a national reputation. These efforts transcended her district and yielded weak ties with her constituency, making her vulnerable to defeat in a district race. In contrast, Greshnevikov had a more constituency-centered populist strategy that won him strong ties within the district. These actions have important consequences for electoral infrastructure. In each election, Greshnevikov built links to the same constituency – the same geographic region, and the same groups within the district. In contrast, Mizulina's district hopping, coupled with party switching, ensured that she targeted a different constituency in each race, working against the provision of information that is at the core of infrastructure.

Explaining District Selection

This work posits that Mizulina and Greshnevikov are exemplars of a large number of candidates who make similar district choices. To understand district selection for all candidates, it is important to begin with the fact that law defined very stark options for candidates: two types of races, one based in districts involving candidates, the other a national contest among

Finding Fit

parties. The choice among these options is driven by factors that we have already seen at work at other points in the campaign cycle: goals, information, resources, and institutions. Further, candidates' district selections have important consequences for the choices that voters face, for election outcomes, and for policy making in the legislature. In short, district selections shape the development of electoral infrastructure. The following discussion develops predictions about district selection, separating factors and predictions that are unique to Russia from those that apply to other transitional democracies.

Redistricting

The process by which district lines are drawn in Russia is extremely obscure. Officially, the Central Election Commission (CEC) set the 1993 district boundaries. Regional authorities (presumably the oblast first secretary and then the governor) were consulted early in the process, and typically suggested appropriate boundaries to the CEC. The 1995 law was very ambiguous, stating, "the electoral districts shall be formed for conduct of elections on the basis of data submitted by the relevant executive bodies of state power and local self-government. The specific boundaries of and amount of electors within each electoral district shall be determined by the corresponding election commission and shall be subject to approval by the corresponding representative body at least sixty days prior to the election."[2] This law also required that the State Duma and the president approve district plans based on a CEC draft.

At one level, Russia's electoral system is a model of stability: The numbers of delegates elected from districts and from the list race have remained constant (and equal) since 1993, despite much debate over alternate schemes.[3] For example, in the period leading up to the 1995 elections, former President Boris Yeltsin strongly pushed for an increase in the number of nominal district seats, with a corresponding reduction in the number of national race seats. This clearly political maneuver was designed to increase the number

---

[2] Ferguson 1995: 6. Debates in parliament showed the deputies to be relatively unconcerned with district boundaries despite the potential effects that the changes could have on their electoral success. Author's interview with Nikolai Petrov, September 26, 1995, and Victor Sheinis, November 20, 1996.

[3] There are a number of good discussions of the selection of the electoral system and subsequent debates. See McFaul 2001: 217–20; Smith and Remington 2001: 105–10; White, Rose, and McAllister 1997: 189–96.

of deputies who were sympathetic to the central state and its reform program. These efforts were blocked by parliamentarians voting according to their policy preferences and district homes (Smith and Remington 2001: 125–33).

This overall stability masks important changes in district size and shape that undermined the accumulation of electoral infrastructure. While the number of districts has been constant, revisions to the electoral law prior to the 1995 elections dramatically altered the boundaries of thirty-three okrugs (districts) and constructed fifty-two new okrugs. These changes shifted districts from rural areas to more urban centers, ostensibly in response to population changes. In political terms, however, these changes strengthened the influence of regional leaders. In 2003, there was unmistakable gerrymandering in the changes made in districts in Bashkortostan, a region noted for electoral corruption and strong support for the national party of power.

A full analysis of the forces shaping legislative districts in Russia and their impact on legislative outcomes is beyond the scope of this work and may be too opaque to report accurately. However, it is important to note that everything we know about redistricting in Russia suggests that this process only exacerbated the tendency against building electoral infrastructure. By forcing some incumbents to run in substantially new districts, the 1995 changes made it tougher for voters in these new districts to form accurate assessments of their incumbent's electoral viability or his or her likely behavior in office. Similarly, candidates in these districts faced the problem of assessing voter preferences in these new districts without the benefit of any past election results. The 1995 changes also forced a number of incumbents to run against each other in the same district, creating a situation where the defeat of some incumbents was inevitable. This development increased turnover in the Duma and within party cohorts, thereby complicating attempts to coordinate behavior or build durable organizations.

Residency Requirements

The lack of residency requirements spawned two types of carpetbagger candidates. First, the combination of portable resources and freedom to select any district allowed some candidates to parachute from Moscow into favorable districts around Russia. This practice began in the 1989 and 1990 elections, when Communist Party of the Soviet Union (CPSU) leaders who resided in Moscow ran in districts around the Soviet Union, betting on their national notoriety and local communist control to secure office. This strategy was also employed by the Moscow-based leaders of small boutique parties, who ran in a friendly district to ensure that they would win office – until the practice was outlawed in 1999, when candidates on the central party list were restricted from running in districts outside Moscow. Even so, 198 Moscow-based politicians ran for office in district races in 1999.

One of the most colorful district shoppers was Nikolai Lysenko, the leader of a small national organization, the National Republican Party of Russia. His party gained ballot access in 1995 and 1999 but received only .40 percent of the vote in 1999. To win a Duma seat, Lysenko migrated across Russia capitalizing on situations of ethnic conflict. In 1993, he ran in Engels, across the river from Saratov's oblast capital, capitalizing on voter anger over Yeltsin's orders allowing Volga Germans to return to Saratov, as well as over the presence of non-Russian black market or mafia figures. During this campaign, Lysenko staged an assassination attempt allegedly by black marketeers from the Caucuses. This stunt provoked the ire of Russian nationalist constituents and garnered much attention. He won the race, but by 1995, having lost the confidence of the voters in Engels, Lysenko migrated to Krasnoyarsk, another hotbed of nationalist sentiment. Just prior to the election, he allegedly blew up his own office in the Duma to gain publicity. He was later arrested, tried, and acquitted of all charges.

As with Lysenko, the presence of national notables profoundly influenced the outcome of many nominal races. For instance, in 1995, the nationalist leader General Boris Gromov unseated the KPRF incumbent Anatoly Gordeev in Saratov's oblast capital. Gordeev's loss was surprising. He was an influential committee chair in the Duma, and worked to build strong district ties by leading regional strike actions on behalf of workers whose wages had not been paid. Still, Gromov's national reputation enabled him to edge out Gordeev by less than 1 percentage point. He did not seek reelection in the district in 1999, although he did run on the Fatherland–All Russia (FAR) national list in the number seven position and secured a seat in the Duma. In 2002, Gromov left his Duma seat to run for governor of the Moscow Region, where he continues to work closely with the UR leader and Moscow mayor, Yury Luzhkov.

In 1999, the pattern of national leaders parachuting into districts turned golden as some of the leading oligarchs won elections in nominal districts far from the capital city. The exiled media magnate, Boris Berezovsky, won a Duma seat from Republic of Karachaevo-Cherkessia, promising to use his influence and wealth to improve the lives of residents. Similarly, the oil magnate Roman Abramovich was elected in Chukotka, a sparsely populated region in the far northeastern corner of Russia. Abramovich later ran and won the governor's office in the region, where he has invested significant amounts of his personal fortune in social programs and also is rumored to have invested heavily in developing the region's mineral and fishing industries.

The more common type of carpetbagger candidate migrated from their oblast capital into an outlying district that encompassed rural areas or smaller cities. In part, this strategy was encouraged by the 1993 election returns, which suggested that candidates in rural districts were weaker and competition was less intense. Prior to 1993, rural districts had been thought to be conservative strongholds because of the tight control that the Communist Party exercised through the collective farm structure. By 1995, some candidates with rural ties, or even those with regional notoriety, began to contest outlying districts. One of the most fascinating of these candidates was Konstantin Kondrat'ev, a professor at the regional agricultural institute and host of a regional television show on agricultural issues. He relied on his former students employed in collective farms across the region to staff his campaign. His students went door to door, spreading leaflets and organizing voter meetings.

The lack of a residency requirement suggests important questions. On the one hand, the fact that candidates need not run for office in their home district implies that they can seek out a district where their chances of winning are maximized – or, put another way, a district where their background, their policy preferences, or their party affiliation is an asset rather than a liability. It is easy to imagine situations where this sort of district shopping leads to a strengthening of linkages between legislators and their constituents, a linkage built on a mutual recognition of shared values. However, it is not clear whether all candidates, or even the majority of candidates, can realistically expect to win districts far from home. The phenomena of well-known notables parachuting into districts may not reflect the central tendency of Russian candidates. For most candidates, simple financial constraints or the non-portability of resources may place strong constraints on their choice of where to run. Consider a candidate with strong ties to a local social movement. Running in a district far on the other side of the country means that the candidate cannot draw on the organization for volunteers or office space. Moreover, the candidate will lose the brand-name value of the organization, as voters in other districts may be unaware of the organization itself or its accomplishments. In the end, this aspect

Finding Fit

of district choice is an empirical question to which we return in the next section.

Candidate Information

Faced with the decision between running on a party list or in a district, the expectation is that at the margin of other factors (such as an interest in party building or a reputation-based connection), as candidates become more confident that they can win in a district, they are less likely to run on their party's list. Put another way, as the district-only lottery becomes more attractive, candidates are less likely to enter a second, party list lottery. Why? Some candidates have a better chance of winning without the party label. For these candidates, affiliation brings significant risk for the future. If the party loses public support during the campaign, or if other candidates from the party or the party leadership take unpopular positions, running on the list could cost a candidate support in his or her district race. If, on the other hand, a candidate believes that his or her chances of winning in a district are relatively poor, then the candidate should be more likely to run on the party list since the increased potential to win outweighs the risks of being identified with the party.

Candidate Resources

The impact of resources on a candidate's district selection depends on whether these resources are independent of a party organization (independent resources) or bound up in the candidate's work within and for a party (connected resources). A candidate's past experiences can translate into both types of resources. For example, a leadership position in a social movement in the early transition period may have no connection to a specific party organization – for example, if the candidate leads a local environmental movement or a loose association of entrepreneurs. At the other extreme, a social movement might be essentially a subsidiary of a political party, such as a pro-reform group whose leadership and members are all members of the local Yabloko organization.

It is possible that even partisan candidates have access to independent resources such as KPRF candidates whose effective leadership or business success under the old regime provided a reason for voters to support them under new rules. Consistent with this logic, the expectation here is that affiliated candidates with independent resources are more likely to run in a nominal district and forego the party list, whereas candidates with connected resources are more likely to run list-only races or in both a nominal district and on the party list. In part these predictions are derived from the lottery example described earlier, where candidates with independent resources do not have to be closely associated with a party in order to win. In addition, close association in the form of a position on the party list carries risks of its own. In addition, connected resources may well be a signal of a candidate's preexisting decision to commit to building a party organization. Candidates with connected resources may also be forced to take a position on their party's list because to do otherwise would be inconsistent with their political history and reputation, or because the party has a measure of control over how these resources are used.

The presence or absence of these resources should also shape a candidate's decision of where to run. In general, most of the resources identified here are regionally if not locally specific. For example, a candidate's reputation due to his or her position in a local elected office is unlikely to extend far beyond the candidate's district lines. As such, a trivial observation would be that candidates who feel that they have name recognition with one set of constituents are likely to run for the Duma where that recognition is concentrated. Such a reputation need not be the product of political experience. Candidates who own businesses, for example, might be inclined to run in districts where voters are familiar with their enterprise. These factors are especially salient for independent candidates, who must rely on their own resources and reputations to win office.

Candidate Goals

Different districts define distinct constituencies with distinct sets of interests. As a result of this variation and the potential it creates to forge distinct ties to voters, candidates who hold different goals (career, policy, party building) will be attracted to different types of districts. Yet, the impact of different goals on district selection differs in important respects to the patterns noted in the analysis of affiliation decisions. As shown in Chapter 5, at the margin of other factors, strong career goals tend to push candidates toward running as independents, whereas candidates interested in party building affiliate at a high rate and candidates with strong policy goals are somewhere in between. Once a candidate decides to join a party, these factors have different effects on their behavior. The decision to affiliate links the candidate to a particular constituency – people who identify with or otherwise associate themselves with the party. Having made this decision, partisan careerists should invest in building the organization by running on the list. (Whether they run in a district as well depends on other factors.) In other words, careerists who affiliate should try to cultivate support for the party by becoming its regional face. Likewise, candidates with strong party-building goals should also run on the list.

The effects of policy goals on district choice are more ambiguous. Once a candidate has affiliated, an interest in enacting good policy may push him or her toward the national list, particularly if those goals strongly overlap with the party's central concerns. However, if the candidate's policy goals stress local issues that are peripheral to the party, or if the candidate's goals are so strong that he or she is unwilling to compromise them, he or she may end up running only in a nominal district. This strategy provides the candidate with the benefit of the party's following without any clear signal about his or her commitment to its platform.

Other Possible Influences

Some obvious factors that might influence district selection are local political ones such as the quality of potential opposition: Who else might run for the seat, and what is his or her chances of winning? In most established democracies, virtually all candidates make calculations along these lines, deciding where and when to run based on the expectation of who is likely to run against them. In the U.S. Congress, for example, the probability that a challenger will run for a seat in the House of Representatives depends on whether the incumbent is safe or vulnerable; in open seats, would-be candidates carefully consider what sort of opposition they might face before making their own decision.

Will candidates make these sorts of calculations in Russia or other transitional democracies? The fact that candidates have an obvious motive to try to find a district where opposition is weak does not imply that they will be able to do so. As discussed earlier, some candidates may be locked into running in their home district because their electoral resources are not portable. Moreover, the uncertainty about voter preferences that is endemic to Russia and other emerging democracies may well make these sorts of calculations impossible. Regardless of their affiliation, candidates may be unable to discern their own prospects for garnering voter support, either in isolation or in light of expectations about what other candidates are likely to do. In the end, whether Russian candidates behave as their counterparts in established democracies in shopping around for a winnable district is an empirical question.

A final question concerns the role of party organizations in shaping candidates' choices of where and how to run for office. As discussed earlier, party leaders may want to spread out strong candidates across many districts and force them to run on the party list as part of a long-term strategy for building support for the party. Alternately, party leaders may want to concentrate strong candidates in districts where the party is strong, as a way of winning seats in the Duma and gaining legislative power. However, in the case of Russia and other transitional democracies, discussion of what party leaders would like their candidates to do may well be premature. First, we must ask, does the party have any control over its candidates? Given their lack of stable organization, electoral resources, and brand names, party leaders in Russia may well act as price takers, allowing candidates to make district choices essentially on their own. Such freedom may be in the interest of individual candidates, but as discussed in Chapter 3, it clearly works against the creation of electoral infrastructure.

The Determinants of District Choice

Three kinds of evidence can be brought to bear to understand how Russian candidates decide where to run. The first is candidates' responses to relevant survey questions. The second is a multivariate analysis that predicts district selection as a function of a candidate's goals, resources, and other factors. The last piece of the puzzle is national data on Russian election outcomes in 1999 and 2003.

In the 1999 survey, candidates were asked a very simple question about the impact that various factors had on their choice of where and how to run. Respondents were asked to rate the importance of a wide range of factors. Table 6.3 reports their responses.

The columns divide candidates on the basis of district selection: independents running in a nominal district, partisans running nominal-only districts, partisans running both in a nominal district and on their party's list, and partisans running only on their party list. The leftmost column describes factors that candidates were asked to evaluate: partisan factors (whether party leaders influenced the candidate's decision), candidate characteristics (whether the candidate's residency or his or her business or

Finding Fit

Table 6.3. *Candidates' Explanations for District Selection, 1999 Duma Elections*

			Partisan Candidates		
	Factor	Independent Candidates	District Only	District and List	List Only
Party	Party Leaders	–	7.0% (6)	12.8% (8)	16.3% (17)
Candidate	Live in District	60.0% (42)	34.1% (29)	29.0% (36)	37.1% (39)
	Business Reputation	58.6% (41)	41.2% (35)	46.8% (29)	30.5% (32)
	Political Reputation	24.1% (19)	29.4% (25)	25.8% (16)	22.3% (24)
District	Good for Independent	27.1% (19)	–	–	–
	Quality of Opposition	0% (0)	0% (0)	0% (0)	1.9% (2)
	Not Controlled by Party or Political Figure	0% (0)	0% (0)	1.6% (1)	0% (0)

Source: Candidate survey conducted by the author.

political reputation was a factor in the candidate's decision), and whether local political factors, such as the expected quality of opposition, influenced the candidate's decision.

Two important political patterns are immediately evident from Table 6.3. First, relatively few candidates reported that party leaders influenced their district selection. Only 7 percent of partisans running district-only races reported party influence. The percentage is slightly higher for candidates running only on a party list or on both ballots, but even here the percentages are quite modest. This finding underscores the weakness in party organizations and echoes the findings in the previous chapters.

The second obvious and significant pattern in Table 6.3 is the relative unimportance of political factors in district selection. Only three partisan candidates reported that their choice was influenced by the expected quality of opposition or the dominance of district politics by a party or political figure. The percentages for independents are significantly higher, but even here, only slightly more than a quarter of these candidates reported that their choice was influenced by the fact that their district was one where an independent had a good chance of winning.

Candidate Strategies and Electoral Competition

Table 6.3 suggests that the lack of a residency requirement for Russian candidates has less of an impact on district selection than intuition and many good stories would suggest. As noted previously, the results for the impact of political factors suggest that relatively few candidates engage in district shopping. Consistent with analyses of candidate entry in Chapter 4, it appears that candidates do not look for sparsely populated districts or for districts in which voters are likely to support them. This lack of strategic thinking about the opposition speaks to the lack of good information about districts and candidates and provides an additional clue about the lack of coordination among candidates and parties as they compete for voter support.

From the perspective of candidates, Table 6.3 shows that residency and reputations (both political and business) loom large for many candidates. In other words, most Russian candidates run in places where they are well-known prior to the campaign – given that their reputations and other resources are not portable, they are unable to look beyond their home districts. Even if their chances of winning their home district were not especially high, they would have little chance of winning elsewhere, even in a district where they are seemingly a better fit. Thus, while the lack of residency requirement might encourage the formation of electoral infrastructure, as candidates seek out districts where they are a natural fit to the majority – and where the majority can appreciate this fact – resource and informational constraints make this strategy impossible for all but a few candidates.

Next, Table 6.4 compares the 1999 results to similar data from the 1995 survey. While this comparison is limited by differences in survey design – in particular, the lack of data on the actual district selection choices that candidates made in 1995 – it still provides important data on the trends in the factors shaping district choices.

As Table 6.4 reveals, the 1999 findings about the unimportance of party leaders and political factors hold for 1995 as well. The sharp difference between the two elections lies in the drop in importance of political experience for district selection. This change may be due to the influx of political amateurs into political competition in 1999.

Table 6.4 also reveals a decline in the perceived value of being an independent candidate in a nominal district between 1995 and 1999. This change could stem from the lack of partisan influence of parties within the district, the perception that voters are less likely to punish partisan district candidates because of their affiliation, or because of a general lack of clear

Finding Fit

Table 6.4. *Comparison of Factors Driving District Selection in 1995 and 1999*

Factor		1995	1999
Party Organization	Party Leaders Influenced Decision	12.0% (10)	9.6% (31)
Candidate Characteristics	Live in District	41.0% (34)	45.3% (146)
	Business Reputation in District	55.4% (46)	42.5% (137)
	Political Reputation in District	65.1% (54)	26.4% (85)
District Factors	Good for Independent	14.5% (12)	5.9% (19)
	Quality of Opposition	0% (0)	.6% (2)
	Not Controlled by Party or Political Figure	–	.3% (1)

Source: Candidate survey conducted by the author.

information about the electoral viability of different candidates. In either case, the trend continued in 2003, with a significant drop in the number of independent candidates running in nominal districts.

Untangling the Factors Behind District Selection: Multivariate Analysis

Up until this point, the analysis has not directly considered the role of the explanatory variables posited in Chapter 3 along with other forces that might influence district selection. Nor has the analysis evaluated these influences controlling for other factors. To accomplish this task, this section reports the results of a series of unordered logistic regressions that explore the importance of different types of resources, goals, and information as determinants of candidates' district choices controlling for partisan affiliation.

Candidates' district choices involved a series of calculations based on a number of factors discussed earlier. To test the predictions regarding the effects of these factors previously outlined, the analysis uses the following model:

$$\text{District-Only} = \beta_1(\text{Constant}) + \beta_2(\text{Fit}) + \beta_3(\text{Campaign HQ}) \\ + \beta_4(\text{Policy}) + \beta_5(\text{Career}) + \beta_6(\text{Party Building}) \\ + \beta_7(\text{Prof. Pol.}) + \beta_8(\text{Pol. Rep.}) + \beta_9(\text{Org. Res.})$$

Candidate Strategies and Electoral Competition

$$+ \beta_{10}(\text{Leg. Leader}) + \beta_{11}(\text{Russian Region})$$
$$+ \beta_{12}(\text{LDPR Member}) + \nu_1$$
$$\text{Both} = \beta_{21}(\text{Constant}) + \beta_{22}(\text{Fit}) + \beta_{23}(\text{Campaign HQ})$$
$$+ \beta_{24}(\text{Policy}) + \beta_{25}(\text{Career}) + \beta_{26}(\text{Party Building})$$
$$+ \beta_{27}(\text{Prof. Pol.}) + \beta_{28}(\text{Pol. Rep.}) + \beta_{29}(\text{Org. Res.})$$
$$+ \beta_{210}(\text{Leg. Leader}) + \beta_{211}(\text{Russian Region})$$
$$+ \beta_{212}(\text{LDPR Member}) + \nu_2$$
$$\text{List-Only} = \beta_{31}(\text{Constant}) + \beta_{32}(\text{Fit}) + \beta_{33}(\text{Campaign HQ})$$
$$+ \beta_{34}(\text{Policy}) + \beta_{35}(\text{Career}) + \beta_{36}(\text{Party Building})$$
$$+ \beta_{37}(\text{Prof. Pol.}) + \beta_{38}(\text{Pol. Rep.}) + \beta_{39}(\text{Org. Res.})$$
$$+ \beta_{310}(\text{Leg. Leader}) + \beta_{311}(\text{Russian Region})$$
$$+ \beta_{312}(\text{LDPR Member}) + \nu_3$$

Because the focus of this chapter, district selection, consists of three choices that cannot be ranked in any logical way, the impact of the various causal factors is estimated using unordered logistic regressions. There are three equations, each with a 0/1 dependent variable that captures a different choice: run in a district-only or not, run in a district and on the list or not, and run only on the list or not. The independent variables are the same in all three equations. Table 6.5 summarizes these predictions, indicating the expected direction of the effect of each factor.

When considering these predictions, readers must bear in mind that district selection occurs at a time when candidates have already affiliated with political parties. As such, at least some of these candidates will have decided to pursue their political ambitions through the party organization. This is particularly true for candidates who are affiliated with existing parties that have a proven track record and some political endurance. With this caveat in mind, the predictions reported in Table 6.5 are straightforward. Strong partisanship drives candidates toward running on the list rather than district-only. This effect is captured by two variables: whether the candidate mounts his or her campaign from the party's headquarters or from the candidate's own resources and whether the candidate holds strong party-building goals. The predicted effect is not all that surprising: Party insiders are less likely to run only in a district and more likely to run on the list. The same is true for candidates with political reputations embedded in

Finding Fit

Table 6.5. *Factors Affecting District Selection*

Variable	Description	Impact on Probability of District Selection		
		District-Only	District and List	List-Only
Candidate Fit with District	Candidate's information about voter preferences (0 = bad fit with candidate 1 = uncertain, 2 = good fit)	+	–	–
Campaign HQ in Party HQ	Candidate's campaign headquarters was located in party headquarters (1 = yes, 0 = no)	–	+	+
Professional Politician	Candidate was a professional politician (0 = no, 1 = yes)	–	+	+
Political Reputation	Candidate had a reputation for being a political activist or political appointee (0 = no, 1 = yes)	–	+	+
Organizational Resources	Candidate heads or holds a leadership position in a social organization (0 = no, 1 = leadership, 2 = head)	–	+	+
Elected Official	Candidate was an elected official (0 = no, 1 = yes)	–	+	+
Career Goal	Candidate's interest in a political career (0 = not important, 1 = important, 2 = very important)	–	+	+
Party Building Goal	Candidate's interest in building a political party (0 = not important, 1 = important, 2 = very important)	–	+	+
Policy Goal	Candidate's interest in enacting good public policies (0 = not important, 1 = important, 2 = very important)	No prediction		

a party organization: These candidates are more likely to run district and list or list-only than candidates who lack this reputation. And controlling for other factors, once affiliated with an existing organization, these candidates are likely to choose strategies that invest in party building over their own probability of winning office – in other words, they are more likely to run just on the list and not in a district.

Consistent with the argument that a "district plus list" strategy allows candidates to hedge their bets, Table 6.5 predicts that politicians with a

Candidate Strategies and Electoral Competition

problematic fit within their district are more likely to choose this strategy.[4] Those candidates who hold the goal of party building are also more likely to run on a list. Once a candidate has affiliated, strong policy goals should also push the candidate toward party-building strategies – toward running on the list. According to a similar logic, once affiliated, partisan candidates with significant resources are more likely to run on the list (with or without running in a district) than their counterparts who lack these resources. This expectation should hold regardless of the type of resources, but political resources should have the strongest effects.

Finally, all of these equations include a regional variable that distinguishes between ethnic Russian and non-Russian regions. Given the lack of information about the value of party labels in ethnic republics, the expectation is that partisans from these regions would be more likely to run only in a district where partisan affiliation need not be the center of the campaign than on a party list or a combination. The equations also include an instrumental variable for legislators from the LDPR: Due to a last-minute snag in the party's registration, most of the party's candidates were able to run in their districts, but did not make it on the list of their proxy, the Zhirinovsky Bloc.

Findings. The expectations in Table 6.5 are largely confirmed by the results in Table 6.6, which reports parameters for each of the three equations. Given the large number of parameter estimates, however, and the essentially relative nature of our predictions about district selection, the analysis here offers an interpretation built on a comparison of the predicted district choices for four hypothetical candidates:

- A candidate with strong policy goals and no resources. In essence, this candidate is a political amateur with strong ideas about what government should be doing.
- A candidate with strong career goals, moderate policy goals, and some independent resources. These parameters describe candidates whose reputations are made outside politics, such as in private enterprise, but who have a strong interest in a political career.

---

[4] This prediction also makes sense from a party-building point of view if the party wants to use local notables to expand the image of the party in the district.

Finding Fit

Table 6.6. *Parameters for District Selection Regressions*

Variables		Logit Parameter (Standard Error)		
		District Only	District + List	List Only
Campaign Variables	Candidate Fit with Constituency	.42** (.25)	−.53** (.25)	.07 (.22)
	Campaign HQ in Party HQ	−1.25*** (.33)	−.04 (.33)	1.1*** (.30)
Candidate Goals	Policy Goal	−.16 (.24)	.06 (.26)	.09 (.22)
	Career Goal	−.77*** (.31)	.77*** (.26)	−.10 (.25)
	Party Building Goal	−.57*** (.22)	.38** (.23)	.20 (.19)
Candidate Background	Professional Politician	−.77** (.45)	.24 (.40)	.37 (.36)
	Political Reputation	−.89** (.40)	.71* (.51)	.45 (.40)
	Organizational Resources	−.32** (.20)	−.03 (.20)	.30** (.18)
	Elected Office	−.11 (.31)	−.57* (.40)	.35* (.26)
	Russian Region	−.84*** (.36)	−.35 (.34)	.82*** (.33)
	LDPR Member	2.05*** (.65)	−1.92** (.88)	−.44 (.56)
	Constant	1.83*** (.70)	−1.48** (.76)	−2.61*** (.67)
	Model Chi Square	58.2	31.3	29.3
	N	252	252	252

Note: *** = sig. at .01, ** = sig. at .05, * = sig at .10, all one-tail.
Source: Candidate survey conducted by the author.

- A candidate with strong career goals, moderate policy goals, and substantial connected resources. In contrast to the previous archetype, this candidate's reputation and resources are bound up in his or her previous political activities – activities that bind the candidate to a party organization.
- A candidate with moderate career and policy goals, strong party-building goals, and substantial connected resources, and who also holds elected office. Such candidates are closely identified with a particular political party and place a high priority on building a party organization.

Candidate Strategies and Electoral Competition

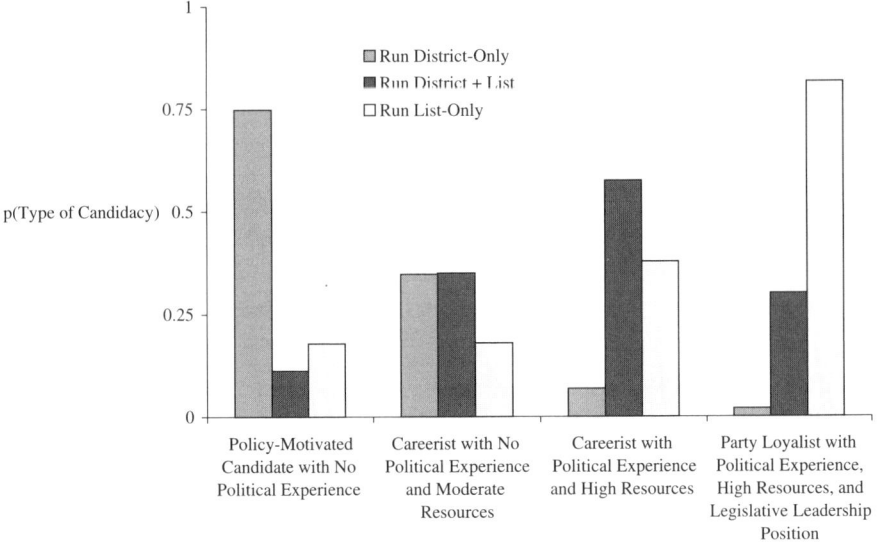

Figure 6.2. Probability of Candidacy Decisions for Different Candidate Types, 1999 Duma Elections

The statistical findings in Table 6.6 are used to calculate the probability that each of these candidates will run only in a district, in a district and on a party list, or only on the party list. The results are depicted in Figure 6.2.

Although many different types of candidates are running for office in Russia, these four archetypes neatly illustrate the factors driving district selection. Policy-motivated amateur partisans, represented by the leftmost bar in Figure 6.2, are most likely to run in a nominal district, with a relatively small probability of running on the party list. This pattern probably reflects two factors. First, these candidates are the least desirable for party leaders looking to assemble a party list that will attract public support. Second, candidates with strong policy goals may be unwilling to make the compromises necessary to get on the party list.

Predictions for the two careerist candidates, shown in the middle of Figure 6.2, also confirm our expectations. The careerist with independent resources has a substantial probability of running a district-only race or in a district race and on the party list, and a much smaller probability of running on his or her party's list. This archetypical candidate has the means to win on his or her own. Such candidates run in a district, where they control

Finding Fit

their electoral fate and where they have a good chance of winning office, regardless of how their party does in the list race. In contrast, the careerist with connected resources has a much higher probability of running both in a nominal district race and on the party list, reflecting his or her inability to abandon the party without losing valuable electoral resources.

Finally, the party-building candidate represented by the rightmost bar in Figure 6.2 has a high probability of running only on the list, and a very small probability of running only in a nominal district race. This combination makes sense: These candidates want to make their party stronger, hence they are happy to help by running on the list. These candidates are also attractive to list builders, given their resources, reputations, and electoral experience. Moreover, since they will likely receive a high position on the party list, they do not need to run in a district to hedge their electoral bet. In essence, these candidates are willing to invest their resources in building the party organization and stake their fate squarely with the party. For the same reasons, these candidates will see little reason to run only in a district race. For them, close ties to the party are desirable, regardless of the consequences. Moreover, given their reputation, voters are likely to see them as strong partisans, even if they try to downplay these ties by avoiding the party list.

Incumbents and District Selection

A final piece of evidence of the impact of district selection on electoral infrastructure considers the results of electoral competition: To what extent are incumbents able to hold the districts they won in a previous election? Put another way, does incumbency matter, in the sense that being an incumbent gives a candidate additional support – more votes – than expected? A finding that incumbents were advantaged would suggest the beginnings of representational linkages between incumbents and groups in the electorate. While these linkages might not be built on policy responsiveness or partisan loyalty – they could be driven by the provision of pork-barrel benefits or effective leadership – they would clearly be an advance over the zero-information beginnings of Russian democracy, where voters knew little about candidates and candidates little about the electorate.

One simple way of assessing incumbent success in elections is to consider the success rate of incumbent legislators in Duma elections: Has it increased or decreased over time? This analysis is not as clear-cut as it is in pure proportional representation (PR) or pure single-member district (SMD) systems. In the Russian case, an incumbent can be drawn from either the

Candidate Strategies and Electoral Competition

Table 6.7. *Success Rates for Russian Incumbents in Nominal (SMD) Districts, 1995–2003*

	1995	1999	2003
Incumbents Running for Reelection in Nominal Districts	77.7% (306)	71.7% (258)	60.5% (236)
Incumbents Reelected in Nominal Districts	31.7% (97)	34.1% (88)	47.5% (113)
Nominal Districts with Winning Incumbent	43.1% (97)	39.1% (88)	50.2% (113)

Source: Data collected by the author from official statistics.

SMD races or the list race. In each election, large numbers of incumbents migrated from the national list to contest a nominal district. This reality provides a second indicator to measure the evolution of infrastructure: the degree to which incumbents run against each other. A final indicator is the likelihood that a district elects an incumbent to the Duma. To assess these indicators, Table 6.7 reports data on the percentage of incumbents running for reelection in a nominal district in the 1995, 1999, and 2003 Russian elections, and their success rates.

Between 1995 and 2003, the percentage of incumbents seeking reelection in nominal districts declined. Yet, even in 2003, the number of incumbents running in districts exceeded the total number of district incumbents – in some districts, two or more incumbents ran against each other for an SMD seat. Some of these contests resulted from redistricted incumbents searching for a more favorable place to run for reelection. However, some of the multiple-incumbent races were the result of list incumbents deciding to seek reelection in a district. Table 6.7 also shows that incumbents' reelection rates in district races continued to rise from 1995 to 2003, although they remain considerably below the U.S. rate of over 90 percent reelection.

At first glance, the trends reflected in Table 6.7 suggest the beginnings of coordination, in the sense that fewer incumbents are running against each other and more are winning office; however, the general trends mask important factors in the accumulation of infrastructure. Districts hopping, moves from list to district races, and the undeniable effect of UR in the increase in reelection rates in 2003 suggest that this trend does not add up to the accumulation of electoral infrastructure. Not all of the winning incumbents represent the same constituencies that they had in a previous

Finding Fit

election. In fact, of the 236 incumbents who ran for reelection in a district in 2003, 173 ran in the district they won in the previous election and 46 percent of them won again. However, among the forty-eight district incumbents who were challenged by another incumbent, only twelve (25 percent) were reelected. Many of these defeats were the result of UR deputies elected on the list in 1999 running in districts where they successfully defeated incumbents standing for reelection. Thus, the increase in vote totals and vote margins across incumbents masks a gap in direct ties between districts and their representatives and a rise in Putin's authoritarian infrastructure – coordination among voters and cooperation among UR candidates based on the parties' increasing reliance on undemocratic methods and cooptation of state resources.

A second piece of evidence about the relative weakness of legislator–constituent ties in contemporary Russia comes from a simple exploratory regression that focuses on incumbents running for reelection in nominal races: their vote percentage, and their probability of winning. The explanatory variables are how many incumbents are in the nominal race, whether an incumbent represented the district prior to the election, and whether the incumbent is a strong partisan, meaning they had not changed their party affiliation since the last election. Table 6.8 reports the results of this analysis.

The critical parameters in these regressions are those for the number of incumbents in the race and for the district incumbent variable – whether the incumbent had represented the district prior to the election. The negative parameter for the "number of incumbents" variable in both regressions points to the substantive impact of the lack of coordination in Russian elections. Running against each other may be an optimal strategy for individual incumbents, since moving to a different district may increase their chances of reelection, even if they must compete against another incumbent. Even so, this behavior works against the accumulation of electoral infrastructure, since incumbents are investing electoral capital in new constituencies rather than building up stable ties in an existing area. The effect is to dilute the signal on incumbency for voters. This argument is most clear in 2003, where the number of incumbents profoundly decreases the potential vote support for any one incumbent but does not hinder the chance that any single incumbent will win the district.

With regard to the district incumbent variable, the important thing to note is that district incumbents do not attract much more support compared to other candidates. In 1999, district incumbents received only about

Table 6.8. *The Impact of District Shopping on Incumbent Success, 1999 and 2003*

	1999		2003	
Variables	Votes (%)	p(win)[1]	Votes (%)	p(win)[1]
N of Incumbents in District	−4.3*** (1.2)	−.35** (.20)	−11.26*** (3.2)	.73 (.57)
District Incumbent	3.1*** (1.8)	.63** (.30)	3.43 (3.12)	.78* (.43)
Independent	.004 (2.2)	−.11 (.43)	6.00 (4.72)	−.17 (.72)
Strong Non-KPRF Partisan	−4.3 (2.9)	−1.6*** (.66)	−5.81 (4.66)	−2.11*** (.69)
Strong KPRF Partisan	6.3*** (2.3)	.31 (.36)	−5.6 (4.26)	.33 (.70)
Constant	24.6 (3.25)	−.27 (.42)	41.87 (4.54)	−.22 (.63)
R^2	.13	.14	.19	.19
N	255	255	225	225

[1] Model estimated using logistic regression.
** = significant at .05, *** = significant at .01.
Source: Collected by the author from official statistics.

5 percent more votes than other types of candidates. In 2003, winning incumbents had an average vote margin of 25.3 percent compared to a margin of 21.4 percent for all non-incumbent winners. This finding remains even after we control for whether an incumbent runs as a partisan or as an independent, or for the level of incumbent challengers in the district.

What is most striking is the lack of coordination among some incumbents and the effect that this has on candidates' ability to win votes. The model shows that when incumbents compete against each other for the same seat, vote totals drop significantly and the cost of running against each other increases with time. A quick look at the data shows that in most cases in 1999, the incumbents going head to head were KPRF candidates against independent incumbents. Yet, in a number of cases, particularly in nationalist areas, an LDPR deputy squared off against a KPRF deputy, or a Yabloko incumbent ran against an NDR incumbent. Thus, even in districts where a party feels as if it has a potential voter base, it often guesses wrong about both its chances and the actions of the opponents. By 2003, this pattern had shifted and UR incumbents tended to face off against independent incumbents and wrest their seats from them. Importantly, in the 2003 election, KPRF candidates were most vulnerable to challenges by other incumbents.

These findings also provide the first indicators about the value of party labels in district races. In short, partisanship does not seem to provide a strong advantage to incumbent candidates even when the party of power (UR) is in the race. Until this point, party labels provide little clear information about a candidate's chances of election. The shifts in partisan effects are extremely interesting in this model. The missing group of candidates or referents here consists of Duma faction members that switch parties. Relative to these candidates, independents are slightly worse off but this effect is not significant. In contrast, non-KPRF partisan incumbents are much less likely to win district-level office than either independents or KPRF incumbents. Change in the KPRF effect foreshadows the problems the party will face in the future. While the party has significant support and party resources to increase a candidate's potential to win votes, the resources are much less effective at securing seats.

These data provide a glimpse into the fragility of linkages that are being formed between voters and their representatives and the difficulty in establishing any type of stable tie to a regionally based electorate. First, relatively few incumbents running in the same single-member district actually are reelected. This means that any given candidate's attempts to build ties are wiped out when he or she loses to a challenger. Moreover, the political party with the clearest message and most identifiable constituency, the KPRF, is actually a liability for experienced candidates. On the whole, the rise in incumbency rates can be attributed more to the growing Kremlin-sponsored authoritarian infrastructure that prompted coordination and cooperation around UR than the accumulation of electoral infrastructure. This trend is likely to increase as the Kremlin works to ensure limited competition in future elections.

The Effects of District Choice on Electoral Infrastructure

Candidates' decisions about where and how to run have a clear impact on electoral infrastructure. By running on a list, partisan candidates lend their name and reputation to the party, and entrust their political career in the party's ability to attract mass support. By running in a nominal district and on the list, partisan candidates place their party brand name before the electorate as a way to structure their choice. In both ways, these choices help to build electoral infrastructure by giving voters information about parties

Candidate Strategies and Electoral Competition

and candidates. In contrast, by running only in a nominal district, candidates sidestep both of these mechanisms, which may help them get elected but works against the accumulation of infrastructure. Electoral infrastructure is also shaped by district shopping, although the effects are complicated. By searching for a district in which they fit well, candidates can help to create strong representational linkages. However, by moving from district to district, and ensuring that voters face an entirely new set of candidates in each election, candidates again work against the accumulation of critical information about their chances of winning and the nature of their electoral support. I return to this theme in Chapter 7.

This analysis has shown that district selection can be explained in terms of candidates' goals, resources, and information. The multivariate analysis shows that candidates make these choices with regard to their own interests, not the advancement of party organizations, constituent interests, or democracy in Russia. In some cases, candidate interests coincide with these larger goals. Candidates whose resources or reputations connect them to party organizations have a stake in the survival of these organizations, and are more likely to run on the party list and thereby help to build the party's brand name and structure voters' choices. And some candidates have an intrinsic desire to build party organizations, perhaps as a vehicle to achieve larger policy goals. To some extent, these candidates subordinate their political careers to the interest of the party organization – put another way, the point is that the interests of these individuals coincide with the interests of the organization.

Leaving these special cases aside, the results about district selection reinforce earlier conclusions about the impact of candidate actions on electoral infrastructure. In particular, they point out the disjuncture between what supporters of Russian democracy would like candidates to do and the actions that the typical candidate sees as being in his or her interests. Consider the provision of information to the electorate and to political elites. One direct source of information deficit comes from frequent redefinition of constituencies so as to undermine existing ties and the meaning of past electoral outcomes. Over the last decade, district boundaries have been redrawn for each of the four competitive elections, first in the Soviet Union and then in the Russian Federation. These changes made it extremely difficult for candidates to learn about their potential constituencies or for parties to target specific constituencies. These changes also made it nearly impossible to determine the relative viability of candidates, a fact that is exemplified by the propensity of Russian incumbents to run against each

Finding Fit

other in nominal races. In addition, constant structural changes also undermined incumbents' efforts to link to constituents on the basis of service, pork, or effective legislation.

Candidates' responses to the opportunity to choose across different districts also undermined the potential to amass information through competition. The liberal entry rules bring together many different kinds of candidates in nominal races – independents, partisans running only in a district race, or partisans running in the district race and on the list. This variation presents voters with very perplexing choices. Moreover, candidates who affiliate with parties may choose to put an alternative label on the ballot next to their names, further proliferating voters' cues. In short, given the district selection options open to candidates, voters face an extremely complex set of choices that would be difficult to sort out even under the best of circumstances.

The impact of candidates' district choices on coordination and cooperation is even clearer than it is on information. The literature on coordination points to the importance of information about the viability of different candidates as a precondition for coordination among voters and among candidates. Clearly, candidates face significant uncertainty around these choices. The most extreme example is the propensity for incumbents to face off against each other rather than to defer to the strongest entrant or shop around for a less competitive district – even if they represent like-minded parties. Although there is some anecdotal information that parties have bargained over the placement of incumbents and other district candidates, these data show that such coordination may be the exception rather than the rule. Moreover, as the regression results illustrate, the willingness of affiliated candidates to run on their party's list is conditional at best. Candidates with independent resources and a good fit with a nominal district tend to run in these districts alone, foregoing a position on the list. Candidates who hold elected office are a notable exception to this pattern, but their number is very low relative to the set of candidates who run under the party label in a typical election.

Finally, these results paint a dismal picture of the role that Russian parties play in shaping the choices that voters face in legislative elections. Many party organizations are bystanders or price takers as candidates decide where and how to run. Rather than operating to shape the set of candidates who run under the party banner, placing candidates in nominal districts and constructing a list with aggregate outcomes in mind, party leaders in Russia appear to take what they can get as candidates pursue their individual interests. The clear outlier in this regard is UR, which used state resources as both incentives and sanctions to ensure that regional elites and government agencies supported the organization. The extension of these tactics to the election of regional legislatures coupled with the appointment of governors will further stifle the emergence of viable opposition candidates.

7

Campaigning for the Duma

MIXED MARKETS, MIXED MESSAGES

During the campaign period, candidates face a final set of decisions to invest in electoral infrastructure. These decisions center on the nature of their appeals to their potential constituents – whether candidates target groups, and whether their campaigns stress issue positions, party platforms, pork, personalized benefits, or their own experiences or character. These decisions have a wide-ranging impact on coordination and cooperation within the constituency. Candidates' campaign strategies can help to identify and forge ties among constituencies or they can further divide or fragment them. Candidates' campaign strategies also shape the information available to voters on election day. They can clearly distinguish themselves from other candidates and explain in detail what they will do in government, or they can blur those distinctions and present voters with very unclear choices. Finally, candidates' appeals can help to define voters' preferences over enduring issues or they can define a referendum that provides little information outside of the current context.

The argument that campaign styles and strategies influence the quality of democracy should not startle anyone. In the United States, a great deal of ink has been used exploring the relationship between negative campaigning and television advertising on citizens' participation rates or attitudes toward the government. In the comparative literature, the debate focuses on the growing use of personalized or leadership appeals to voters rather than strong party platforms and the effect of this change on representation and stability. The argument in this chapter builds on these approaches to understand how campaign strategies influence the accumulation of electoral infrastructure. The empirical analysis takes aim at two questions. First, how do candidates choose campaign strategies in contemporary Russia, in elections marked by weak parties, many sources of material resources, and considerable uncertainty about voter preferences and candidate viability? Second, what are the implications of these choices for the creation of electoral infrastructure, ranging from framing voters' choices to coordination and cooperation within party organizations? The analysis focuses on candidates' appeals during the campaign period: Do they stress their personal characteristics, issue positions, or a party platform? I also consider the coherence of campaigns run by partisan candidates: To what extent do candidates from the same party target the same groups or emphasize the same issues?

This approach complements two different strands of existing studies of campaign strategies. Analyses of parties' positions show that on the party system level, organizations adopt very different positions on issues, and that these positions appear to be stable over time.[1] This finding is hopeful in the sense that it suggests the potential for clear information for voters and the possibility for coordination and cooperation within party organizations. However, a closer look at behavior within party organizations is less convincing. The data reveal that while the mean assessments of party elites are quite stable, there is tremendous variance within party organizations, rendering them statistically indistinguishable. Moreover, party programs tend to be amorphous and vague, providing little information to the electorate.

Parties' campaign advertising underscores this finding. In her analysis of television and campaigns in post-Soviet Russia, Sarah Oates (forthcoming: 325) finds that parties' use of free time and paid advertising increasing relies on images and personalities over issue positions. Campaigns were marked by confusing ads of dancing apples, talking cows, women daydreaming about the LDPR leader Vladimir Zhirinovsky, and, finally, ambitious democratic leaders in their private plane.

The problem of unclear messages and personality-based campaigns was particularly acute within the "centrist" parties of power. By 2003, the UR campaign message was "Together with the President," and its web site invoked Ronald Reagan, asking voters to contemplate whether they were better off today than they had been four years ago. Its paid advertising followed Roger Ailes' formula for promoting Richard Nixon in 1968, relying

---

[1] These findings are based on surveys of political party elites that I conducted with Professor Herbert Kitschelt (Kitschelt and Smyth 2002; Smyth 2002; Smyth forthcoming).

heavily on "happy" images of a contented and diverse Russia at work and play against a backdrop of patriotic music.

These trends together with the general weakness of party organizations in transition demand a different approach to studying campaigns and their effects on political development. In the context of a stable party system in which party discipline assures appeals based on a party program and citizens voting based on stable party affiliations, questions about campaign appeals and targeting decisions are not meaningful, for there is usually little variance to explain. In Russia, however, the weakness of many party organizations and the lack of stable partisan ties among voters bring campaign appeals and strategies to the fore, both as an explanation of election outcomes and as a source and indicator of electoral infrastructure. As in previous chapters, the goals of this analysis are to understand how candidates frame their appeals to voters and to assess the consequences of these decisions for the development of effective democracy. The explanatory variables are the same as those employed in previous chapters: candidates' goals, resources, and information, as well as their district selection.

The argument proceeds in three sections. The first section develops a framework to assess candidates' decisions to present appeals based on their personal characteristics, personal issue agenda, or partisan agenda. The second section tests this framework using the 1999 Russian candidate survey. While there is some issue-based campaigning in Russia, the data also reveal serious coordination and cooperation problems among candidates and within parties. Many candidates eschew issues and party platforms, choosing instead to emphasize their personal background or characteristics. The third section employs spatial models to highlight one of the central implications of this electoral chaos: an inability to draw inferences about voter preferences from election outcomes.

Coordination and Cooperation Dilemmas in Electoral Campaigns

As the evidence in the previous chapters illustrate, the combination of pervasive uncertainty, nascent, weak political organizations, and a particular set of electoral institutions in contemporary Russia combine to create numerous coordination and cooperation dilemmas in the campaign period. These dilemmas are reinforced by a variety of factors mentioned in previous chapters, including the tendency of candidates to enter contests in large numbers, run as independents, and refuse to run on their party's list, as well as the

Table 7.1. *Candidate Assessments of Fairness of Duma Elections, 1999*

Statement	Agree	Unsure	Disagree
Elections conducted fairly?	22.1% (71)	25.2% (81)	52.8% (170)
Elections have become dirtier?	63.4% (204)	26.4% (85)	10.3% (33)

Source: Candidate survey conducted by the author.

proliferation of independent electoral resources and the relative absence of strong party-building goals among candidates. In this regard, the politics of transitional Russia is simply a more extreme version of that of other transitional systems.

Before turning to an exploration of campaign structures and strategies, it is important to note the widespread perception among Russian candidates that corruption and coercion still mar the Russian campaign process. Table 7.1 summarizes 1999 candidates' responses to questions about the fairness of the electoral process.

Over half of the candidates in 1999 perceived the election process to be unfair and a quarter more were unsure. Even more striking is that almost two-thirds of candidates in the survey believed that the election process had become dirtier or more biased with time. These responses must be viewed with some caution, since they may reflect the candidates' natural propensities to blame forces outside their control for their losses. Even so, the large number of candidates who made similar claims during the campaign period suggests that even before the election began, candidates faced tremendous obstacles in the campaign period. By all accounts, these obstacles grew in 2003 as the Kremlin consolidated its control of national and regional media outlets and used these resources to dominate the airwaves.[2] Although Russian elections were perennially marked by state abuse of the media in its own favor, for the first time election observers noted that this manipulation was profound enough to undermine the process.

Not surprisingly, Russian candidates also agree that the resources available to them were not sufficient to mount an effective campaign. Their responses to a question about campaign resources are summarized in Table 7.2.

[2] For a final report by the OSCE election observation team, see http://www.osce.org/documents/odihr/2004/01/1947en.pdf, accessed October 21, 2004.

Campaigning for the Duma

Table 7.2. *Candidate Assessments of Campaign Funding, 1999 and 1995*

Election	Had Sufficient Funds	Unsure	Needed More Money
1995	6.0%	1.2%	92.8%
	(5)	(1)	(77)
1999	7.5%	21.7%	70.8%
	(24)	(70)	(228)

Source: Candidate survey conducted by the author.

As the numbers indicate, the overwhelming message is that the resources available to candidates were not viewed as being sufficient. Again, these responses may reflect candidates' reluctance to blame their defeat on factors within their control, but on the whole they speak to the frustrations that face most candidates, both partisan and independent. In a sense, this frustration is no surprise, as these candidates were trying to win office despite a profound lack of electoral infrastructure, which in turn complicates the task of identifying potential supporters and winning their votes in a relatively short time span.

Resources took on an entirely new meaning in the 2003 election and profoundly shifted the electoral landscape as the Kremlin worked on a number of fronts to generate a monopoly over electoral resources. These activities took two forms. The first was to deprive the opposition of resources. The arrest of some of the oligarchs hit Yabloko and other liberal organizations directly at a critical period in the lead-up to the campaign. Similarly, the Kremlin's intervention in the Duma through the UR faction deprived the KPRF of critical organizational and pork-barrel resources that had been critical in previous campaigns. The second strategy was to centralize and control state resources to support UR. As the previous chapters suggest, increased Kremlin control over the federal structure deprived key regional leaders of their own resource portfolios and transferred these to UR candidates and regional party organizations. Governors even lent their own reputations to the party's efforts. Kremlin control of the media also strongly influenced the race. On the whole, it is difficult to imagine that UR candidates lacked effective support if they desired it. In fact, UR's increasing monopoly over all government resources not only attracted a large number of quality candidates, in the post-election period it provided strong incentives for independents to join the organization once the Duma was in session, securing a two-thirds majority for the party in the legislature.

Candidate Strategies and Electoral Competition

Campaign Organization and Activity

Absent strong party organizations, Russian campaigns tend to be run on a lick and a promise, with candidates cobbling together support, space, expertise, and materials from a wide range of sources. Finding campaign offices to conduct interviews was almost always a challenge. They were located in the basements of schools and universities, factory offices, and private apartments. Even party headquarters were often difficult to locate, and were cramped and ill equipped to reach out to voters. Because of this variation, the actual physical space that a candidate or party occupied during the campaign was telling. Without fail, LDPR regional headquarters were well appointed, and the parties of power were all well equipped and filled with paid campaign staff. In contrast, Yabloko's regional headquarters were almost always inadequate, dark, and lacking in personnel and fundamental office equipment. To formalize these impressions, the survey asked candidates about key organizational features of their campaign, from the location of headquarters to the nature of the staff. Table 7.3 presents some results.

Candidates are broken up by party affiliation (independents, candidates from established parties [parties that held legislative seats at the time of the campaign], and candidates from all other parties) and by their district choice. The data provide some insights into how the opportunity to run in different constituencies influences candidates' behavior. Four factors deal directly with the relationship between candidates and party organizations: the location of campaign headquarters, the source of campaign funds, the level of paid staff, and use of work-related resources. Not surprisingly, independent candidates are much more likely to use structures and resources from nonpartisan sources. Among partisans, the data show differences across both party organizations and where candidates from those parties run. Nominal district candidates are more likely to have headquarters independent of party organizations than those running on the list. Moreover, those candidates are also more likely to fund their own campaigns.

The interesting finding here is that partisans running out of established parties are more likely to self-finance than those running with new parties. This finding reflects differences among candidates rather than parties. From interviews across the party spectrum, it seemed clear that this was not a finding limited to the pro-market parties. Some KPRF candidates also subsidized the party, although most seemed to rely on the organization. The 1999 SPS organization in Chelyabinsk was a telling example of this phenomenon. The organization was run by very motivated and

Table 7.3. *Measures of Campaign Organization and Activity, 1999*

		Partisan: New Party			Partisan: Established Party		
Variables	Independent	Nominal-Only	Nominal and List	List-Only	Nominal-Only	Nominal and List	List-Only
Campaign HQ at Home or Workplace	59.6% (41)	47.1% (16)	32.3% (10)	25.0% (11)	41.2% (21)	12.9% (4)	3.3% (2)
Campaign Funded by Self, Family, Friends, CEC	31.3% (22)	38.2% (13)	64.5% (26)	20.4% (9)	54.9% (28)	67.7% (21)	39.3% (24)
No Paid Staff	61.4% (43)	55.9% (19)	58.1% (18)	77.3% (34)	21.6% (11)	32.3% (10)	54.1% (33)
No Polling of Electorate	32.9% (23)	41.2% (14)	45.2% (14)	61.4% (27)	27.4% (14)	16.1% (5)	29.5% (18)
Resources from Work (Phones, Fax, Space, etc.)	91.3% (64)	85.3% (29)	74.3% (23)	38.6% (17)	78.4% (40)	35.5% (11)	41.0% (25)
Campaign Flyers "Important" or "Very Important"	45.7% (32)	32.4% (11)	24.8% (8)	38.6% (17)	37.3% (19)	38.7% (12)	44.3% (27)
Door-to-Door Campaigning "Important" or "Very Important"	67.1% (47)	55.9% (19)	88.9% (26)	65.9% (29)	51.0% (26)	74.2% (23)	62.3% (38)
"Well-Known" in District Prior to Campaign	28.6% (20)	14.7% (5)	22.6% (7)	31.8% (14)	35.3% (18)	45.2% (14)	34.4% (21)

Source: Candidate survey conducted by the author.

hardworking college students who had little contact with the party's district candidates in the region. The same pattern is reflected in the use of work resources for campaign purposes. Again, independents rely heavily on these resources to pursue their campaign strategies. Partisans running in nominal districts also use work resources on a regular basis. In contrast, those running on the list tend to use these resources less frequently.

Table 7.3 shows some of the important differences between established and new parties. Established parties are much more likely to have paid campaign staff, although this staff seems to be concentrated in the nominal races rather than in the party list race.[3] Established parties also seem to have higher rates of polling. Here it is important to note the relatively frequent use of polls in both the list race and in nominal districts, particularly in face of observations in Chapter 4 about the lack of strategic withdrawals at the end of the campaign period. For the average candidate, uncertainty about voter preferences may be essentially irresolvable, even after considerable polling, a situation that leaves many candidates with a nontrivial chance of winning the election. Established parties also attract more candidates who are well-known in their districts prior to the campaign period.

In terms of campaign strategy, there are also a few surprising similarities across candidates in different parties and electoral contexts. Independent candidates are marginally more likely to stress campaign fliers than their partisan counterparts, although established party candidates also use this tactic. The same is true for door-to-door campaign efforts. Again, independent candidates and those running on the party list are more likely to use door-to-door efforts to build support, while nominal district candidates are slightly less likely to rely on these methods. These tactics stand in contrast to efforts to reach voters through television and radio, where established party candidates have a clear advantage.

These data provide preliminary evidence of differences in campaign tactics and organizations across candidates and party organizations. Not surprisingly, list candidates are most closely tied to party organizations, whereas partisan district candidates supplement party resources and structures with other sources. Consistent with the discussion in Chapter 5 of the disparity in resources across party organizations, differences between

---

[3] One explanation is that the responses refer to staff who are under a candidate's personal control, thus list candidates from a party do not report on individuals who are controlled by the central party organization, and whose job it is to elect the entire list.

candidates for established parties and new parties also reveal more organizational support for candidates from established parties.

Interviews with candidates during all three campaign periods underscore the variation in candidates' campaign strategies and its consequences for party development. During the 1993 campaign in Saratov Oblast, Russia's Choice candidates repeatedly complained that the regional party chief and candidate for the Federation Council had turned the relatively well-funded and well-organized party headquarters into his own personal campaign headquarters. In 1999, a regional party leader in Chelyabinsk argued that the key nominal district candidate in the region used more than 75 percent of the funds available for the whole campaign for his own race. Time and again, it was clear that the party list race and lesser candidates' campaigns suffered at the expense of prominent regional leaders.

At the same time, some candidates clearly invested in party building during the campaign period. These candidates, mostly from the LDPR and KPRF, as well as from smaller policy-based organizations such as the Social Democrats and the Ecological Party, KEDR worked hard to build a campaign organization aimed at supporting the party list. These decisions have important implications for the potential for coordination in the future.

In all, these data highlight why it is difficult for small parties to survive beyond a single election or grow in support between elections. Many appealing candidates run as independents. Those who join parties often maintain a significant degree of independence from the party. Some partisan candidates use their party's resources without reinvesting in the organization. The next sections explore another piece of the campaign equation, the types of appeals that different candidates make during the campaign period. This evidence speaks to the same point. A large number of partisan candidates do not promote the party's platform, instead stressing personal vote or individual issue appeals.

Different Constituencies, Different Messages: Predicting Campaign Appeals

The evidence suggests wide variation on candidates' appeals to voters – the message that candidates send to attract support. Besides shaping the information available to voters, candidates' appeals have important implications for electoral infrastructure. Insofar as candidates emphasize personal characteristics, then elections become isolated contests hinging on idiosyncratic factors that vary from place to place and from election to election. Similar concerns arise even if candidates focus on issues, as there is no guarantee that the same issues will be raised in different campaigns or contests.

Most studies of Russian elections focus on the electoral strategies of political parties: their media strategies, campaign platforms, and placement of candidates in single-member districts. This chapter focuses on candidates' appeals both within parties and outside of the party structure. Survey respondents were asked about the nature of their appeal to voters: whether they emphasized their personal background, name, and characteristics; their personal policy preferences; or their party's platform.

The analysis in this section explains the variation in these choices using the same set of explanatory factors used in previous chapters: candidates' goals, information, resources, and choices regarding where and how to run for office (district selection). In this chapter, a candidate's choice of where to run becomes part of the explanation of which electoral strategy a candidate pursues. Likewise, candidates' partisanship shifts from something to be explained to something that explains subsequent behavior.

These factors have somewhat different effects on this final set of campaign strategy decisions than the effects observed in previous chapters. As discussed at length in previous chapters, Russia's mixed electoral system acts as a sorting mechanism that divides candidates into partisans and independents as well as nominal and list races. The first task in this section is to specify how this variation shapes campaign appeals. Do partisan candidates who run in nominal districts adopt different campaign strategies than their fellow party members who run in the district? Are independents' strategies distinct from partisans' strategies in nominal districts? The findings in previous chapters suggest the following hypotheses:

- H1: Compared to independents, partisans are less likely to make personal appeals, and less likely to make personal issue appeals.
- H2: Partisans who run in a district will be less likely to make platform appeals and more likely to make personal or issue appeals than partisans who run solely on the party list.

In other words, as a result of institutional incentives, candidates should sort themselves in terms of their campaign appeals. The result in a typical district, with both partisans and independents, is that candidates offer voters a wide variety of appeals, leaving voters with the complicated task of deciding which one(s) they prefer. There is also the danger that candidates present so many conflicting signals to voters that it is difficult to discern the value of

Campaigning for the Duma

any single one or infer from election outcomes which one – if any – voters respond to as they cast their votes.

Previous findings also suggest that the information available to candidates about potential constituencies and their rivals should shape their campaign strategies, although not in the ways we expect in established systems. For instance, most studies of affiliation in established systems assume that candidates hold common beliefs about the structure of constituent preferences over policy and therefore the viability of different contestants and messages. In game theoretic terms, the requirements for shared knowledge are rigorous: 1) Each player is fully aware of the rules of the game and the utility functions of the players; and 2) each player is aware that others are aware of this information. As I have argued in previous chapters, this assumption does not necessarily hold for all Russian candidates or for candidates in other transitional systems. The question is, how does the lack of shared knowledge influence candidates' strategic decisions?

The predictions about the nature of campaign appeals given varying levels of information are very straightforward. In general, candidates who know more about their constituents' issue preferences should stress issues in the campaign – that is, information should translate into a clear sense of which issue positions will be electorally useful. Conversely, candidates who are uncertain about voter preferences should stress personal characteristics or professional attributes. Those who are most certain about voters' preferences should affiliate with political parties who can target these constituencies and stress party platforms.

- H3: Regardless of affiliation, candidates with good information about voter preferences should be more likely to make issue appeals and less likely to make personal appeals than candidates with poor information.

Finally, the discussion of candidate motivations and the effects they have on behavior as shown in previous chapters suggests an important prediction about the impact of goals on appeal decisions:

- H4: Regardless of affiliation, candidates who hold strong policy goals are more likely to make issue-based appeals and less likely to make personal appeals than candidates who do not have such goals. Similarly, candidates with strong party-building goals are more likely to make partisan appeals and less likely to make personal appeals.

The logic underlying these propositions is simple: Motivations color candidates' appeals to the electorate because they change the probability that

Candidate Strategies and Electoral Competition

any single strategy will advance their efforts to achieve those goals. While we expect that these appeals will be shaped by the electoral imperative, we do not expect that the desire to get elected will drown out all other factors.

The last prediction about the content of campaign appeals concerns the influence of independent or personal vote resources on campaign appeals:

- H5: For independents, access to resources should increase personal appeals and reduce issue appeals. For partisans, access to resources should increase personal and issue appeals and reduce platform appeals.

Simply put, as candidates have more of a following among their constituents and the means to activate their supporters, they are less likely to rely on generic appeals and will instead place more emphasis on what is unique about their personality or experiences. Hence, resource availability should lead independents away from issue appeals and toward personal appeals. Similarly, partisans with resources should be less likely than their resource-poor colleagues to emphasize their party's platform and more likely to emphasize issues and personal characteristics.

Explaining Mixed Messages

This section tests the hypotheses about campaign appeals using a multivariate analysis of the 1999 survey. The analysis follows the approach used in the other empirical chapters by employing a multinomial logistic analysis, where each equation measures the probability that a candidate uses a particular campaign appeal: personal, issues, or party platform (usually referred to simply as partisan appeals). In all, parameters will be estimated for three equations:

$$
\begin{aligned}
\text{Personal} = {} & \beta_{11} + \beta_{12}(\text{Policy Goal}) + \beta_{13}(\text{Party-Building Goal}) \\
& + \beta_{14}(\text{Resources}) + \beta_{15}(\text{Resources*Independent}) \\
& + \beta_{16}(\text{Information}) + \beta_{17}(\text{District}) + \beta_{18}(\text{District/List}) \\
& + \beta_{19}(\text{Independent}) + \beta_{110}(\text{Russian}) + \upsilon_1 \\
\text{Issues} = {} & \beta_{21} + \beta_{22}(\text{Policy Goal}) + \beta_{23}(\text{Party-Building Goal}) \\
& + \beta_{24}(\text{Resources}) + \beta_{25}(\text{Resources*Independent}) \\
& + \beta_{26}(\text{Information}) + \beta_{27}(\text{District}) + \beta_{28}(\text{District/List}) \\
& + \beta_{29}(\text{Independent}) + \beta_{210}(\text{Russian}) + \upsilon_2
\end{aligned}
$$

Campaigning for the Duma

Table 7.4. *Variables in Analysis of Campaign Appeals*

Variables		Description
Dependent Variables	Personal	Did candidate emphasize personal characteristics or name in campaign (1 = yes)
	Issues	Did candidate emphasize personal issue preferences in campaign (1 = yes)
	Platform	Did candidate emphasize party platform in campaign (1 = yes)
Independent Variables	Policy	Candidate's policy goals
	Party Building	Candidate's interest in helping to build a party organization
	Resources	Summary indicator of candidate's personal vote resources (0 = none, 1 = some, 2 = substantial)
	Russian	Did candidate run in a Russian region (1 = yes)
	Information	Quality of candidate's information on voter preferences (0–4 scale, high = more information)
	District	Did candidate run as partisan in a single-member district (1= yes)
	Independent	Did candidate run as independent (1= yes)
	District/List	Did candidate run as partisan in district and on party list (1 = yes)

$$\text{Platform} = \beta_{31} + \beta_{32}(\text{Policy Goal}) + \beta_{33}(\text{Party-Building Goal}) \\ + \beta_{34}(\text{Resources}) + \beta_{35}(\text{Information}) + \beta_{36}(\text{District}) \\ + \beta_{37}(\text{District/List}) + \beta_{38}(\text{Russian}) + v_3$$

The variables in these equations are described in Table 7.4.[4] As in previous chapters, the hypotheses developed in the previous section will be tested first by assessing the statistical significance or insignificance of various parameter coefficients in the regression results, and then by comparing predictions about campaign appeals for different hypothetical candidates.

---

[4] Note that all of the candidates in the sample will be used to estimate the personal and issue appeal equations; the platform equation will be estimated only with partisans, as independent candidates cannot make platform appeals. For the same reasons, the platform equation does not include the independent variable or the resources-independent interaction.

Candidate Strategies and Electoral Competition

Table 7.5. *Candidates' Campaign Themes, 1999*

Variables Theme	Personal Characteristics	Issues	Party Platform
Policy Goals	.35**	.19	.09
	(.22)	(.20)	(.24)
Party-Building Goals	−.84***	.03	.93***
	(.21)	(.17)	(.22)
Personal Vote	.36**	.40***	−.42***
	(.17)	(.15)	(.17)
Personal Vote Independent	.24	−.96***	–
	(.32)	(.32)	
District Information	−.69***	.89***	−.21
	(.28)	(.26)	(.32)
Partisan Running District-Only	−.16	.94***	−1.14***
	(.36)	(.33)	(.36)
Partisan Running District/List	−.32	.69***	−1.09***
	(.43)	(.36)	(.42)
Independent	.49	2.63***	–
	(.49)	(.52)	
Russian Region	.32	.21	−.32
	(.34)	(.30)	(.36)
Constant	−1.25***	−2.32***	1.57***
	(.58)	(.54)	(.59)
Chi Square	57.3	48.0	45.6
N	322	322	252

Note: ** = $p < .05$, *** = $p < .01$.
Source: Candidate survey conducted by the author.

Table 7.5 reports results the parameter coefficient estimates for all three equations. The parameter coefficient estimates are consistent and in general strongly supportive of all five hypotheses. In particular, the estimates partly confirm hypothesis one (independents are more likely to make issue appeals; the differences for personal appeals are in the right direction but not statistically significant). Hypothesis two is entirely confirmed (partisans running in a district are more likely to make issue appeals and less likely to make platform appeals). The estimates strongly confirm hypothesis three (increased information about voters increases issue appeals and decreases personal appeals). Hypothesis four is partly confirmed (strong party-building goals lead to increased issue and platform appeals and fewer

Campaigning for the Duma

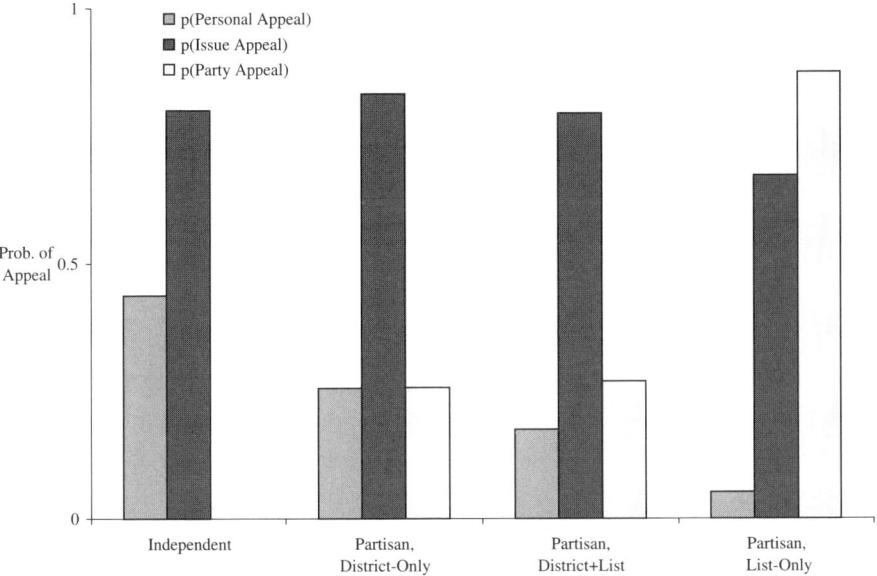

Figure 7.1. The Impact of Affiliation and District Choice on Campaign Appeals

personal appeals, but the pattern does not hold for policy goals). The estimates strongly confirm hypothesis five (access to resources increases personal appeals by independents and reduces platform appeals, whereas the reverse is true for partisans).

As in the previous analyses, the parameters themselves provide only partial insight into the impact that these factors have on campaign appeals. The next step is to illustrate these effects using comparisons across hypothetical candidates. Figure 7.1 begins by illustrating a question central to hypotheses one and two: What is the variation in appeals across partisans and independents and between partisans who make different district selection choices?[5]

As the figure shows, an independent candidate is more likely than any of the affiliated candidates to make an individual appeal (rather than an

---

[5] In this and all other figures, the hypothetical candidate is the "experienced careerist" seen in other chapters – a candidate with political experience and high resources (note that this explanation of campaign appeals does not include career goals). Using this hypothetical candidate to interpret the parameters does not bias the interpretation, as similar graphs could be constructed for the other hypothetical candidates described in previous chapters.

issue-based appeal). Moreover, among the partisans, individual appeals are most likely from district-only candidates, less likely from candidates running in a district and on the list, and least likely from list-only candidates.

The probability of issue appeals is relatively high for all candidates, reinforcing the picture of a cacophony of campaign messages from candidates in Duma elections. It is important to note that the open-ended question asking candidates to list the three most important issues facing their constituents yielded very little consensus beyond a desire for lower unemployment rates. Some candidates stressed correcting a backlog of wage arrears. Others stressed reforming education or healthcare systems. Still others focused on the environment. Against this backdrop, the analysis suggests the possibility for coordination dilemmas among candidates in district races who focus on different messages and cooperation dilemmas within a party organization, where some candidates stress alternatives to the party message or personal characteristics along with the party platform. The former situation complicates voters' calculations about which candidate they prefer; the latter creates uncertainty about the content of the party brand name.

Finally, the probability of platform messages among partisan candidates moves in the opposite direction from individual appeals, being lowest among district-only candidates and highest among list-only candidates. While the list candidates were relatively loyal to the party platform, a significant plurality is predicted to dilute the list message with personal and issue appeals. Moreover, the other findings suggest that the most viable partisan candidates tend to avoid investment in their party's brand.

To interpret the meaning of the statistical analysis further, Figure 7.2 illustrates the relationship between information and appeals as predicted in hypothesis three. The impact of information on appeals is profound. In the figure, information levels vary from the lowest possible value to the highest. Increased information dramatically lowers the probability of personal appeals and dramatically increases the probability of issue appeals for both independent and partisan candidates. Particularly important here is the observation that partisan candidates with high levels of information who run in nominal districts are much more likely to stress their personal issue platforms in addition to party platforms and personal characteristics. That is, even the most experienced and qualified partisans do not invest in shoring up their party's platform during the campaign period. This finding underscores how individual candidates' decisions have undermined the process of party building and in particular, the development of party brand-name labels.

Campaigning for the Duma

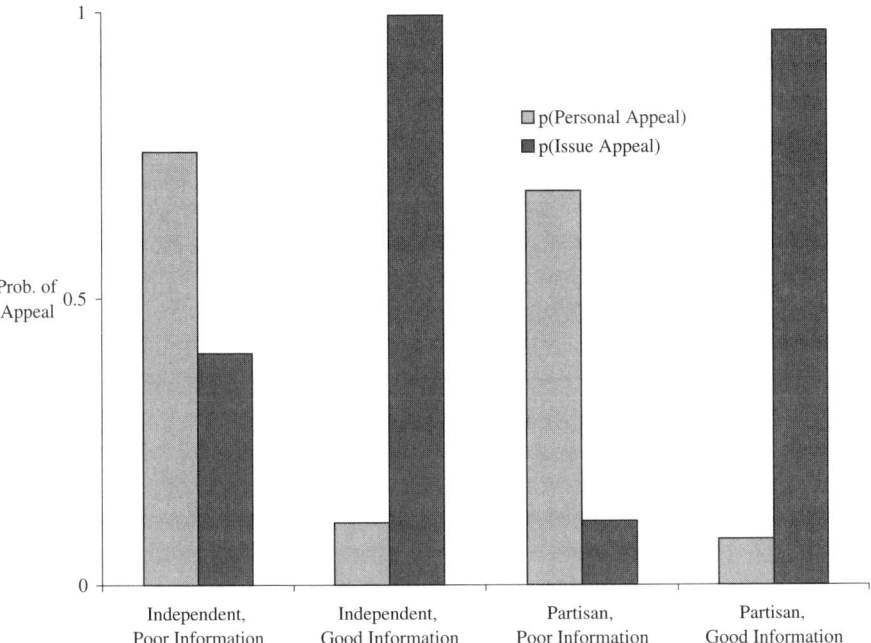

Figure 7.2. The Impact of District Information on Campaign Appeals

Figure 7.3 shows the impact of party-building goals on campaign appeals – the leftmost candidate has the lowest level of party-building goals, while the rightmost candidate has the highest level. Moreover, the leftmost candidate is assumed to run district-only, while the rightmost candidate runs on the district and the list. This presentation follows from the finding in Chapter 6 that candidates who hold party-building goals are more likely to run on the party list.

The finding in this figure is consistent with common-sense expectations. As the figure indicates, the difference in goals (and district selection) does shape campaign appeals. While all candidates make some sort of issue appeals, party-centered candidates are much more likely to make a partisan appeal, and have a much lower probability of making a personal appeal than candidates who hold career goals or even specific policy goals. The finding that partisans are slightly more likely to stress their own issue appeals over the party platform once again underscores the potential for disagreement within the organization and within a Duma faction once the party takes office.

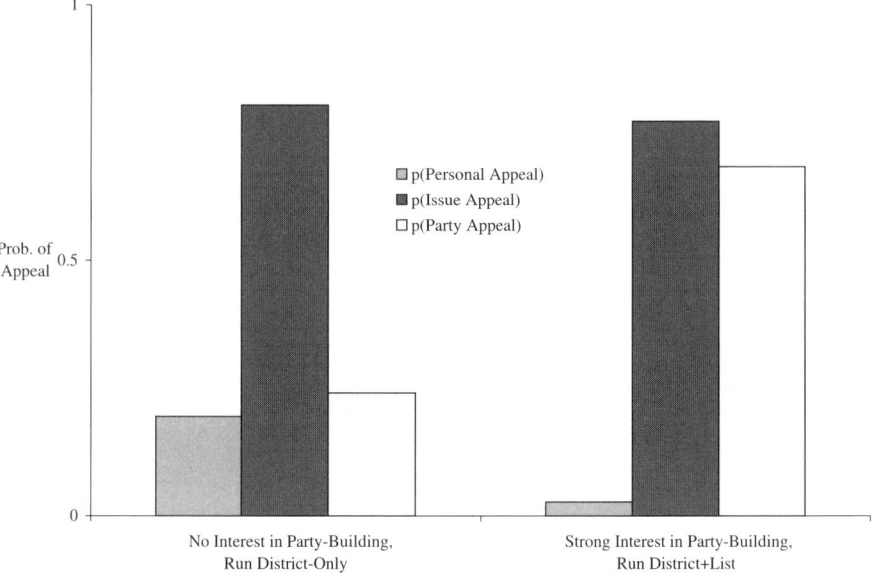

Figure 7.3. The Impact of Goals on Campaign Appeals

Finally, Figure 7.4 illustrates how various types of resources influence campaign strategies. Two pairs of candidates are shown: an independent and a partisan. For each candidate, the graph gives the predicted appeals given that they have no personal vote, and given that they have the highest amount of personal vote. The variation parallels the earlier discussion and hypothesis five: As resources increase, independents are more likely to make personal appeals and less likely to make issue appeals. The same effect is seen for partisans making personal appeals, but increased resources also lower the probability that a partisan will make a party-based appeal. Put another way, Figure 7.2 shows that access to information dramatically decreases candidates' propensities to focus on their personal characteristics. In contrast, Figure 7.4 shows that the impact or resources is smaller. The data show a significant plurality of partisan candidates who stress personal characteristics in their campaign, demonstrating persistent cooperation dilemmas within party organizations.

The findings for the effects of personal votes are significant and strong across all types of candidates regardless of district choice. Candidates with personal votes are more likely to stress individual appeals, either in the form

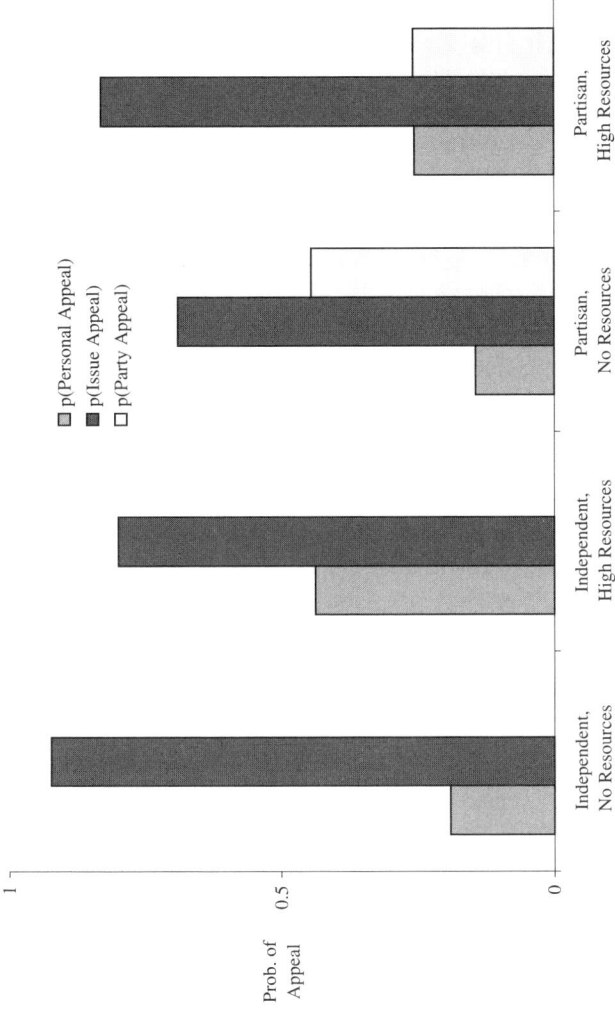

Figure 7.4. The Impact of Resources on Campaign Appeals

183

of personal characteristics or particularistic issue appeals. For partisans, this change occurs at the expense of support for the platform. The strength and consistency of this finding are particularly interesting since the measure does not capture many potential resources that exist outside of the public eye in Russia. These results support the notion that parties do not yet hold a monopoly over relevant resources, and that the lack of a monopoly has important consequences for candidates' behavior both before and during the campaign.

Political Parties, Issues, and Target Constituencies

This section considers the coherence of campaign strategies among partisans from the same party in Russian elections. That is, to what extent do candidates running from the same party emphasize the same or similar issues? Do they target the same groups? If parties are organizing around programmatic appeals, individual members should be targeting specific groups with consistent messages. In addition, individual party organizations should be distinguishing themselves by using specific messages to target different constituencies. Table 7.6 reports on the target audiences of different party organizations in the 1999 election. To simplify the presentation, the table includes data only on a subset of established political parties.

For each party, the table reports the percentage of candidates who reported they had targeted a particular group of potential supporters during the campaign.[6] The rightmost column reports on the central tendency of each party's candidates, using an arbitrary 50 percent cutoff.[7] The first remarkable finding is that without fail, all candidates target pensioners. This finding strongly confirms extended conversations I've had with candidates since 1993. The logic for targeting pensioners was different for each party. For instance, in 1995 the Democratic Choice of Russia (DVR) party leader in Chelyabinsk showed me letters from elderly voters who remembered the success of the New Economic Program (NEP) period and pledged their support for reform parties. During the next election, the same organization was stressing the costs of Stalin's terror and the impact of mass graves being excavated outside of the city on older voters' partisan preferences.

---

[6] Some candidates mentioned other groups that are omitted because the percentage of candidates who mentioned them was relatively low (less than 15 percent of the sample).

[7] The 50 percent mark was intended to be a relatively low threshold to capture the trends in party development.

Table 7.6. Central Tendencies in Group Appeals of Established Russian Parties, 1999

Party	Government Workers	Private Industry	Pensioners	Kolkhoz Members	Youth	Intelligentsia	Central Tendency (Excluding Pensioners)
KPRF (25)	56.0% (14)	12.0% (3)	100% (25)	28.1% (7)	28.1% (7)	24.6% (6)	Government workers
LDPR (17)	5.9% (1)	5.9% (1)	100% (17)	0% (0)	5.9% (1)	0% (0)	None
Yabloko (18)	38.9% (7)	61.1% (11)	100% (18)	5.6% (1)	72.3% (13)	33.3% (6)	Private industry, youth
NDR (18)	22.2% (4)	44.4% (8)	100% (18)	5.6% (1)	44.4% (8)	11.1% (2)	None
FAR (28)	32.1% (9)	14.3% (4)	100% (28)	28.6% (8)	25.2% (7)	7.1% (2)	None
Unity (20)	15.0% (3)	75.0% (14)	100% (20)	5.0% (1)	35.0% (7)	15.0% (3)	Private industry
SPS (17)	29.4% (5)	64.5% (11)	100% (17)	0% (0)	88.2% (15)	52.4% (9)	Private industry, youth, intelligentsia
All Established Parties (143)	20.0% (43)	36.4% (52)	100% (144)	12.6% (18)	40.6% (58)	19.6% (28)	

Source: Candidate survey conducted by the author.

Candidate Strategies and Electoral Competition

The KPRF organizations talked almost exclusively about the high cost of reform on pensioners, and told heart-wrenching stories of extreme poverty among the elderly in their regions. The LDPR stressed the patriotism of those who had fought in or endured World War II. Moreover, all parties recognized that pensioners had extremely high turnout rates in an era where general turnout was declining. In contrast, no parties specifically targeted the rural populations in the regions included in the study.

Beyond pensioners, parties tend to fall into two categories: Either there is no central tendency in targeting (LDPR, NDR, FAR), or they target roughly the same groups, private industry and youth (Unity, Yabloko, SPS). The lone exception is the KPRF, whose candidates target workers in state enterprises and in the state apparatus. At best, this table gives only weak support to the proposition that partisans are presenting a coherent message, one that describes their party as distinct from all the others.

Table 7.7 takes this analysis a step further by reporting the data on the issues emphasized by partisans from different parties. Candidates were asked to mention whether or not they stressed a number of issues in their campaign. Again, a 50 percent cutoff is used to define a central tendency in a party organization. The clear trend in the table is the consistent importance of regional issues (issues specific to the district or the oblast) for all candidates. While this finding might not surprise analysts, it is another piece of evidence that party organizations are not largely linking salient national issues to salient regional issues – a key talking point for the mixed electoral system. Moreover, candidates who target the same audiences may in fact be making very different appeals.

The exceptions to this rule are the KPRF, Yabloko, and Unity. As the table indicates, a majority of KPRF candidates campaigned on both national issues – constitutional amendments and government performance – and on regional issues. These positions are consistent with the party's status as the organized opposition to the government. Yabloko's candidates stressed constitutional amendments and issues related to center–regional relations. Not surprisingly, Unity's candidates did not campaign on issues relating to power shifts or government performance. They did, however, stress center–regional relations.

Overall, the picture in Table 7.7 is of elections in which some candidates focus on national issues while most candidates emphasize regional concerns. In other words, while Russia appears to have a national party system that is arrayed on a right-left scale in terms of political and economic reform, candidates' appeals to voters at election time stress regional

Table 7.7. *Central Tendencies in Issue Appeals of Established Russian Parties, 1999*

Party	Constitutional Amendments	Government Performance	President–Parliament	Center–Region	Regional or Local Issues	Central Tendency
KPRF	64.0%	68.0%	40.0%	40.0%	76.0%	Constitution, performance,
(25)	(16)	(17)	(10)	(10)	(19)	regional issues
LDPR	29.4%	35.3%	11.8%	5.9%	58.2%	Regional issues
(17)	(5)	(6)	(2)	(1)	(10)	
Yabloko	50.0%	27.8%	27.8%	50.0%	88.3%	Regional issues
(13)	(9)	(5)	(5)	(9)	(15)	
NDR	27.8%	22.2%	33.3%	38.9%	94.4%	Regional issues
(13)	(5)	(4)	(6)	(7)	(17)	
FAR	42.9%	35.7%	17.9%	25.0%	85.7%	Regional issues
(23)	(12)	(10)	(5)	(7)	(25)	
Unity	10.0%	30.0%	5.0%	60.%	100%	Center–region,
(20)	(2)	(6)	(1)	(12)	(20)	regional issues
SPS	5.9%	47.1%	24.5%	47.1	100%	Regional issues
(17)	(1)	(8)	(4)	(8)	(17)	
All Established Parties	33.3%	39.2%	24.5%	37.8%	86.0%	
(143)	(48)	(56)	(35)	(54)	(123)	

Source: Candidate survey conducted by the author.

issues. This regional focus in elections complicates voters' inferences about what candidates will do about national policy concerns, as well as their judgments about who should be held responsible for regional issues. Thus, the party system itself perpetuates uncertainty within the electoral arena. The disconnection between the national and local levels also highlights the dangers of drawing conclusions about the nature of Russian politics (or that of any democracy) from conversations with candidates and elites in the party headquarters. Election outcomes may hinge on a very different set of factors.

This focus on the difficulty of resolving uncertainty has important implications for the debate over the applicability of different theories of party development to the Russian case. Given the lack of political organization, cleavage structures, and other types of information available to party entrepreneurs in the national arena, it is unlikely that imposition of parties from the top will occur quickly. A wholesale incorporation of large social groups as Seymour Martin Lipset and Stein Rokkan (1967) observed in Western Europe is not likely to occur in Russia since political learning in the face of new institutions is not sparking the formation of stable collective identities.

Russia seems destined to follow the more lengthy route posited by James Schlesinger (1966: 1994). He argues that candidate learning about the benefits of party organizations hinges on developing shared information about their overlapping constituencies. This information is uncovered over time through elite interaction in the campaign and legislature. As this work suggests, the route toward revealing this information may be circuitous and may come from sources such as economic shocks or state intervention in the electoral process – events that do not bode well for democratic consolidation. Moreover, Russian campaigns have not been opportunities for exploring underlying similarities across regional constituencies, but rather occasions of fragmenting these constituencies and highlighting differences. The analysis here adds to this conventional wisdom by highlighting the proliferation of candidates and candidates' messages at the district level and within party slates.

This explanation for party development in Russia echoes John Aldrich's (1995) work on the U.S. case (see also Cox 1997), where presidential candidates have strong incentives to link district constituencies in order to secure national office. These incentives are weaker in Russia, where the presence of non-affiliated district deputies allows the president to generate a stable legislative majority based on the support of a minority coalition that won seats in the list race, and a pork- or personal goods–based coalition among district-based independents. This strategy avoids the potential problem of creating a nationally based political organization that could be used to challenge the president in the future. It also maintains a distinction between the constituencies represented in the executive and the legislature, enabling the president to avoid popular accountability. As such, Putin or another president may distance himself from the Duma while actually encountering very little opposition to his or her legislative program if he or she is able to provide the resources for independent and partisan district candidates to follow through on their campaign promises. This is not simply an academic argument. It is extremely telling that Putin handed control of key pork-barrel committees in the Duma over to the independent deputies groups nearly two years before the 2003 elections.

This analysis shows that both candidates and voters are likely to face the problem of having to collect, digest, and disentangle a great deal of information in the course of a campaign. This information comes at them from all sides: national parties' television campaigns, party leaders' personal appeals, regional party organizations' mobilization efforts, and individual candidates in the district. It also takes a number of different forms: a stress on regional issues, national issues, party platforms, or candidates' personal attributes. It seems inevitable that these dissonant signals will affect the long-term aggregation of electoral infrastructure and stymie the development of effective electoral democracy.

The Accumulation of Infrastructure: The Problem of Inference

The multivariate analysis presented earlier reveals systematic differences in campaign appeals as a function of affiliation and district selection, information, resources, and candidate goals. What difference, then, does variation in campaign appeals make? Of course, candidates' actions during the campaign are likely to affect election outcomes, as candidates search for appeals that will gain support from voters. However, given the focus here and in the transition literature on information and the consequences of uncertainty, it is appropriate to ask whether variation in campaign appeals impacts electoral infrastructure – in particular, the information available regarding voter preferences.

The answer is yes. This section shows that the appeals that candidates use shape the inferences that we can draw from election returns. In other words, variation in appeals can influence whether candidates and other elites are able to resolve their uncertainties concerning voter preferences as democratization proceeds and elections occur. In general, the transition literature assumes that a series of free and fair elections will, over time, educate candidates as to what voters want and for what they are willing to vote. Discussions of founding elections often assume a lack of coordination at the entry period that leads to a large number of contestants (Gunther 1989; O'Donnell and Schmitter 1986). The expectation is that information generated by founding elections quickly provides incentives to form strong, stable parties. A simple example shows how these inferences can be short-circuited if candidates' appeals are based upon their personalities or personal issue positions rather than uniformly focused on partisan platforms.[8]

The example is constructed from a spatial model of voting, where candidates' expected behavior in office and the preferences of each voter are modeled as points on a single policy or issue dimension. In general, a voter is expected to vote for the candidate whose expected behavior in office – a point in the space – comes closest to the voter's ideal point, or the point that summarizes the voter's policy preferences. The winning candidate is the one who attracts the largest number of votes.

To understand how campaign appeals and other facets of elections in transition can distort the process of inference, I relax a central assumption of spatial models: Rather than assuming that voters evaluate candidates solely in terms of their policy positions, I allow for a mix of personal vote and policy appeals. While the standard assumptions are appropriate for established democracies, everything we know about elections in Russia and other transitional regions suggests that this assumption is true only sometimes, if not rarely. In particular, in a world where candidates are unsure of the electoral attractiveness of different records, backgrounds, or promises, and where parties do not control ballot access, the way is open for those who gain votes via their personal vote rather than promises concerning policy-related issues or a recitation of their party's platform.

To see the implications of these changes, consider Figure 7.5, where seven candidates run for office with platforms as shown. The figure also gives the distribution of voter preferences, which is skewed to the right, meaning that there are more pro-reform voters in the district (for example,

---

[8] The example does not control for variation in messages among party members, such as those presented in Tables 7.6 and 7.7, but such variation will only magnify the problems discussed here.

Campaigning for the Duma

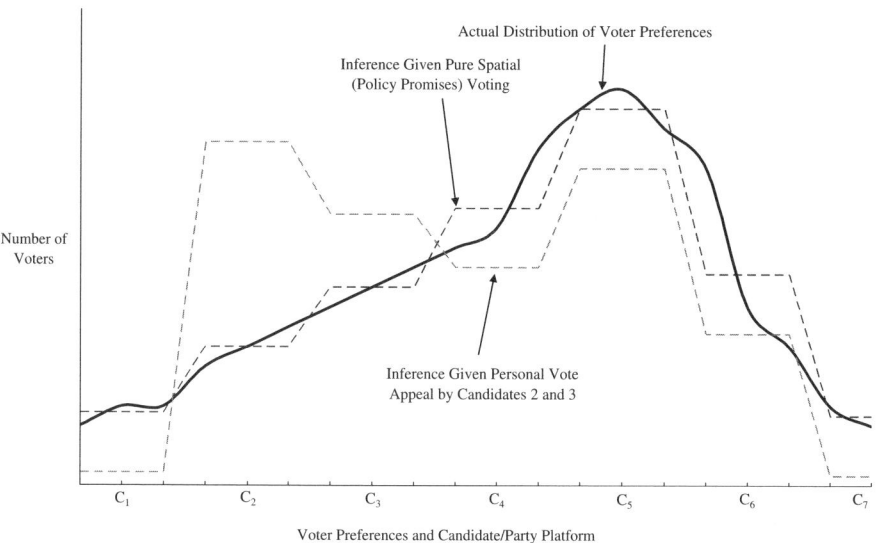

Figure 7.5. The Impact of Personal Votes on Inferences About Voter Preferences

supporters of SPS or Democratic Russia) than die-hard advocates of the status quo (for example, KPRF supporters). The dotted lines will be explained shortly.

Suppose an observer knows the location of the candidate's platform but does not know the distribution of other voters' preferences. Can he or she evaluate election returns to make an educated guess of what the distribution looks like? Such an inference is possible given information on how voters vote – what criteria they use to make their decision. To begin with, suppose that voters in the district behave as classical spatial voters, meaning they each vote for the candidate whose platform is closest to their ideal point. This assumption characterizes a world where candidates' appeals are cast in terms of policy outcomes, usually a party platform that they are bound to support if elected. If everyone votes this way, the candidates will receive votes as described in Table 7.8

As the table indicates, given pure spatial voting, candidate five would win the election with 28.5 percent of the popular vote. Moreover, an observer could use these results to estimate the distribution of voter preferences; this estimate is labeled in Figure 7.5. Although this estimate does not perfectly match the actual distribution, it is not too far off. In particular, even one election's worth of data allows an observer to learn about the right-wing

Candidate Strategies and Electoral Competition

Table 7.8. *Hypothetical Inference Example*

Candidate	Votes Received Given:	
	Pure Spatial Voting	Spatial Voting and Personal Vote
1	5.5%	1.0%
2	10.5%	26.0%
3	15.0%	20.5%
4	21.0%	16.5%
5	28.5%	24.0%
6	16.0%	11.5%
7	3.5%	0.5%

skew in voter preferences, and to estimate the shape of the distribution (how many left-wing voters, how many centrists, and so on) fairly closely. Thus, if the real world matched the assumptions – pure spatial voting, known candidate platforms – then it would be safe to assume that repeated elections, even a small number of them, would tell candidates everything they needed to know about voter preferences. Put another way, given these assumptions, elections could function as a source of electoral infrastructure for transitional democracies.

Of course, the real world need not match the spare assumptions of spatial theory. Suppose that candidates two and three receive support (20 percent of the electorate for candidate two, 10 percent for candidate three) from some voters in the district not because of their platforms, but because of their personal vote appeals, with the remaining votes determined by the spatial logic described previously. Assume that voters who support these candidates because of their personal vote are drawn uniformly from across the political spectrum – in effect, they are voting for the candidate as an individual, not because of the policy choices that voters expect the candidates to make if elected.

The rightmost column of Table 7.8 shows the election results given the personal votes assumed here. Now candidate two wins the election, with the former winner, candidate five, in second place. Suppose our hypothetical observer still assumes that voters are voting on issues, and uses these new returns to estimate what the distribution of voter preferences looks like. This revised judgment is shown in Figure 7.5. As the table shows, this new inference is quite different from the earlier one. It is also significantly different from the true distribution – rather than seeing the district as a bastion of right-wing voters, our observer would conclude that the district is sharply divided, with slightly more left-wing voters as compared to those on the right.

While Table 7.8 describes a hypothetical example, it illustrates why repeated elections may not provide electoral infrastructure to candidates and other elites. The example resonates with a number of examples, including the fate of Elena Mizulina, Anatoli Gordeev, or Nikolai Lysenko discussed in previous chapters. It also captures the effect of a number of UR incumbents entering races against sitting incumbents in 2003. Simply put, when some candidates campaign on non-policy terms – and when this fact is not well known to observers – inferences about voter preferences based on election returns may bear only a scant resemblance to reality. This problem becomes worse if candidates' platforms are not well known, or if the number and identity of candidates with personal vote resources vary across elections, or if the magnitude of these resources is unknown. A different set of candidates with different mixes of personal and spatial voter support will almost certainly dramatically alter outcomes and inferences. This is not to say that election returns never provide any information. The point is that they cannot be seen as a reliable mechanism for resolving the uncertainty that is endemic in many democratic transitions.

These findings also point out the difficulty in understanding the value of party labels as a tool to forge durable ties with voters, underscoring the low value of party labels as information. Studies of mass partisanship found greater than expected levels of party attachments in the early period of Russian elections, then a leveling off of reported partisanship in 1999 and 2003. The elite side of the equation, candidates' willingness to invest in electoral infrastructure, suggests a possible explanation for this behavior (Smyth forthcoming). It is difficult for durable partisanship to emerge when the cast of characters changes from election to election, messages are indistinct, and personalities shape vote choices. It is also difficult for voters to assess organizations such as the LDPR that promise one set of policies and support an entirely different set of policies in the Duma. Similarly, voters may lose interest in an opposition organization such as the KPRF that is essentially shut out of the policy process and entirely ineffective no matter how strongly they share the organization's policy preferences.

To some degree, Russia's mixed electoral systems, combined with decentralized and fragmented resource endowments, bear responsibility for the lack of infrastructure accumulation. The mixed system enables candidates to avoid parties altogether or partisans to run in districts and use the party label selectively. These options define the opportunity cost of the system – resources that might have been invested in political party organizations that go to individual candidates.

In comparative context, it is important to highlight the effects of this system on the long-term evolution of the political system. The mixed electoral system, one of a growing number of such systems governing elections in emerging democracies, has alternately been assessed as providing Russia with the potential for this "best of both worlds" in terms of representation and hindering the formation of representative structures such as parties. These two sets of predictions describe very different political equilibria or steady states that may emerge in response to the incentives codified by the electoral structure.

Optimists argue that mixed electoral systems will yield great benefits once Russian politicians adapt to the new system and invest in building a stable political party system. Underlying this work is the assumption that repeated elections, even those that are introduced in the context of great uncertainty, will quickly produce a stable party system. Conversely, pessimists argue that Russia's political structure – from the super-presidential mode of executive–legislature relations to the internal structure of legislature, to electoral laws – does not provide incentives to build a stable party system capable of transforming the mixed law into a mechanism of government responsiveness. Moreover, they stress the costs of instability for the long-term success of the democratic project.

The critical difference between these views rests on the capacity of the political party system to ensure coordination and cooperation among like-minded candidates, to reconcile issue concerns, and to unify voters at all levels. A necessary condition for all of these actions is the provision of reliable information about voter preferences, in the nation as a whole and in each nominal district. Without such information, parties do not know which appeals will attract voter support – and candidates do not know which party brand name will resonate with their electorates. What happens if elections proceed without such information? As the example here illustrates, democratic consolidation cannot be bootstrapped by itself – elections may not yield the information needed for consolidation.

The Russian case shows that unstable or volatile electoral democracies are vulnerable to populist appeals that are backed by effective leadership. The lack of coordination and cooperation within electoral parties can have devastating effects on the capacity of the opposition to withstand the power of a strong president. In part, this disarray in the party system can be traced back to the candidates' strategies in the campaign period that fail to identify winning electoral appeals or generate clear and consistent messages from individual party organizations. In this environment, a powerful president can build non-partisan coalitions in the legislature and sideline existing opposition. He or she can also bestow an organization with the president's own reputation, as Putin did with Unity in 1999 and to a greater extent with United Russia in 2003. Neither party was challenged to come up with a viable issue-based electoral platform by coherent opposition that articulated an alternative vision of governance, so the parties could safely pursue amorphous campaigns that succeeded as much because of their weakness of their alternatives as they did because of their own power.

The Meaning of Elections in New Democracies

The lasting result of the mixed system adopted in Russia in 1993 is that candidates are led to campaign strategies that contribute very little to electoral infrastructure. Not only does the electoral system create the opportunity for candidates to run on personal vote appeals, it complicates this information with a heady dose of partisan competition. This combination undermines the ability of candidates or parties to learn over time and begin to make decisions that yield issue-based partisan competition. In reality, candidates' choices preclude the programmatic organization of parties, and, in some cases, impede the construction of party organizations. Indeed, the analysis offered in this chapter demonstrates that within electoral coalitions, many party members have no real interest in developing a coherent party organization or party platform that could constrain their future behavior. The relative incoherence of issue emphasis and messages targeting partisans only confirms this diagnosis.

These behaviors have implications for how we should interpret election returns in Russia and other transitional regimes. Perhaps the most devastating effect of the mixed system on the accumulation of electoral infrastructure is the cacophony of signals present in the campaign period. This complexity results from interactions among the electoral process, uncertainty, and a variegated set of candidates with disparate goals and disparate levels of alternative resources. As a result, a large number of independent and partisan contestants, rooted in very different constituencies and broadcasting very different appeals, populate nominal elections. Perversely, this abundance of information can decrease the value of all other signals, perpetuating uncertainty.

Candidate Strategies and Electoral Competition

The persistence of contradictory messages, appeals, and themes in Russian elections is contrary to theories of founding elections that posit competition as a relatively quick mechanism to clarify the relative power of competing parties and their appeals. The analysis here shows that uncertainty, institutions, personal votes, weak parties, and the stress on policy goals can all hinder the accumulation of information that enables elections to function as mechanisms of responsiveness within nascent democracies. At best, elections held under these conditions are likely to prolong the consolidation period. At worst, they make the regime vulnerable to exogenous shocks and demagogic appeals that can derail the democratization project entirely, either putting it on a path toward unconsolidated democracy, a neo-authoritarian regime, or a full-scale reversal toward authoritarianism.

8

Democrats, Democratic Transitions, and Russian Democracy

The period following founding elections, usually referred to as democratic consolidation, is distinct from the other periods of political transition. Electoral competition generates a new focus for political action, one where winning votes is the gateway to policy outcomes or power. Elections can profoundly transform the relative influence of individuals and groups as well as political resources that survived the authoritarian regime or emerged in the democratization period. Elections can also provoke the emergence of new actors or the dissolution of existing ones. As a result of these shifts, the politics of the post-election period is distinct from the previous liberalization and democratization periods.

Conventional wisdom argues that the politics of early electoral contests tends to be fierce and unpredictable, followed by a period of learning or adaptation, as individual and collective actors decode the new system and the effects of their own strategies in pursuit of political goals. We expect that these processes strengthen democratic governance. Yet, the Russian case illustrates that candidates' adaptations to electoral institutions need not generate investment in electoral infrastructure or democratic development. Russian candidates were extremely adroit at choosing strategies that protected their own interests in the electoral process, but did not lead to a successful democracy.

At the national level, the Russian case demonstrates that the outcomes of consolidation periods also can be surprising and lead to a long period of instability or an outright failure to solidify representative and accountable democracy. The evidence presented here shows that three factors – candidates' strategies, electoral infrastructure, and successful consolidation – are linked. Chapter 2 used a crossnational analysis of consolidation in postcommunist states to show that elite commitment to democratic rules, strong

Candidate Strategies and Electoral Competition

international incentives backed with significant benefits such as membership in the European Union, and regime structures that promote elite integration foster successful consolidation after founding elections. These findings are bolstered by the evidence presented in the subsequent chapters, which showed that high levels of electoral uncertainty, personalistic institutional structures, and widely dispersed political resources lead candidates to choose strategies that undermine the accumulation of electoral infrastructure.

Put more broadly, the analysis here illuminates the conditions under which electoral competition is likely to work to strengthen new democracies and when it is likely to provoke individuals to act contrary to that goal. In this concluding section, the implications of the theoretic framework and the evidence presented throughout the book are extended to explain the evolution of Russian politics and then to explore the implications for theories of democratic transition: the role of candidates, parties, institutions, and political uncertainty in shaping new regimes.

Russian Democracy: Past, Present, and Future

Political developments in Russia following the 2003–2004 election cycle led to a consensus among political analysts that elections did not propel Russia toward democratic consolidation. Russia is not unique in this regard. As Chapter 2 shows, Russia is one of a handful of postcommunist countries that have failed to consolidate new democratic regimes even after a number of rounds of competitive elections. Russia represents a larger, geographically dispersed set of cases that continue to struggle with the instability and disarray that mark transitional politics and leave the regime vulnerable to sudden change. These cases raise fundamental questions: Under what conditions do elections provide elite actors with incentives to invest in collaborating to build electoral infrastructure? Or more specifically, having begun the democratic transformation with high hopes, why is Russia failing to live up to expectations?

The case for growing authoritarianism in Russia is relatively clear-cut. Almost two years after the 2003 elections, President Putin's United Russia organization controls a remarkable two-thirds of the seats in the lower house of the State Duma. Only fifteen independent deputies remain in parliament. Opposition parties are in disarray, forced continuously to reinvent themselves in search of their voices. Putin himself received 70 percent of the vote in the first round of the March 2004 presidential elections. His nearest rival, the Communist candidate Nikolai Kharitonov, received just under 14 percent. Effectively, these outcomes obliterated the checks and balances structure in the constitution, enabling Putin to alter existing institutional structures to concentrate power in the executive. Importantly, while these outcomes illustrate significant coordination and cooperation among voters and elites, they do not signal the growth of electoral infrastructure, since collaboration was predicated on coercion, manipulation of electoral rules, and the illegal use of state resources in favor of the party of power.

The findings presented in the empirical chapters illuminate the conditions that make the concentration of executive power in Russia possible and even attractive in the wake of the ineffectiveness of the Yeltsin regime. The weakness and volatility across the party system and within individual organizations reflect the profound lack of electoral infrastructure over the course of the first decade of Russia's democratic experiment, generating incentives and opportunities for alternative gatekeepers and other state actors to enter the electoral fray. The result was a broad but weak political opposition to executive power.

Arguably, the regime structure put in place in response to the 1993 constitutional referendum was aimed at diminishing existing and potential opposition to the center, and the empirical chapters show that this strategy was effective. But the institutional structure itself could not deliver executive autonomy. To achieve this end, Putin needed to marginalize regional and legislative opposition – a goal he realized through institutional change and electoral manipulation.

As discussed in the text, a relatively small core political party, Unity, which emerged from the Kremlin's direct intervention into electoral politics in 1999, enabled Putin to concentrate power in the executive branch. Such state intervention in elections was by no means a new tactic. Since 1993, state intervention has taken a number of forms: the initiation of new state-sponsored parties; alteration of electoral rules and regulations; the use of state resources behind the scenes; and even the perpetuation of vote fraud.

The list of party organizations sponsored by the state since 1993 is quite long, and includes the creation of both Kremlin-based parties and organizations that comprised "friendly opposition." Unity is unique from its predecessors in two regards. First, it succeeded in surpassing expectations in 1999. Second, Unity is the only party of power to increase its vote share in a second election. Unity was also distinct from previous parties of power in other ways. The party's late start and its utter lack of policy content generated a perception of centrism that set it apart from the staunchly pro-market, pro-Western positions of the right organizations such as Russia's Choice and SPS. In addition, unlike Our Home Is Russia, Unity was directly connected to an increasingly popular national leader, Putin, who emerged as the front-runner in the 2000 presidential election over the course of the 1999 campaign. As such, Putin was the expected purveyor of all sorts of state resources. This combination of executive support and centrism garnered Unity a second-place finish in 1999 and established the legislative party faction as an important instrument of control within the State Duma. In a final distinction from other organizations, the party's faction increased its roster and marginalized legislative opposition over the course of its first term.

In addition to building parties, the Kremlin routinely engaged in other forms of state intervention in elections. The biased use of the state media, including the national smear campaign against the leaders of the Fatherland organization in 1999, has been the most visible manipulation of the electoral process, although the Yeltsin regime used similar tactics in previous races. This observable activity is just the tip of the iceberg. There have been repeated Kremlin-backed initiatives to change the electoral apparatus, ranging from redistricting to revamping the electoral commissions and rewriting the election law and the law on political parties. There have even been rumors and some evidence of state-orchestrated vote fraud.

The 2003 election marked a high watermark in the level of state intervention on behalf of the United Russia organization. Kremlin intervention in this election provoked international nongovernmental organizations (NGOs) engaged in democracy assistance and election observation to declare the process compromised. The effect of media domination was more profound than in 1999 given the concentration of resources within state hands. The presence of federal and regional officials on the UR candidate roster suggested increased use of state resources to promote the organization. There were also more ominous interventions, including the use of courts and electoral commissions to remove strong opposition candidates and intimidation by the tax police. Together, these efforts made UR appear to be invincible. Elites flocked to join the party and voter response was overwhelming.

After the 2003 elections, the Kremlin intensified its efforts to engineer new rules that favor the consolidation of the party of power. In the wake of the terrorist attack in Beslan, President Putin initiated far-reaching reforms of the electoral system, federal structure, and regional electoral process. Both the State Duma and the regional legislatures overwhelmingly supported his proposals. These changes will further extend the party of power's control over electorally relevant resources while eliminating sources of potential opposition. Proportional representation electoral rules will establish strong gatekeeping functions for political parties while high barriers to entry will make it difficult for new parties to form. Abolishing direct election over regional governors will deprive them of a personal electoral base and shift control of political careers to the Kremlin. Changes in electoral rules at the regional level will increase UR's penetration across the Federation and preclude the emergence of new organizations or new leadership. In short, these reforms mimic the strategy that kept Mexico's PRI party organization safely in control of that country for nearly six decades.

These coercive strategies and institutional changes are not just insurance against potential opposition. Voter surveys demonstrate that a good deal of the party's support stemmed from Putin's own reputation as an effective and honest leader. To date, events such as the protests against benefits reform and bungled responses to the terrorist attacks on the Nord-Ost theater and on the school in Beslan have not undermined that reputation, but the president remains vulnerable to unpredictable events and an almost intractable set of economic and social reforms looming on the horizon.

The solution to this problem is to substitute some type of party organization for the personal reputation of its leader – a difficult task under any conditions. UR continues to struggle with growing pains as it seeks to establish control over the regions. Partisan accord at the federal level masks significant divisions within the party of power across regions. More importantly, having eliminated effective opposition, the president used his own party as the scapegoat for policy missteps. Most recently, the Kremlin blamed the Duma (and indirectly the party) for poorly implemented social reforms. To hedge its bets, the administration has embarked on a new round of institution-building efforts to construct potential alternatives, or at least friendly opposition, to United Russia for future elections.

One year before the next election cycle, the debate over the durability of United Russia is under way again, masking the authoritarian infrastructure that made the emergence of the organization possible. This infrastructure extends beyond the party organization itself and it is easily transferable to the next electoral context. The Kremlin derives a great deal of power through the appointment of regional governors; election rules that enable small, core parties similar to Unity to establish control over regional legislatures; the willingness to use coercion in the guise of the courts, election commissions, and the tax police; and the concentration of electoral resources, including economic resources at the center. Focusing on the nature and composition of infrastructure suggests that a sudden shift back toward democracy is unlikely in the Russian Federation absent a strong impulse from outside the current political system.

Toward a New Theory of Democratic Consolidation

Although this analysis has focused on Russia, the aim is to develop general insights into the last stages of democratic transitions. At the most general level, the results suggest that understanding the behavior of candidates – how they make decisions, and the consequences of these decisions for electoral infrastructure – helps to explain the character of transitions in other nations, particularly those that began their democratic experiment as Russia did, without agreements, preexisting political organizations, or legacies that structured early competition.

Building on this insight, both the approach and the evidence used in this work provide a fresh look at the causes of a new wave of neo-authoritarian regimes emerging across the globe. Neo-authoritarian or hybrid regimes are defined as systems that feature democratic institutions, including elections, but extremely limited societal control of government (Karl 1995; Levitsky and Way 2002; Zakaria 1997). Similarly, in the narrower set of post-Soviet cases, the euphoria over the imposition of democratic regimes has given way to a more realistic view of the prospects for effective democracy in the near term, if at all. These countries share the common trait of having competitive elections without effective democracy in terms of social control over policy outcomes and the absence of effective checks on strong national leaders.

The Advantages of a Candidate-Centered Approach

By focusing on candidates, this book offers a new approach to understanding the apparent disconnect between repeated elections and democratic development in some new democracies. While candidates and their strategies are not the only variables needed to explain consolidation – the analysis in Chapter 2 shows that international democracy assistance and mass responses to elite efforts also matter – the evidence presented here highlights the fundamental role that candidates play in the consolidation process. The focus on candidates provides a new microlevel view into why elections matter, both in terms of immediate outcomes and in terms of long-term

Democrats, Democratic Transitions, and Democracy

system development, allowing us to assess more accurately when elections matter for the outcome of transition and how they matter.

The post-Soviet cases illustrate three broad responses to electoral competition. The Central Asian cases introduced elections in the face of authoritarian regimes and strong authoritarian infrastructure. In these cases, elections had little effect on the patterns of governance or in enhancing popular control over government. At the other extreme are cases such as Poland and Hungary, in which significant electoral infrastructure existed at the point of founding. As a result, the electoral process became a mechanism to solidify these relationships over varying time periods. The middle ground is occupied by those cases such as Albania, Romania, and Russia, in which elections may provide the catalyst for democratic consolidation or may contribute to a reemergence of authoritarianism. The candidate-centered approach can distinguish among these cases and shed light on the emergence of either electoral or authoritarian infrastructure.

A candidate-centered approach also suggests the conditions under which the past, the authoritarian legacy, and the struggles during the democratization period influence the trajectory of consolidation. The authoritarian legacy is critical when resource monopolies or strong political coalitions survive the regime transformation and remain vital for electoral competition. In these cases, the legacy of the past strongly influences post-transition outcomes. The legacy of the democratization period is predominant when robust contingent consent bargains or cleavage structures emerge to provide electoral infrastructure. These patterns provide strong impulses to guide candidates' decisions. Importantly, assessments of these networks and the resources and information that they provide to party leaders, candidates, and voters may be elusive because their relative strengths rely on internal cohesion and shared perceptions that are often difficult to capture, particularly if analysts focus on collective actors such as political parties. The candidate perspective is one way to shed light on the viability of these factors and assess their future impact on early elections.

Conversely, when neither strong coalitions nor concentrated resources emerge from the past, institutional incentives to amass information and coordinate and cooperate in pursuit of shared goals are likely to be critical to explain outcomes. Institutions that allow candidates to participate without investment in collective goods such as party organizations are likely to push the project off track. Put another way, absent mechanisms that impose electoral infrastructure on political contestants in the early stages of democracy, these participants may not take the actions needed to produce it.

Candidate Strategies and Electoral Competition

Taken to their logical conclusion, these findings offer a new description of the process of pushing democratic transitions toward consolidated democracy. Often democratization is conceptualized as a cumulative process, with emphasis on institutional learning or adaptation, the formation of social capital, and gradual party development. These terms imply a single, smooth trajectory from start to finish. The analysis here suggests that that the processes of transition and consolidation should not be characterized in these terms. Regime transitions can be punctuated, with no progress for long periods of time. Change need not be gradual; a system can be abruptly jolted from one equilibrium to another. Exogenous shocks can derail or propel movement toward democracy. Even with competitive elections, democratic consolidation can regress as well as progress. Endpoints can range from effective democracy to authoritarian revival, with semi-authoritarianism coming in somewhere between these outcomes. Candidates, through their decisions in electoral campaigns, play a key role in shaping these trajectories.

Focusing on candidates and the long-term consequences of their decisions moves the analysis of elections and democratic transitions beyond assessments that are framed in terms of specific individuals, winners and losers, or the presence or absence of political parties. Absent shared information, coordination, and cooperation, these measures may capture short-term outcomes, but will mask the long-term developments or the trajectory of change, and lead to misguided use of democracy assistance and to poor advice about the best strategies to coax a democratic regime into full operation. In contrast, the candidate-centered approach takes the focus off the success or failure of "democrats" and shines a light squarely on the emergence of democratic processes.

Political Parties and Consolidation

Does this focus on candidates imply that party organizations are irrelevant to the study of transitions in Russia or elsewhere? No modern democracy exists without political parties and it is undeniable that political parties play a significant role in democratic governance. Parties fulfill a number of important functions, from linking voters to their representatives to solving collective action problems in the legislature. But what about the roles that parties play in new democracies? Theories of the relationships between parties and democratic development tend to follow thinking about elections and democracy. Both are assumed to be essential, therefore they must be universally beneficial in a new regime.

The discussion in earlier chapters reveals that there is tremendous variation in the number and nature of party organizations in new democracies. The organizational logics of parties can range from shared issue positions, to patronage, to outright coercion. Parties may be nationally or regionally based. Internal discipline may be strong or weak. Party systems may be multiparty, two-party, fragmented, polarized, or volatile. These differences suggest that it is imperative to establish the types of parties and party systems that contribute to democratic consolidation and those that do not, and why.

The findings in this book provide tentative clues about the types of parties that foster successful democratic consolidation. For parties to contribute to democratic development, they must embody the other components of electoral infrastructure: information about voters' preferences, policy alternatives, and candidates' positions and coordination among voters and candidates in pursuit of common goals. The findings also point to why information and coordination absent political parties may not be sufficient to sustain new democracies. The institutions of party organization provide important support for opposition candidates – jobs when they are out of office, a focal point for future activity, and a ready alternative to the governing party in times of crisis or collapse. All of these features ensure the support for a viable opposition in the face of strong national leaders.

This argument implies that the roles that parties play in initial elections and in the larger process of consolidation depend heavily on their internal structures and the rules governing electoral competition. Parties are most influential when they have gatekeeping power over electoral competition, when they monopolize electoral resources. Under these circumstances, parties become important vehicles for ambitious office seekers to pursue political goals. Conversely, when ballot access is broadly available and resources are dispersed, parties play some role in electoral outcomes – as they did in the Russian case – but may not be decisive.

The analysis also stresses that party organizations in transitional democracies such as Russia look and operate very differently than their established counterparts. Such nascent organizations may not control candidate recruitment; they may not control electoral resources; they may be unable to force candidates to campaign on the same platform; they may not be able to deter entry by individuals who refuse to affiliate with a party organization, or prevent their partisans from switching to another organization. As such, our assumptions about the roles that parties play in incorporating and channeling elite and mass interests must reflect the actual capacities of different organizations.

Finally, it is critical for future work to examine the ways in which the focus on parties or particular elements of parties may provide a misleading measure of political development in periods of transition. In studies of Russia, there have been significant debates regarding the relationship between parties and democratic development. The discussion emerged among scholars studying different aspects of parties and party systems to predict future outcomes (Smyth forthcoming). Those looking at the emergence of mass partisanship in the 1990s interpreted the greater than expected level of partisan attachment as a harbinger of democratic success, while at the same time those examining organizational structure predicted more pessimistic outcomes. This debate raises fundamental questions about the sequencing, measurements, and implications of party development that provide the basis for future work.

Political Institutions and Consolidation

My study adopts a choice-theoretic institutional approach to the study of transitions, and expands that approach to include factors that compete with new institutions in transitional regimes: candidates' strategies, alternative resources, informal institutions such as patronage, and coercive efforts to manipulate or evade electoral regulations. One of the central conclusions of this analysis is that for all the newness of democratic competition, Russian candidates respond predictably to incentives, choosing strategies aimed at their political goals, even when their responses do not always produce optimal collective outcomes. As this work shows, Russia's electoral system operates as a sorting mechanism that drives certain candidates toward affiliating with parties, running in nominal districts, and appealing to voters on the basis of the party platform, but drives others to run as independents and to cultivate a personal vote.

The findings of this study support the general principle that electoral institutions have a fundamental effect on the character of elections, election outcomes, and ultimately the success or failure of democratic transitions. It underlines what many scholars already recognize, that electoral rules are not deterministic but interact with the larger political context to shape outcomes. As the business of democracy assistance grows and spreads to

Democrats, Democratic Transitions, and Democracy

new cultures, it is critical to begin to understand more deeply how electoral rules interact with different contexts in order to predict their short- and long-term effects on political development. Again, this work provides some guidance by integrating factors normally relegated to cultural studies (such as cleavages) and rational choice arguments (the nature of shared information) with institutional arguments to explain electoral results.

Three caveats are critical for conclusions about the effects of institutions in transitional settings. First, the analysis of candidate behavior in contemporary Russia also shows that the effects of electoral institutions during transitions can be highly contextual and sensitive to small details. As Olga Shvetsova (1999) warns, the conditions that characterize transitional elections are likely to magnify the effects of relatively minor institutional regulations, including the threshold for representation, the relationship between tiers of seat allocation, and hybrid systems. For example, in Russia the absence of a linkage mechanism between the list and district races for the Duma has profound implications for the strategic decisions made by candidates and party organizations. The results presented in Chapter 4 showed that provisions allowing the transfer of signatures between a party's list and district candidates increased incentives for candidate entry. Moreover, the mixed system gave party organizations a strong incentive to run candidates in as many districts as possible, in order to put a local face on the party label, which also contributed to the proliferation of candidates. This work suggests a renewed focus on the range of electoral structures that influence patterns of coordination within the new regime. These can include electoral administration procedures that enhance electoral transparency and forge elite commitment to the electoral process.

In addition, more attention should be paid to the interactions between electoral regulations and other regime structures. In Russia, parliamentary elections preceded the presidential contest by a few months. As a result, potential presidential candidates saw parliamentary elections as an opportunity to build a national reputation and political organization that would aid a run for the presidency. A number of parties were formed on that basis. The lack of linkage between national and regional elections further undermined incentives for candidates to cooperate to build party organizations and coherent party platforms. Again, a crossnational study would clarify the conditions under which strong presidents are able to intervene in electoral politics. Looking beyond constitutional structure to explore the timing of presidential, legislative, and national elections, the nature of parliamentary and presidential coalitions, and the disjuncture between national and regional election rules would also clarify their broader effects on patterns of coordination and cooperation within the electoral arena.

Likewise, the de facto federal structure in Russia had important implications for the dispersion of electoral resources and the preservation of Soviet-era patronage. Coupled with electoral rules that provide ballot access to independent candidates, the federal system helps to proliferate candidates, generate mixed messages in the campaign period, and siphon resources from party organizations.

Finally, Gerard Alexander (2001) argues that transitions are marked by greater than expected rule changes, negating the explanatory power of the institutional. The Putin administration's restructuring of the Russian system is an excellent example of this phenomenon. Yet, it is equally true that even though the institutions put in place in 1993 were vulnerable in the long term, their short-term effects were measurable and significant. Moreover, it is critical to understand that not all institutional changes alter outcomes or the trajectory of political development. Changes that favor one group over another in the long term may also provide greater transparency that assures long-term commitment to those rules. Thus, rather than getting bogged down in a debate over whether or not institutions matter in transition, it is imperative to study when and how they matter in different contexts. As noted earlier, this study suggests that the structure of institutional incentives matters most when elections are introduced in an absence of electoral infrastructure since the rules provide important incentives to invest in building that infrastructure or not.

The Impact of Uncertainty on Democratic Consolidation

Most scholars agree that political uncertainty is the hallmark of regime transition. They are less united in how they define uncertainty, capture the variation in types and levels of uncertainty across transitional regimes, or study the effect of uncertainty on political behavior. Some scholars focus on the ambiguity surrounding regime survival. Others focus on individual uncertainty over the value of their skills and jobs in the new economy. Still others focus on actors' capacities to understand the new rules, the degree to which those rules will be enforced, or their effects on other actors.

In Russia, uncertainty in the new electoral regime stems both from the nature of the old regime and the rapid and chaotic wholesale transformation that Russia experienced between 1991 and 1993. The revolutions carried

Democrats, Democratic Transitions, and Democracy

out under the guise of democratic transition in the postcommunist states were really two profound transitions that transformed both the economic and political systems of these states. This simultaneous change generated enormous ambiguity for all political actors and potential actors, from voters to entrepreneurs to leaders of the old regime. Not only did citizens have to determine the value of their old skills and assets in a new economy, they were faced with the need to calculate their political interests in a new competitive regime structure. Similarly, political leaders faced the task of determining the value of their own political resources, their likely opposition, and the changes in both that were likely to occur in the short term. Everything, from the boundaries of class divisions to the composition of the new elite, is in flux during a dual transition. In terms of electoral politics, the difficulty in these situations is not that politics is complex; rather, it is that high levels of uncertainty nullify the shortcuts that structure political interactions in established systems.

This type of uncertainty is distinct from uncertainty over regime survival and the impact of new rules and regulations. In their study of democracy and economic development, Adam Przeworski and his coauthors (2000) make a very useful distinction between uncertainty over whether or not the regime will survive and uncertainty about the likelihood that any single candidate or party will win seats in the legislature. Many scholars, including Przeworski (1986), underscore the latter type of uncertainty as essential to democratic regime survival, since uncertainty over electoral outcomes is a fundamental element in convincing contestants to comply with democratic rules and to encourage opposition participation. It is this uncertainty that generates choice.

This study of Russia offers a new interpretation of the role of uncertainty in transitional elections and its impact on regime survival and demonstrates the linkage between the two types of uncertainty identified by Przeworski. The empirical focus of the study is on the lack of shared knowledge in elections: what voters want from government, what strategies will win voter support, the nature of electoral opponents, and the value of parties' brand labels. The analytic chapters show that these sources of uncertainty influence candidates' strategies: Many hopeless candidates competed for Duma seats; they were reluctant to invest in parties that might not endure through the next round of competition, and they ran away from party platforms in the campaign period. These strategies weakened the potential for political opposition to build durable institutions to protect them if they did lose an election. The sum of these decisions undermined the accumulation of electoral infrastructure and, in particular, perpetuated the lack of information from election to election.

The more general point is that the amount of electoral infrastructure available at the point of founding elections varies tremendously. In Western Europe, well-integrated trade unions provided strong cues about the relative strength of party organizations, the potential sources of electoral resources, and voters' demands. In contrast, in the postcommunist states, the legacy of the Soviet system together with dual economic and political transitions undermined basic cleavages from class to ethnicity, and left politicians with little to go on when formulating their strategies. In the case of Russia, this lack of information was carried through a number of elections, yielding electoral volatility and weak opposition organizations.

In the end, this book shows that uncertainty in transition is not something that is inevitably resolved by the imposition of a new regime structure or repeated electoral competition. Nor is it inevitable that uncertainty will decline in a steady and predictable manner. Even new democracies that have relatively positive democracy scores can be plagued by electoral volatility that undermines the policy process and leaves the regime vulnerable to external shocks such as scandal and economic crises that can stall or even derail the new regime.

Conclusion

The evidence presented here argues that elections, the hallmark of democratic governance, can actually undermine the development of an effective and representative democracy. The solution is not to abandon or delay elections in new regimes but to think systematically about how to structure competition and provide democracy assistance to enable elections to perform two key functions: integrate elites into the new system and incorporate mass interests through investments in electoral infrastructure.

The postcommunist cases illustrate how elections can work to deepen democracy but also how they can derail democratic experiments. The startling successes of democracy in Romania and Albania speak to the power of the electoral process to overcome the obstacles of authoritarian legacies. More recently, the role of elections and election fraud in mobilizing the Ukrainian opposition testifies to the power of elections to spark political change. Conversely, electoral volatility hindered consolidation in Lithuania. And the focus of this work, the Russian Republic, illustrates how elections can generate conditions that lead to authoritarian revival.

Democrats, Democratic Transitions, and Democracy

These latter cases illustrate that elections are not a panacea for struggling regimes. Rather, the capacity of elections to fulfill the promise of democratic deepening relies not on the good intentions of leaders or hopes of voters but on the context in which they are held, the rules that govern competition, and the right kind of international assistance – all aimed at providing incentives to individual politicians to invest in electoral infrastructure.

Appendix A

THE SAMPLE

The work began with the idea that all candidates are important to the electoral process – even those whose candidacies are futile. The reasoning emerges from the assumption that candidates' strategic decisions are interactive, that at each point in the campaign process, decisions are made in light of the actions taken by other contestants. A fundamental goal of the work was to capture the effects of these interactions. To achieve this goal within the limits of comparative research, the survey did not randomly sample national candidates, but rather sampled as extensively as possible within case study regions. The regions included in the initial survey were Kostroma, Saratov, Yaroslav'l, and Chelyabinsk. In 1999, the sample regions were expanded to include five ethnically defined republics: Bashkir, Chuvash, Komi, Tartarstan, and Udmurt. The empirical work in this book concentrates on the 1999 data to provide the most extensive comparison among candidates, including a comparison of behavior in Russian regions and the ethnic republics.

The regions included in the study were first identified in 1994. The ethnic republics were chosen to mirror conditions within the first set of Russian regions, but also to provide some variation in the level of titular citizens in each region. These initial regions were selected based on variation on key indicators that were identified as crucial determinants of electoral behavior in Russia and elsewhere. These included region size, population, rural population, percent of pensioners, employment in industry, unemployment, the size of regional budgets, and titular population. All of these data are available upon request.

In addition, I looked at political indicators such as the number of electoral districts in each region, ranging from one in Kostroma and Komi to six in the Bashkir Republic. I was also interested in ensuring variation on key

Appendix A

Table A.1. *Response Rates in Case Study Regions, 1999*

Region	Number of Candidates	Number of Respondents	Percent of Total Candidates
Chelyabinsk Oblast	106	72	68
Kostroma Oblast	25	20	80
Saratov Oblast	67	57	85
Yaroslavl Oblast	56	38	68
Bashkir Republic	42	33	79
Chuvash Republic	36	22	61
Komi Republic	25	14	56
Tartarstan	63	43	68
Udmurt Republic	31	23	74

indicators of voter preferences: support for the regional governor in the first round of the regional elections; support for the president in 1996; support for party organizations in parliamentary elections; and finally, party activity within the regions. On all of these indicators, the regions showed strong variation, including variation in whether or not they were consistent over time in their political opinions. Again, all of these data are available upon request.

Response rates for the survey were quite high, ranging from 56 percent of all candidates running for office in the Komi Republic to 85 percent of candidates running in Saratov Oblast. The response rates for the survey are presented in Table A.1.

The response rates do not appear to be biased in favor of any type of candidate; the pool includes winners, high government officials, and entrepreneurs. The response rates also do not overrepresent candidates running in the oblast capital. Special care was taken to include candidates from Moscow or other areas who ran in these districts, so they are also represented in the sample.

Appendix B

THE CANDIDATE SURVEY

This appendix details the survey questions used to construct the variables used in the analysis of candidate behavior, with particular attention to questions asked in the 1999 round (the 1995 survey is similar, but omits some questions as discussed in the text). Questions that were not used in the analysis, as well as those capturing basic demographic information (interview number, region), are omitted for space considerations.

Block 1: Demographic Information

1.01. Do you consider yourself a professional politician?
   1. Yes
   2. No
   3. Hard to answer
1.02. Do you own your own business or part of a business?
   1. Yes
   2. No
   3. Hard to answer
1.03. How much of your time during each week would you say you spend doing political work?
   1. 100 percent of my time
   2. 75 percent of my time
   3. 50 percent of my time
   4. 25 percent of my time
   5. Less than 25 percent of my time
   6. Hard to answer

Appendix B

Block 2: Activity in Parties, Blocks, or Societal Organizations

2.01. Why did you want to join a party organization (asked only of partisans)?
   1. Party leaders invited you to become a candidate with the support of their party.
   2. You wanted to join the party in order to run on the party list.
   3. You wanted the party to support you in your single-member district race.
   4. The party was popular in your district.
   5. The party was able to give you financial and material support for your campaign.

Block 3: General Political Experience

3.01. Did you have a position in the structure of the CPSU (check all that are appropriate)?
   1. In the apparat of the Central Committee (TSK) of the CPSU
   2. In the apparat of the republic-level CPSU
   3. In the Obkom
   4. In the Gorkom or Raikon
   5. In the primary party organization
   6. I didn't hold such a position.

Block 4: Experience as a Candidate

4.01. Were you elected to a Soviet before 1989 (select all appropriate answers)?
   1. Supreme Soviet SSSR
   2. Supreme Soviet RSFSR
   3. Oblast soviet
   4. Supreme Soviet of an autonomous republic
   5. City soviet
   6. Raion soviet
   7. Other
   8. Was never elected
4.02. Did you run for oblast office or city office?
   1. Yes
   2. No

The Candidate Survey

4.03. Were you in a leadership position in that Duma?
   1. Yes
   2. No
4.04. Did you run for office in an oblast or city soviet in 1995 or 1996?
   1. Yes
   2. No
4.05. Were you in a leadership position in that oblast or city duma?
   1. Yes
   2. No
4.06. Following are listed several reasons that people might use to explain their participation in electoral competition. Please indicate which were very important for your decision and which were not important the first time you ran for office (1–4 scale: 1 = very important, 2 = important, 3 = not important, 4 = hard to say).
   1. Further democratic reform
   2. Change your life/build a political career
   3. Make policy you consider important
   4. Create or strengthen the party
   5. Strengthen your position at work
   6. Gather experience for future political work
   7. Change the direction of reform in Russia
   8. Other
4.07. In general, would you say that elections are conducted fairly in your oblast?
   1. Yes
   2. No
   3. Hard to answer
4.08. Thinking of candidates in your oblast for all elections, would you say that election technologies have become dirtier since 1990?
   1. Yes
   2. No
   3. Hard to answer

Block 5: Electoral Experience

5.01. Did you run for national parliamentary office in 1995?
   1. Yes
   2. Tried to register on the ballot but could not

Appendix B

        3. Thought about it and decided against running
        4. Didn't run and didn't think about running – if answer is 3 or 4, skip to 6.01
5.02. If you ran on the party list, what list did you run on?
        1. National list
        2. Regional list
5.03. Which organization nominated you to run for office (if the candidate ran as an independent, skip to question 6.01)?
        1. Party or bloc
        2. Other societal organization
        3. Work collective
        4. Group of voters in place of residence
5.04. What was the name of the party or societal organization with which you were affiliated in 1999?
        1. Central party organization (show list)
        2. Regional party organization (add name)
        3. Hard to answer

Block 6: The 1999 Campaign

6.01. Which organization nominated you to run for office in 1999?
        1. Party or bloc
        2. Other societal organization
        3. Work collective
        4. Group of voters in place of residence
6.02. Where did you run for office?
        1. In a single-member district
        2. In a single-member district and on the party list
        3. Only on the party list
6.03. What was the name of the party or societal organization with which you were affiliated in 1999 (record the name of the party or organization)?
6.04. Where was your campaign headquarters located?
        1. In your home
        2. At your place of work
        3. At the party or bloc organization headquarters
        4. At another societal organization that gave you help
        5. Had no headquarters
        6. Other

The Candidate Survey

6.05. How many people on your campaign staff received wages?
1. 1–5
2. 6–10
3. 11–20
4. 21–30
5. 31–50
6. Over 50
7. No paid workers

Please indicate how important the following people were for your campaign. Indicate whether 1) you did not use these advisors; or they were 2) very helpful; 3) helpful; 4) not helpful; 5) hard to say.

6.06. Pollsters
6.07. Specialists on television and other press
6.08. Press secretary
6.09. Political advisors
6.10. Help from Western NGO groups

6.11. Candidates often use resources from their job to aid their campaign effort. Which of these resources did you use in your campaign? (Please include all relevant answers.)
1. Didn't use work resources
2. Help from coworkers
3. Help from employees to campaign door to door or hand out information
4. Printing, photocopier
5. Computer, fax, video equipment
6. Office help
7. Help with arranging meetings with voters
8. Other

Which of the following sources of financial help were most important for your campaign? Please indicate whether 1) there was no such source; 2) the source was very important; 3) important; 4) not important; 5) hard to say.

6.12. Your own funds
6.13. Party funds
6.14. Help from a local commercial structure
6.15. Help from a central commercial structure
6.16. Help from the Central Election Commission
6.17. Help from voters
6.18. Help from friends and colleagues

Appendix B

6.19. Did you have enough money to run your campaign?
   1. Yes
   2. No
   3. Hard to say

How did you run your campaign? What activities were important to reach your voters? Please indicate whether 1) you did not use the tactic listed or 2) the tactic was very important; 3) important; 4) not very important; or 5) hard to answer.

   6.20. Speak on the radio
   6.21. Speak on television
   6.22. Get coverage in newspapers
   6.23. Meet with groups of voters
   6.24. Meet personally with voters – door-to-door campaigning
   6.25. Meet with collective organizations
   6.26. Place ads in mass media
   6.27. Distribute flyers

6.28. From this list, please identify which groups you considered important to your campaign.
   1. Workers in government industry
   2. Workers in private industry
   3. Pensioners
   4. Kolkhozniks
   5. Private businesspeople
   6. Directors of government enterprises
   7. Youth
   8. Ethnic groups
   9. Intelligentsia
   10. Members of trade unions
   11. Members of independent trade unions
   12. Women's groups
   13. Military personnel
   14. Unemployed
   15. Other
   16. Targeted campaign at all voters
   17. Hard to answer

6.29. Do you feel that you were well-known in your district before the campaign?
   1. Yes

The Candidate Survey

    2. No
    3. Hard to say

6.30. How much would you say you know about the issue positions or political demands of the constituents in the district?
   1. I have a good understanding of the positions of constituents in my district.
   2. I feel I understand the positions of more than half my district.
   3. I feel I understand the positions of half of my district.
   4. I feel I understand the positions of less than half of my district.
   5. I simply don't know much about the positions of constituents in my district.

6.31. What do you consider to be the basis for your reputation in your district?
   1. Economic activity/business
   2. I held elected office in that district prior to this election.
   3. I held an appointed political office in that district prior to this election.
   4. I was a political activist in the district prior to this election.

The following is a list of several reasons that a person would choose a particular district. Why did you choose to run in that district? Please indicate whether each reason was 1) very important; 2) important; 3) not important; or 4) hard to answer.

    6.32. Local party leaders selected the district.
    6.33. Party leaders in the center selected the district.
    6.34. I live in that district.
    6.35. People in the district know me by my work.
    6.36. People in the district know me by my political activities.
    6.37. The district was best suited for an independent candidate.
    6.38. There were fewer potential opponents in that district.
    6.39. The district was not controlled by any political leader or party.

6.40. To what did you want voters to pay attention in your campaign?
   1. Individual qualities
   2. Your political platform
   3. Your party's platform
   4. Your name

How important were the following types of issues in your campaign strategy?

    6.41. Issues regarding constitutional amendments

Appendix B

 6.42. Issues regarding the performance of the current government
 6.43. Issues regarding the balance of power between the president and parliament
 6.44. Issues regarding the balance of power between the regions and the center
 6.45. Issues specific to my region
 6.46. Issues specific to a particular group of voters within my region

Appendix C

VARIABLES CONSTRUCTED FROM SURVEY DATA

Affiliate (did the candidate affiliate with a political party)
- 1 V5.01 = 1 (Partisan)
- 0 Otherwise (Independent)

Campaign HQ (was the candidate's HQ located in the party HQ)
- 0 HQ99 = 1, 2, 3, 4, 5, 6 (no)
- 1 HQ99 = 3 (yes)

Career Goal (candidate's interest in a political career: higher = stronger)
- 0 V4.15 = 3, 4
- 1 V4.15 = 2
- 2 V4.15 = 1

Center (did the candidate affiliate with NDR, Fatherland, Unity, Yabloko)
- 1 Constructed from V5.13 (yes)
- 0 Otherwise (no)

Dirty (have elections become dirtier since 1990)
- 1 V4.29 = 1 (yes)
- 0 Otherwise (no)

District Information (candidate's information about voters: higher = better information)
- 0 V6.47 = 0, 5
- 1 V6.47 = 4
- 2 V6.47 = 3
- 3 V6.47 = 2
- 4 V6.47 = 1

Appendix C

District Selection (how did candidate run for office)

    0 Affiliate = 0 (independent)
    1 Affiliate = 1 and V6.02 = 1 (partisan, district-only)
    2 Affiliate = 1 and V6.02 = 2 (partisan, district, and list)
    3 Affiliate = 1 and V6.03 = 3 (partisan, list-only)

Door (did candidate campaign door to door extensively)

    1 V6.40 = 1 (yes)
    0 Otherwise (no)

Elected Leader (did the candidate hold a leadership position in the city government or legislature)

    0 Otherwise (no)
    2 V4.03 = 1 or V4.08 = 1 or V4.11 = 1 (yes)

Established Party (did the candidate affiliate with a party that had Duma seats prior to 1999)

    1 Left = 1, Center = 1, or Right = 1 (yes)
    0 Otherwise (no)

Fair (candidate assessment of the fairness of elections)

    1 V4.29 = 1 (fair)
    0 Otherwise (not fair)

Fit (candidate with district: higher = better fit)

    0 V6.49 = 0 and District Information = 5
    1 District Information = 0, 1, 2, 3, 4
    2 V6.49 = 1 and District Information = 5

Flyers (did the candidate make extensive use of campaign flyers)

    1 V6.43 = 1 (yes)
    0 Otherwise (no)

Issues (which issues did the candidate emphasize during the campaign – multiple responses coded)

    0 None
    1 V6.61 = 1 (constitutional amendments)
    2 V6.61 = 1 (performance of current government)

Variables Constructed from Survey Data

   3 V6.65 = 1 (president–parliament relations)
   4 V6.66 = 1 (center–region relations)
   5 V6.67 = 1 (regional or local issues)

Issue Appeals (did the candidate emphasize personal policy preferences during the campaign)

   1 V6.58 = 3 (yes)
   0 Otherwise (no)

Join (reasons for wanting to join party – coded multiple times if necessary)

   1 V2.03 ne 0 (party leaders recruited)
   2 V2.04 ne 0 (wanted to run on the list)
   3 V2.05 ne 0 (wanted party support in the district race)
   4 V2.06 ne 0 (party popular in my district)
   5 V2.07 ne 0 (party could give material or financial support)

Known (was the candidate well-known prior to campaign)

   1 V6.46 = 1 (yes)
   0 Otherwise (no)

Left (did the candidate affiliate with the KPRF)

   1 Constructed from V5.13 (yes)
   0 Otherwise (no)

New (did the candidate affiliate with a new party)

   1 Affiliate = 1 and Center, Left, Right = 0 (yes)
   0 Otherwise (no)

Organizational Resources (candidate's organizational resources: higher = more resources)

   1 V3.21 = 2 (member of leadership of the organization)
   2 V3.21 = 1 (leader of the organization)
   0 Otherwise (no)

Own Business (did the candidate own a business)

   2 V1.3 = 1 (yes)
   0 Otherwise (no)

Appendix C

Party-Building Goal (candidate's interest in building party: higher = stronger goal)

    0 V4.17 = 3, 4
    1 V4.17 = 2
    2 V4.17 = 1

Personal (did the candidate emphasize personal characteristics in the campaign)

    1 V6.58 = 1, 4 (yes)
    0 Otherwise (no)

Platform (did the candidate emphasize the party platform during the campaign)

    3 V6.58 = 3 (yes)
    0 Otherwise (no)

Policy Goal (candidate's interest in enacting good policy: higher = stronger goal)

    0 V4.16 = 3, 4
    1 V4.16 = 2
    2 V4.16 = 1

Poll (did the candidate hire a pollster)

    1 Otherwise (yes)
    0 V6.22 = 1 (no)

Professional Politician (did the candidate consider himself or herself a professional politician)

    1 V1.2 = 1, 2 (yes)
    0 Otherwise (no)

Reform (candidate's interest in democratic reform: higher = stronger goal)

    0 V4.18 = 3, 4
    1 V4.18 = 2
    2 V4.18 = 1

Variables Constructed from Survey Data

Reputation (what was the candidate's reputation – coded multiple times)

    0 Otherwise (none)
    1 $V6.48 = 1$ (business)
    2 $V6.48 = 2$ (elected offices)
    3 $V6.48 = 3$ (political activist)
    4 $V6.48 = 4$ (political appointee)

Resources (summary of the candidate's personal vote resources)

    Variable equals maximum of Elected Leader, Organizational Resources, Soviet-Era Position and Own Business

Reverse Reform Goal (candidate's interest in reversing reforms: higher = stronger goal)

    0 $V4.20 = 3, 4$
    1 $V4.20 = 2$
    2 $V4.20 = 1$

Right (did the candidate affiliate with Democratic Russia, SDS)

    1 Constructed from V5.13 (yes)
    0 Otherwise (no)

Russian Region (region of the candidate's district/regional list)

    5 Region $= 3, 4, 8, 9$ (Russian)
    0 Otherwise (Non-Russian)

Select (candidate's reasons for district selection – coded multiple times if necessary)

    1 $V6.50 = 1$ or $V6.51 = 1$ (party leaders selected)
    2 $V6.52 = 1$ (live in the district)
    3 $V6.53 = 1$ (business reputation)
    4 $V6.54 = 1$ (political reputation)
    5 $V6.55 = 1$ (district good for an independent)
    6 $V6.56 = 1$ (quality of opposition)
    7 $V6.57 = 1$ (district not controlled by an organization or leader)

Appendix C

Self-Fund (did the candidate get campaign funds only from self, family, and friends)

    1 V6.29 = 4, V6.30 = 4, V6.31 = 4, V6.32 = 4, V6.33 = 4 (yes)
    0 Otherwise (no)

Soviet-Era Position (did the candidate have a position in Soviet-era government or party)

    1 V4.06 = 1, or V3.24 = 5 (midlevel position)
    2 V4.01 = 1, V4.02 = 1, V4.03 = 1, V4.04 = 1, V3.24 = 1, V3.24 = 2, V3.24 = 3, or V3.24 = 4 (high-level position)
    0 Otherwise (no position)

Staff (did the candidate have a paid staff)

    0 V6.17 = 7 (no)
    1 Otherwise (yes)

Sufficient (did the candidate have sufficient resources for the campaign)

    0 V6.35 = 1 (yes)
    1 Otherwise (no)

Target (which groups did the candidate target – up to five responses coded)

    0 No groups targeted
    1 V6.45 = 1 (government workers)
    2 V6.45 = 2, 5 (workers in private industry)
    3 V6.45 = 3 (pensioners)
    4 V6.45 = 4 (kolkhozniks)
    5 V6.45 = 7 (youth)
    6 V6.45 = 9 (intelligentsia)

Work Resources (did the candidate use resources from place of work in the campaign)

    1 Otherwise (yes)
    0 V6.27 = 1 (no)

Appendix D

SAMPLE AND VARIABLE CONSTRUCTION FOR ANALYSIS IN CHAPTER 2

Ideally, this study would include all of the postcommunist cases. However, I excluded Serbia and Montenegro since the constitution was not adopted until 2003 near the end of this study. I also excluded Bosnia and Uzbekistan, and Turkmenistan because it was not possible to collect the necessary data for those cases. Twenty-two cases are included in the study: Albania, Armenia, Azerbaijan, Belarus, Bulgaria, Croatia, Czech Republic, Estonia, Georgia, Hungary, Kazakhstan, Kyrgyzstan, Latvia, Lithuania, Macedonia, Moldova, Poland, Romania, Russia, Slovakia, Slovenia, and Ukraine.

The Dependent Variable

The dependent variable is measured as a country's Freedom Score (the average of the political rights and civil liberties components of the scale) in 2003. Alternative specifications of the model using a 0 (unconsolidated), 1 (consolidated), or 1 (unconsolidated), 2 (partially consolidated), or 3 (authoritarian) using logistic regression yield the same results but raise technical problems when calculating the robustness of the parameters.

Cultural Variables

WVS (measure of popular support for the old regime). To measure popular affect toward the old regime, I used the WVS question number 163 drawn from the 1999–2001 wave. The question was worded as follows:

People have different views about the system for governing this country. Here is a scale for rating how well things are going: 1 means very bad; 10 means very good.

Appendix D

Where on this scale would you put the political system as it was under the communist regime?

1	2	3	4	5	6	7	8	9	10	99
Bad									Very good	Don't know

The percentages used in the regression reflect responses between six and ten on a ten-point scale.

The Central Asian cases are not included in the WVS project. To incorporate Kazakhstan and Kyrgyzstan, I used available data garnered from a different set of questions but collected at the same time as the WVS data. The series of three questions asked respondents whether they would like to return to the Soviet Union due to 1) political reasons; 2) economic reasons; or 3) social reasons. The response was a simple yes or no. To make the questions comparable, I averaged across the three questions. Both surveys were commissioned by USAID and conducted by the Almaty-based Central Asian polling agency Brif in June 1999. The Kyrgyz survey draws on 1,200 respondents from two cities, and the Kazakh survey consists of 1,219 respondents from ten cities. For more on Brif and its survey methodology, see www.brif.kz. I am grateful to Eric McGlinchey for these data points.

Postsov. This is a 0 (former communist but not Soviet state) or 1 (former Soviet state) dummy variable.

Economic Variables

Growth. This variable measures the total real growth in gross domestic product (GDP) from founding elections until 2002. The data are collected from the World Bank Development indicators on-line, accessed through the Penn State library system. I also used a number of other economic indicators, such as the change in GDP per capita, average real growth and average change in real growth over this period. All data was collected from the same source. None of these alternative measures changed the parameter coefficient.

Political Variables

PPI. The presidential powers index is a scale variable measuring the relative strength of presidents. The power index is highly correlated with the Hellman-Frye-Tucker index that is frequently cited in the literature.

Sample and Variable Construction for Chapter 2

However, it includes more cases and was updated until 2004. Scores in the regression reflect measurement in 2003. The data are drawn from a larger data set of political institutions: Klaus Armingeon and Romana Careja, *Comparative Data Set for 28 Post-Communist Countries, 1989–2004*, Institute of Political Science, University of Berne, 2004. Accessed at http://www.ipw.unibe.ch/mitarbeiter/ru_armingeon/CPD_Set_en.asp.

FHfounding. These are the Freedom House political rights index scores in the year of the founding elections. The scores constitute a proxy for the procedural and commitment elements of consolidation definitions. The four-part checklist for the scale measures: electoral process, political pluralism and participation, functioning of government, and additional political rights questions.

Yearsfounding. To measure the expectation that consolidation is a process of learning or trial and error, this variable measures the years since the founding elections.

Works Cited

Aldrich, John. *Why Parties?* Chicago: University of Chicago Press, 1995.
Alexander, Gerard. "Institutions, Path Dependence, and Democratic Consolidation," *Journal of Theoretical Politics*, 13, 3, 2001: 249–70.
Almond, Gabriel A., and Sidney Verba. *The Civic Culture: Political Attitudes and Democracy in Five Nations, an Analytic Study*. Boston: Little, Brown, 1965.
Ames, Barry. *The Deadlock of Democracy in Brazil*. Ann Arbor, MI: University of Michigan Press, 2001.
Ansolabehere, Stephen, James M. Snyder, Jr., and Charles Stewart III. "Old Voters, New Voters, and the Personal Vote: Using Redistricting to Measure the Incumbency Advantage," *American Journal of Political Science*, 44, 1, 2000: 17–34.
Bahry, Donna, Cynthia Boaz, and Stacy Burnett Gordon. "Tolerance, Transition and Support for Civil Liberties in Russia," *Comparative Political Studies*, 30 August 1997: 484–510.
Bianco, William, and John Aldrich. "A Game-Theoretic Model of Party Affiliation of Candidates and Office-Holders," *Mathematical and Computer Modeling*, 16, 2, 1992: 103–15.
Black, Gordon S. "A Theory of Political Ambition: Career Choices and the Role of Structural Incentives," *American Political Science Review*, 66, 1, March 1972: 144–59.
Brader, Ted, and Joshua A. Tucker. "The Emergence of Mass Partisanship in Russia, 1993–96," *American Journal of Political Science*, 45, 1, January 2001: 69–83.
———. "It's Nothing Personal? The Appeal of Party Leaders and the Development of Partisanship in Russia," unpublished manuscript.
Bratton, Michael. "Deciphering Africa's Divergent Transitions," *Political Science Quarterly*, 112, 1, 1997: 67–93.
Buckley, Cynthia, and Regina Smyth. "The Ties That Bind: The Importance of Region in the Construction of Social and Political Citizenship," in Blair Ruble and Nancy Popson, eds., *Fragmented Spaces: Russian Regions in Transition*. Baltimore, MD: Johns Hopkins University Press, 2001.
Bunce, Valerie. "Rethinking Recent Democratization," *World Politics*, 55, 2, 2003: 147–92.

———. "Comparative Democratization: Big and Bounded Generalizations," *Comparative Political Studies*, 33, 6–7, August–September 2000: 703–34.

———. "Regional Differences in Democratization: The East Versus the South," *Post-Soviet Affairs*, 14, 3, July–September 1998: 187–211.

———. "Should Transitologists Be Grounded?" *Slavic Review*, 54, 1, Spring 1994: 111–27.

Bunce, Valerie, and Maria Csanadi. "Uncertainty in the Transition: Post-Communism in Hungary," *European Politics and Society*, 7, 2, 1993: 240–75.

Cain, Bruce E., John A. Ferejohn, and Morris P. Fiorina. "The Constituency Service Basis of the Personal Vote for U.S. Representatives and British Members of Parliament," *American Political Science Review*, 78, 1, 1984: 110–25.

Calvo, Enesto, Abal Medina, and Juan Manuel. "Institutional Gamblers: Majoritarian Representation, Electoral Uncertainty, and the Coalitional Costs of Mexico's Hybrid Electoral System," *Electoral Studies*, 21, 3, September 2002: 453–71.

Canon, David T. *Actors, Athletes, and Astronauts: Political Amateurs in the United States Congress*. Chicago: University of Chicago Press, 1990.

Carey, John M., and Matthew Soberg Shugart. "Incentives to Cultivate a Personal Vote: A Rank Ordering of Electoral Formulas," *Electoral Studies*, 14, 4, December 1995: 417–39.

Carothers, Thomas. "The End of the Transition Paradigm," *Journal of Democracy*, 13, 1, January 2002: 5–21.

Cheibub, Jose Antonio. "Minority Governments, Deadlock Situations, and the Survival of Presidential Democracies," *Comparative Political Studies*, 35, 3, April 2002: 284–312.

Clark, Elizabeth Spiro. "Why Elections Matter," *Washington Quarterly*, 23, 3, 2000: 27–40.

Clem, R. "Urban-Rural Voting Differences in Russian Elections, 1995–1996: A Rayon Level Analysis," *Post-Soviet Geography and Economics*, 38, 7, 1997: 379–95.

Colaresi, Michael, and William R. Thompson. "The Economic Development-Democratization Relationship: Does the Outside World Matter?" *Comparative Political Studies*, 36, 4, May 2003: 381–403.

Collier, David, and Steven Levitsky. "Democracy with Adjectives: Conceptual Innovation in Comparative Research," *World Politics*, 49, 3, 1997: 430–51.

Collier, Ruth Berins. *Paths Toward Democracy. The Working Class and Elites in Western Europe and South America*. Cambridge, UK: University of Cambridge Press, 1999.

Colton, Timothy J. *Parties, Citizens, and Democratic Consolidation in Russia*. Presented at Ten Years After the Collapse of the Soviet Union: Lessons and Perspectives, 13–14 October 2000b, Princeton, NJ: unpublished manuscript.

———. *Transitional Citizens: Voters and What Influences Them in the New Russia*. Cambridge, MA: Harvard University Press, 2000a.

———. "Economics and Voting in Russia," *Post-Soviet Affairs* 12, 4, 1996a: 289–318.

———. "From the Parliamentary to the Presidential Election: Russians Get Real About Politics," *Demokratizatsiya*, 4, 3, 1996b: 371–9.

———. "The Politics of Democratization: The Moscow Election of 1990," *Soviet Economy*, 6, 4, 1990: 285–344.

Works Cited

Colton, Timothy J., and Jerry F. Hough, eds. *Growing Pains: Russian Democracy and the Election of 1993*. Washington, DC: Brookings Institution Press, 1998.

Colton, Timothy J., and Michael McFaul. *Popular Choice and Managed Democracy*. Washington, DC: The Brookings Institution Press, 2003a.

———. "Russian Democracy Under Putin," *Problems of Post-Communism*, 50, 4, July/August 2003b: 12–21.

———. "Reinventing Russia's Party of Power: 'Unity' and the 1999 Duma Election," *Post Soviet Affairs*, 16, 3, July–September 2001: 201–24.

Colton, Timothy, and Henry Hale. "Context and Party System Development: Voting Behavior in Russian Parliamentary Elections in Comparative Perspective." Paper presented at the Annual Convention of the American Political Science Association, 3 September 2004. Chicago: unpublished manuscript.

Cox, Gary. *Making Votes Count: Strategic Coordination in the World's Electoral Systems*. New York: Cambridge University Press, 1997.

———. "Centripetal and Centrifugal Incentives in Electoral Systems," *American Journal of Political Science*, 34, 4, November 1990: 903–35.

———. *The Efficient Secret: The Cabinet and the Development of Political Parties in Victorian England*. Cambridge, UK: Cambridge University Press, 1987.

Cox, Gary W., and Matthew McCubbins. *Legislative Leviathan: Party Government in the House*. Berkeley, CA: University of California Press, 1993.

Dahl, Robert. *Polyarchy: Participation and Opposition*. New Haven, CT: Yale University Press, 1971.

Diamond, Larry. "Thinking About Hybrid Regimes," *Journal of Democracy*, 13, 2, April 2002: 21–35.

———. *Developing Democracy: Toward Consolidation*. Baltimore, MD: Johns Hopkins University Press, 1999.

———. "Illusions About Consolidation," *Journal of Democracy*, 7, 2, 1996: 34–51.

Diamond, Larry, and Richard Gunther, eds. *Political Parties and Democracy*. Baltimore, MD: Johns Hopkins University Press, 2001.

DiPalma, Guiseppe. *To Craft Democracies: An Essay on Democratic Transitions*. Berkeley, CA: University of California Press, 1990.

Downs, Anthony. *An Economic Theory of Democracy*. New York: Harper and Row, 1957.

Duverger, Maurice. *Political Parties: Their Organization and Activity in the Modern State*. New York: Wiley, 1966.

Easter, Gerald M. "Preference for Presidentialism: Postcommunist Regime Change in Russia and the NIS," *World Politics*, 49, January 1997: 184–211.

Ekiert, Grzegorz, and Stephen Hanson. *Capitalism and Democracy in Central and Eastern Europe*. New York: Cambridge University Press, 2003.

Ekiert, Grzegorz, and Jan Kubik. "Contentious Politics in New Democracies: East Germany, Hungary, Poland and Slovakia, 1989–93," *World Politics*, 50, 4, July 1998: 574–581.

Elster, Jon, Claus Offe, and Ulrich K. Pruess. *Institutional Design in Post-Communist States: Rebuilding the Ship at Sea*. New York: Cambridge University Press, 1998.

Works Cited

Evans, Geoffrey, and Stephen Whitfield. "The Evolution of Left and Right in Post-Soviet Russia," *Europe-Asia Studies*, 50, 6, September 1998: 1023–43.

———. "Identifying the Bases of Party Competition in Eastern Europe," *British Journal of Political Science*, 23, 1993: 521–48.

Ferguson, Gary. *IFES Russian National Survey Regional Profiles*. Washington, DC: International Foundation of Electoral Systems (IFES), 1995.

Ferrera, Federico, and Erik S. Herron. "Going It Alone? Strategic Entry Under Mixed Electoral Rules," 2003, unpublished manuscript. Available at http://www.ku.edu/~herron/, accessed June 2004.

Fish, M. Steven. *Democracy from Scratch: Opposition and Regime in the New Russian Revolution*. Princeton, NJ: Princeton University Press, 1996.

———. "The Advent of Multipartism in Russia, 1993–95," *Post-Soviet Affairs*, 11, October 1995: 340–83.

Fowler, Linda. *Political Ambition: Who Decides to Run for Congress*. New Haven, CT: Yale University Press, 1989.

Frye, Timothy. "The Perils of Polarization: Economic Performance in the Post-Communist World," *World Politics*, 54, 3, April 2003: 308–37.

———. "A Politics of Institutional Choice: Post-Communist Presidencies," *Comparative Political Studies*, 30, 5, October 1997: 523–52.

Geddes, Barbara. "A Game Theoretic Model of Reform in Latin American Democracies," *American Political Science Review*, 85, 1991: 371–92.

Gelman, Vladimir, and Grigorii V. Golosov. "Regional Party System Formation in Russia: The Deviant Case of Sverdlovsk Oblast," *Journal of Communist Studies and Transition Politics*, 14, 1–2, March–June 1998: 31–62.

Gibson, James L. "Social Networks, Civil Society, and the Prospects for Consolidating Russia's Democratic Transition," *American Journal of Political Science*, 45, 1, 2001: 51–68.

Golosov, Grigory V. "From Adygeya to Yaroslavl: Factors of Party Development in the Regions of Russia, 1995–1998," *Europe-Asia Studies*, 51, 8, 1999a: 1333–65.

———. "History Reports Itself: How the Fatherland – All Russia Alhance is Nothing New, *Russian Election Watch*, 2 September 1999b: 14–15.

Grzymala-Bussa, Anna. "Political Competition and the Politicization of the State in East Central Europe," *Comparative Political Studies*, 36, 10, December 2003: 1123–47.

———. *Redeeming the Communist Past: The Regeneration of Communist Successor Parties in East Central Europe*. Cambridge, UK: Cambridge University Press, 2002.

Grzymala-Busse, Anna, and Abby Innes. "Great Expectations: The EU and Domestic Political Competition in East Central Europe," *East European Politics and Societies*, 17, 1, 2003: 64–73.

Gunther, Richard. "Electoral Laws, Party Systems and Elites: The Case of Spain," *American Political Science Review*, 89, 3, 1989: 835–58.

Hale, Henry. *Elections, Parties and Democratization in Russia*. New York: Cambridge University Press, 2005.

Works Cited

———. "Why Not Parties? Supply and Demand on Russia's Electoral Market," *Comparative Politics*, forthcoming.

———. "Will Elections Erode Russia's Democracy?" *Fletcher Forum of World Affairs*, 24, 1, 2000: 123–31.

Hanson, Stephen E. "Instrumental Democracy: The End of Ideology and the Decline of Russian Political Parties," in V. Hesli and W. Reisinger, eds., *Elections, Parties and the Future of Russia*. New York: Cambridge University Press, 2004: 163–85.

———. "Ideology, Uncertainty, and the Rise of Anti-System Parties in Post-Communist Russia," *Journal of Communist Studies and Transition Politics*, 14, March–June 1998: 98–127.

———. "The Leninist Legacy and Institutional Change," *Comparative Political Studies*, July 1995: 306–14.

Haspel, Moshe, Thomas Remington, and Steven Smith. "Electoral Institutions and Party Cohesion in the Russian Duma," *Journal of Politics*, 60, 2, 1998: 417–39.

Herron, E. S. "Mixed Electoral Rules and Party Strategies: Responses to Incentives by Ukraine's Rukh and Russia's Yabloko," *Party Politics*, 8, 6, 2002: 719–34.

Hewett, Ed A. "Perestroyka and the Congress of People's Deputies," *Soviet Economy*, 5, 1, 1989: 47–69.

Higley, John and Richard Gunther, eds. *Elites and Democratic Consolidation in Latin America and Southern Europe*. Cambridge, UK, and New York: Cambridge University Press, 1992.

Hinich, Melvin J., and Michael C. Munger. *Ideology and the Theory of Political Choice*, Ann Arbor, MI: University of Michigan Press, 1994.

Hough, Jerry F., Evelyn Davidheiser, and Susan Goodrich Lehman. *The 1996 Russian Presidential Election*. Washington, DC: Brookings Institution Press, 1996.

Huntington, Samuel. *The Third Wave: Democratization in the Late Twentieth Century*. Norman, OK: University of Oklahoma Press, 1991.

———. *Political Order in Changing Societies*. New Haven, CT: Yale University Press, 1968.

Ishiyama, John T. "Candidate Recruitment and the Development of Russian Political Parties, 1993–1999", *Party Politics*, 7, 2001: 387–412.

———. "Candidate Recruitment, Party Organization and the Communist Successor Parties: The Cases of the MSzP, the KPRF and the LDDP," *Europe Asia Studies*, 52, 5, 2000: 875–96.

———. "Political Parties and Candidate Recruitment in Post-Soviet Russian Politics," *Journal of Communist Studies and Transition Politics*, 15, 4, 1999: 41–69.

———. "Electoral Systems Experimentation in the New Eastern Europe: The Single Transferable Vote and the Additional Member System in Estonia and Hungary," *East European Quarterly*, 29, 1996: 486–507.

———. "Founding Elections and the Development of Transitional Parties: The Cases of Estonia and Latvia, 1990–1992," *Communist and Post-Communist Studies*, 26, 1993: 277–99.

Ishiyama, J. T., and R. Kennedy. "Superpresidentialism and Political Party Development in Russia, Ukraine, Armenia and Kyrgyzstan," *Europe-Asia Studies*, 53, 8, December 2001: 1177–99.
Ishiyama, John T., and Sahar Shafqat. "Party Identity Change in Post-Communist Politics: The Cases of the Successor Parties in Hungary, Poland and Russia," *Communist and Postcommunist Studies*, 33, 4, 2000: 439–55.
Johnston, R. J., and C. J. Pattie. "Campaigning and Split-Ticket Voting in New Electoral Systems: The First MMP Elections in New Zealand, Scotland and Wales," *Electoral Studies*, 21, 4, December 2002, 583–600.
Jones Luong, Pauline. *Institutional Change and Political Continuity in Post-Soviet Central Asia: Power, Perceptions, and Pacts*. Cambridge, UK, and New York: Cambridge University Press, 2002.
Jowitt, Kenneth. "Dizzy with Democracy," *Problems of Post-Communism*, 43, 1, January/February 1996: 3–8.
Karl, Terry Lynn. "The Hybrid Regimes of Central America," *Journal of Democracy*, 6, 3, July 1995: 72–87.
Karl, Terry Lynn, and Phillipe Schmitter. "What Democracy Is . . . and Is Not," *Journal of Democracy*, 2, 3, Summer 1991: 75–89.
Katz, Richard. *Democracy and Elections*. London: Oxford University Press, 1997.
Key, V. O. *Southern Politics in State and Nation*. New York: Knopf, 1949.
Kingdon, John W. *Candidates for Office: Beliefs and Strategies*. New York: Random House, 1968.
Kitschelt, Herbert. "Linkages Between Citizens and Politicians in Democratic Polities," *Comparative Political Studies*, 33, 6/7, August/September 2000: 845–79.
_____. *The Logics of Party Formation*. Ithaca, NY: Cornell University Press, 1989.
Kitschelt, Herbert, et al. *Post-Communist Party Systems: Competition, Representation, and Interparty Collaboration*. Cambridge, UK: Cambridge University Press, 1999.
Kitschelt, Herbert, and Regina Smyth. "Programmatic Party Cohesion in Emerging Postcommunist Democracies: Russia in Comparative Context," *Comparative Political Studies*, 35, 10, December 2002: 1228–56.
Kopstein, Jeffrey, and David Reilly. "Geographic Diffusion and the Transformation of the Post-Communist World," *World Politics*, 53, 2000: 1–37.
Kovalev, V. "The Quasi-Party System in the Regions: The Case of the Republic of Komi and the Overall Situation in Russia," *Russian Politics and Law*, 39, 2, December 2001: 45–64.
Kubicek, Paul. "Delegative Democracy in Russia and Ukraine," *Communist and Post-Communist Studies*, 27, 4, 1994: 443–61.
Levitsky, Stephen L., and Lucan A. Way. "The Rise of Competitive Authoritarianism," *Journal of Democracy*, 13, 2, April 2002: 51–65.
_____. "Autocracy by Democratic Rules: The Dynamics of Competitive Authoritarianism in the Post–Cold War Era," October 2002, unpublished manuscript.
Lijphart, Arend. *Electoral Systems and Party Systems: A Study of Twenty-Seven Democracies, 1945–1990*. Oxford, UK: Oxford University Press, 1995.

Works Cited

Lijphart, Arend, and Beverley Crawford, eds. *Liberalization and Leninist Legacies: Comparative Perspectives on Democratic Transitions*. Berkeley, CA: International and Area Studies, 1997.

Lijphart, Arend, and Carlos Waisman, eds. *Institutional Design in New Democracies*. Boulder, CO: Westview Press, 1996.

Linz, Juan. "The Perils of Presidentialism," *Journal of Democracy*, 1, Winter 1990: 51–69.

Linz, Juan, and Alfred Stepan. *Problems in Democratic Transition and Consolidation: Southern Europe, South America, and Post-Communist Europe*. Baltimore, MD: Johns Hopkins University Press, 1996.

Linz, Juan J., and Arturo Valenzuela, eds. *The Failure of Presidential Democracy*. Baltimore, MD: Johns Hopkins University Press, 1994.

Lipset, Seymour Martin. "Some Social Requisites of Democracy: Economic Development and Political Legitimacy," *American Political Science Review*, 53, 1, 1959: 69–105.

Lipset, Seymour Martin, and Stein Rokkan. "*Cleavage Structures, Party Systems, and Voter Alignments: An Introduction,*" in Seymour Martin Lipset and Stein Rokkan, eds., *Party Systems and Voter Alignments: Cross National Perspectives*. New York: Free Press, 1967, pp. 1–64.

Mainwaring, Scott. "Electoral Volatility in Brazil," *Party Politics*, 4, 1998: 523–46.

———. "Presidentialism, Multipartism, and Democracy: The Difficult Combination," *Comparative Political Studies*, 26, 2, 1993: 198–228.

———. "Politicians, Parties, and Electoral Systems: Brazil in Comparative Perspective," *Comparative Politics*, 24, 1, October 1991: 21–44.

Mainwaring, Scott, and Timothy Scully, eds. *Building Democratic Institutions: Party Systems in Latin America*. Stanford, CA: Stanford University Press, 1995.

Mainwaring, Scott, and Matthew Soberg Shugart, eds. *Presidentialism and Democracy in Latin America*. Cambridge, UK: Cambridge University Press, 1997a.

———. "Juan Linz, Presidentialism, and Democracy: A Critical Appraisal," *Comparative Politics*, 29, 4, July 1997b: 449–72.

Mayhew, David R. *Congress: The Electoral Connection*. New Haven, CT: Yale University Press, 1974.

McAllister, Ian, and Stephen White. "The Mixed Member Electoral System in Russia." Paper available at: http://www.russiavotes.org/.

McFaul, Michael. "The Fourth Wave of Democracy and Dictatorship, Noncooperative Transitions in the Postcommunist World," *World Politics*, 54, 2, 2002: 212–44.

———. *Russia's Unfinished Revolution: Political Change from Gorbachev to Putin*. Ithaca, NY: Cornell University Press, 2001.

———. "Russia's 1999 Parliamentary Elections: Party Consolidation and Fragmentation," *Demokratizatsiya*, 8, 1, 2000: 5–23.

———. "The Perils of a Protracted Transition," *Journal of Democracy*, 10, 2, 1999: 4–18.

———. *Russia's 1996 Presidential Election: The End of Polarized Politics*. Stanford, CA: Hoover Institution Press, Stanford University, 1998a.

———. "Uncertainty, Institutional Design and Path Dependency During Transitions: Cases from Russia," 1998b: unpublished manuscript.

———. "Russian Electoral Politics After Transition: Regional and National Assessments," *Post-Soviet Geography and Economics*, 38, 9, 1997: 507–49.

———. "Russia Between Elections: The Vanishing Center," *Journal of Democracy*, 7, 2, 1996a: 90–104.

———. "Russia's 1996 Presidential Elections," *Post-Soviet Affairs*, 12, 4, 1996b: 318–50.

———. "State Power, Institutional Change, and the Politics of Privatization in Russia," *World Politics*, 47, 2, January 1995: 210–43.

———. "Russia's Choice: The Perils of Revolutionary Democracy," in Timothy J. Colton and Jerry F. Hough, eds., *Growing Pains: Russian Democracy and the Election of 1999*. Washington, DC: Brookings Institution Press, 1993.

McFaul, Michael, Nikolai Petrov, and Andrei Ryabov, eds., with Elizabeth Reisch. *Primer on Russia's 1999 Duma Elections*. Moscow, Washington, DC: Carnegie Endowment for International Peace, Carnegie Moscow Center, 1999.

Michels, Robert. *Political Parties: A Sociological Study of the Oligarchical Tendencies of Modern Democracy*. Gloucester, MA: P. Smith, 1978.

Miller, Arthur H., Gwyn Erb, and Vicki L. Hesli. "Emerging Party Systems in Post-Soviet Societies: Fact or Fiction?" *Journal of Politics*, 62, 2, 2000: 455–90.

Miller, Arthur H. and T. F. Klobucar. "The Development of Party Identification in Post-Soviet Societies," *American Journal of Political Science*, 44, 4, 2001: 667–86.

Moser, Robert G. *Unexpected Outcomes: Electoral Systems, Political Parties, and Representation in Russia*. Pittsburgh, PA: University of Pittsburgh Press, 2001.

———. "Independents and Party Formation: Elite Partisanship as an Intervening Variable in Russian Politics," *Comparative Political Studies*, 37, 2, 1999: 147–66.

Motyl, Alexander. "Structural Constraints and Starting Points: The Logic of Systemic Change in Ukraine and Russia," *Comparative Politics*, 29, 4, July 1997: 433–447.

Munck, Gerardo, and Carol Skalnik Leff. "Modes of Transition and Democratization: South America and Eastern Europe in Comparative Perspective," *Comparative Politics*, 29, 1997: 343–62.

Myagkov, Mikhail, and Peter Ordeshook. "The Trail of Votes in Russia's 1999 Duma and 2000 Presidential Elections," *Communist and Postcommunist Studies*, 34, 3, 2001: 353–70.

Myagkov, M., P. Ordeshook, and A. Sobyanin. "The Russian Electorate, 1991–1996," *Post-Soviet Affairs*, 13, 2, 1997: 134–66.

Norris, Pippa. "Legislative Recruitment," in Lawrence Le Duc, Richard G. Niemi, and Pippa Norris, eds., *Comparing Democracies: Elections and Voting in Global Perspective*. Thousand Oaks, NJ: Sage Publications, 1996.

Oates, Sarah. Forthcoming. *Tuning Out Democracy: Television and Elections in Russia*.

———. "The 1999 Russian Duma Elections," *Problems of Post-Communism*, 47, 3, 2000: 3–14.

Works Cited

O'Donnell, Guillermo. "Horizontal Accountability in New Democracies," *Journal of Democracy*, 9, 1998: 112–26.
———. "Illusions About Consolidation," *Journal of Democracy*, 7, 2, April 1996: 34–51.
———. "Delegative Democracy," *Journal of Democracy*, 5, January 1994: 55–69.
O'Donnell, Guillermo, and Philippe Schmitter. *Transitions from Authoritarian: Tentative Conclusions About Uncertain Democracies*. Baltimore, MD: Johns Hopkins University Press, 1986.
Ordeshook, Peter C. "Institutions and Incentives," *Journal of Democracy*, 6, 2, April 1995: 46–60.
Ostrow, Joel M. "Conflict-Management in Russia's Federal Institutions," *Post Soviet Affairs*, 18, 1, January 2002: 49–70.
———. *Comparing Post-Soviet Legislatures: A Theory of Institutional Design and Political Conflict*. Columbus, OH: Ohio State University Press, 2000.
Panebianco, Angelo. *Political Parties: Organization and Power*. Cambridge, UK: Cambridge University Press, 1988.
Piattoni, Simona, ed. *Clientelism, Interests, and Democratic Representation: The European Experience in Historical and Comparative Perspective*. New York: Cambridge University Press, 2001.
Popkin, Samuel L. *The Reasoning Voter: Communication and Persuasion in Presidential Campaigns*. Chicago: University of Chicago Press, 1991.
Project on Political Transformation and the Electoral Process in Post-Communist Europe, University of Essex, 2003.
Przeworski, Adam. *Democracy and the Market*. Cambridge, UK: Cambridge University Press, 1991.
———. "Some Problems in the Study of Transition to Democracy," chapter 2 in Guillermo O'Donnell, Phillippe C. Schmitter, and Lawrence Whitehead, eds., *Transitions from Authoritarian Rule: Comparative Perspectives*. Baltimore, MD: Johns Hopkins University Press, 1986.
Przeworski, Adam, Michael E. Alvarez, Jose Cheibub, and Fernando Limongi. *Democracy and Development: Political Institutions and Well-Being in the World 1950–1990*. Cambridge, UK: Cambridge University Press, 2000.
Przeworski, Adam, and Fernando Limongi. "Modernization: Theories and Facts," *World Politics*, 49, 2, 1997: 155–83.
Przeworski, Adam, Susan C. Stokes, and Bernard Manin. *Democracy, Accountability, and Representation*. New York: Cambridge University Press, 1999.
Rae, Douglas W. *The Political Consequences of Electoral Laws*. New Haven, CT: Yale University Press, 1967.
Randall, Vicky, and Lars Svasand. "Political Parties and Democratic Consolidation in Africa," *Democratization*, 9, 3, Autumn 2002: 5–29.
Ratiani, Natalia, and Olga Tropkina. "Senators May Be Elected Soon: The Federation Council Is on the Threshold of Crucial Reforms," *Izvestiya*, June 22, 2004.
Reisinger, William M., Arthur H. Miller, and Vicki L. Hesli. "Ideological Division and Party-building Prospect in Post-Soviet Russia," in Matthew Wyman,

Stephen White, and Sarah Oates, eds., *Elections and Voters in Post-Communist Russia*. Northampton, MA: Edward Elgar, 1999: 136–66.

———. "Political Norms in Rural Russia: Evidence from Public Attitudes," *Europe-Asia Studies*, 47, 6, 1995a: 1025–42.

———. "Public Behavior and Political Change in Post-Communist Societies," *Journal of Politics*, 57, 4, November 1995b: 941–70.

Reisinger, William, Arthur H. Miller, Vicki L. Hesli, and Kristen Maher. "Political Values in Russia, Ukraine and Lithuania: Sources and Implications for Democracy," *British Journal of Political Science*, 24, 2, April 1994: 183–223.

Remington, Thomas F. *The Russian Parliament: Institutional Evolution in a Transitional Regime, 1989–1999*. New Haven, CT: Yale University Press, 2001a.

———. "Putin and the Duma," *Post-Soviet Affairs*, 17, 4, December 2001b: 285–308.

Remington, Thomas F., and Steven S. Smith. "Theories of Legislative Institutions and the Organization of the Russian Duma," *American Journal of Political Science*, 42, 2, 1998: 545–72.

———. "Political Goals, Institutional Context, and the Choice of an Electoral System: The Russian Parliamentary Election Law," *American Journal of Political Science*, 40, 1996: 1253–79.

Riker, William. "The Two-Party System and Duverger's Law: An Essay on the History of Political Science," *American Political Science Review*, 74, 4, December 1982: 753–66.

Robinson, Neil. "Classifying Russia's Party System: The Problem of 'Relevance' in a Time of Uncertainty," *Journal of Communist Studies and Transition Politics*, 14, 1–2, March–June 1998: 159–78.

Rohde, David W. "Risk-Bearing and Progressive Ambition: The Case of Members of the United States House of Representatives," *American Journal of Political Science*, 23, 1, February 1979: 1–26.

Rose, Richard, William Mishler, and Christian Haerpfer. *Democracy and Its Alternatives: Understanding Post-Communist Societies*. Baltimore, MD: Johns Hopkins University Press, 1998.

Rose, Richard and Neil Munro. *Elections Without Order*. New York: Cambridge University Press, 2003.

Samuels, David J., and Matthew Soberg Shugart. "Presidentialism, Elections and Representation," *Journal of Theoretical Politics*, 15, 1, January 2003: 33–60.

Schattschneider, E. E. *Party Government*. New York: Holt, Rinehart and Winston, 1942.

Schedler, Andreas. "Taking Uncertainty Seriously: The Blurred Boundaries of Democratic Transition and Consolidation," *Democratization*, 8, 4, 2001: 1–22.

Schlesinger, Joseph A. *Political Parties and the Winning of Office*. Ann Arbor, MI: Michigan University Press, 1994.

———. *Ambition and Politics*. Chicago: Rand McNally, 1966.

Schmitter, Phillippe. "Parties Are Not What They Once Were," chapter 2 in Larry Diamond and Richard Gunther, eds., *Political Parties and Democracy*. Baltimore, MD: Johns Hopkins University Press, 2001, 67–89.

Works Cited

Schmitter, Philippe C., and Terry Lynn Karl. "The Conceptual Travels of Transitologists and Consolidologists: How Far to the East Should They Attempt to Go?" *Slavic Review*, 53, 1, 1994: 173–85.

Schumpeter, Joseph A. *Capitalism, Socialism, and Democracy*. London: Allen and Unwin, 1954.

Shevtsova, Lilia. "Russia's Hybrid Regime," *Journal of Democracy*, 12, 4, 2001: 65–70.

———. "Can Electoral Autocracy Survive?" *Journal of Democracy*, 11, 3, 2000: 36–8.

Shvetsova, Olga. "Resolving the Problem of Pre-Election Coordination: The 1999 Parliamentary Election as Elite Presidential 'Primary,'" in V. Hesli and W. Reisinger, eds., *Elections, Parties and the Future of Russia*. New York: Cambridge University Press, 2004.

———. "A Survey of Post-Communist Electoral Institutions: 1990–1998," *Electoral Studies*, 18, 1999: 397–409.

Shugart, Matthew Soberg. "The Inverse Relationship Between Party Strength and Executive Strength: A Theory of Politicians' Constitutional Choices," *British Journal of Political Science*, 28, 1, January 1998: 1–29.

———. "Executive–Legislative Relations in Post-Communist Europe," *Transition*, 2, 25, December 1996: 6–11.

Shugart, Matthew Soberg, and John M. Carey. *Presidents and Assemblies: Constitutional Design and Electoral Dynamics*. New York: Cambridge University Press, 1992.

Shugart, Matthew Soberg, and Martin P. Wattenberg, eds. *Mixed-Member Electoral Systems: The Best of Both Worlds?* Oxford, UK: Oxford University Press, 2001.

Smith, Steven S., and Thomas F. Remington. *The Politics of Institutional Choice: The Formation of the Russian State Duma*. Princeton, NJ: Princeton University Press, 2001.

Smyth, Regina. "Partisans Without Parties," *Comparative Politics*, forthcoming.

———. "Building State Capacity from the Inside Out: Parties of Power and the Success of the President's Reform Agenda in Russia," *Politics and Society*, 30, 4, December 2002: 555–78.

Stepan, Alfred and Cindy Skach. "Constitutional Frameworks and Democratic Consolidation: Parliamentarism Versus Presidentialism," *World Politics*, 46, October 1993: 1–22.

Stoner-Weiss, Kathryn. "The Limited Reach of Russia's Party System: Underinstitutionalization in Dual Transitions," *Politics and Society*, 29, 3, 2001: 385–414.

Taagepera, Rein. "Effective Magnitude and Effective Threshold," *Electoral Studies*, 17, 1998: 393–404.

Taagepera, Rein, and Matthew Shugart. *Seats and Votes: The Effects and Determinants of Electoral Systems*. New Haven, CT: Yale University Press, 1989.

Tarrow, Sidney. "The Italian Party System: Between Crisis and Transition," *American Journal of Political Science*, 21, 2, May 1977: 193–223.

Thames, Frank C., Jr. "Legislative Voting Behavior in the Russian Duma: Understanding the Effect of Mandate," *Europe-Asia Studies*, 53, 6, September 2001: 869–84.

Works Cited

Tsygankov, Andrei. "Manifestations of Delegative Democracy in Russian Local Politics: What Does It Mean for the Future of Russia?" *Communist and Post-Communist Studies*, 31, 4, 1998: 329–41.

White, Stephen, Richard Rose, and Ian McAllister. *How Russia Votes*. Chatham, UK: Chatham House, 1997.

Yargomskaya, M. "Effect of the Electoral System on the Electoral Strategies of Duma Elections," in V. Gelman, G. Golosov, and E. Melshkina, eds., *The Second Electoral Cycle in Russia, 1999–2000*, Moscow: Ves Mir (in Russian), 2002.

Zakharia, Fareed. "The Rise of Illiberal Democracy," *Foreign Affairs*, 76, November–December 1997: 22–41.

Index

Agrarian Party of Russia, 98, 135
Aldrich, John, 8, 39–40, 107, 188
Alexander, Gerard, 208
Ambition theory, 72, 92–3
   political amateurs, 93–4
Ames, Barry, 41
Armenia, 41, 82
Authoritarian infrastructure, 64, 70, 129,
   159, 161, 201, 203
Ayatskov, Dmitry, 86, 99

Bianco, William, 107
Bunce, Valerie, 24, 32

Campaign organizations, 170–2
Campaign strategies, 165, 174–5
   effect of goals on, 181
   effect of resources on, 181–4
   explanation of, 176–80
   implications for electoral infrastructure,
      193–4
   partisan appeals, 166–7
Candidate pool, 73, 76–8
Candidate resources. *See* Electoral
   resources
Candidate survey, 45–6, 213
Candidates' goals, 57–9, 145–6
Candidates' strategies, 46–8
Canon, David, 57, 93
Central Asian states, 20, 25, 29, 203,
   230
Chelyabinsk oblast, 73, 92–3, 170, 173, 184,
   213
Chernomirdin, Victor, 112

Colton, Timothy, 129
Communist legacy, 7, 24, 26, 32, 67, 85,
   203
Communist Party of the Russian Federation,
   111, 124, 137, 161, 169, 186
Communist Party of the Soviet Union, 62,
   142
Connected resources. *See* Electoral
   resources
Corruption, 168
Cox, Gary, 37–8, 59–60, 100, 107, 175

Dahl, Robert, 6, 9, 36, 235
Democracy assistance, 200, 204, 206, 210
Democracy, definitions of, 6–7
Democratic Choice of Russia, 84, 112,
   139
Democratic consolidation, 1–2
   choice theoretic explanations, 27, 41–2
   consolidation scores, 17–20
   impact of uncertainty, 208–10
   patterns of, 20, 203
   role of elections in, 4–5, 8–10
   role of political parties, 204–6
   in the Russian Federation, 198–202
   structural explanations, 23–7
Democratic deepening, 7, 9, 16, 35
Diamond, Larry, 6, 9
District selection, 131–2
   carpetbaggers, 142–5
   effect of party organizations, 135–7
   explanation, 151–6
   incumbents and, 157–61
   patterns over time, 133–4

Index

Duverger's Law, 50, 53, 72, 88, 91–2
  mechanical effect, 88
  psychological effect, 88
  underlying assumptions, 89

Electoral infrastructure, 3, 5, 35, 42–3, 161
  cooperation, 39–41
  coordination, 37–9
  information, 35–7, 54, 184–8
  partisan affiliation, 128–30
  as a product of candidates' strategies, 69–70, 127–8, 161–4, 189–93
Electoral resources, 59–61, 168
  partisan resources, 61–5, 107–10
  personal vote resources, 65–8
Electoral rules, 49–52, 78, 81–2
  effect on electoral infrastructure, 194–5
  electoral threshold, 52–3
  reform of, 79, 200–1
  residency, 12, 79, 132, 142, 144, 150
  strategic entry, 38–9, 50
  strategic voting, 38–9, 50, 88, 91
  strategic withdrawal, 95–9
European Union, 10, 25–6, 29–31, 33, 236
Evans, Geoffrey, 23

Fatherland–All Russia, 63, 98, 112, 200
Founding elections, 190, 196–8, 210
Freedom House, 14, 16–17
Frye, Timothy, 35

Geddes, Barbara, 57
Gorbachev, Mikhail, 7, 94
Gordeev, Anatoly, 90, 143, 193
Greshnevikov, Anatoly, 139–40
Gromov, Boris, 90, 143
Grzymala-Busse, Anna, 67
Gunther, Richard, 41

Haerpfer, Christian, 23
Hale, Henry, 67, 129
Hanson, Stephen, 67
Hungary, 5, 20, 41, 79, 82, 203
Huntington, Samuel, 1, 9, 20, 40
Hybrid regime, 202

Incumbents, campaign strategies of, 159–61
Independent candidates, 41, 44, 46, 84, 105, 119, 127–9, 150
Independent resources. *See* Electoral resources
Ishiyama, John, 81, 84, 107, 124

Katz, Richard, 8
Key, V. O., 34
Kingdon, John, 53
KPRF, 185

Levitsky, Stephen, 25
Liberal Democratic Party of Russia, 7, 64
Limongi, Fernando, 36
Linz, Juan, 6, 9, 23–5, 67, 115
Lipset, Seymour Martin, 24, 188
Lithuania, 41, 74, 79, 82, 210
Lysenko, Nikolai, 96, 143, 193

Mainwaring, Scott, 41
Mass media, use in campaigns, 62, 108, 166, 168, 200
Mass partisanship, 128–9, 193, 206
Mayhew, David, 57
McFaul, Michael, 28, 84
Mironov, Oleg, 96–7
Mizulina, Elena, 138–40, 193
Motyl, Alexander, 24

Oates, Sarah, 62, 166
O'Donnell, Guillermo, 72
O'Keeffe, Georgia, 14
Oligarchs, 65, 87, 112, 143–4, 169
Our Home Is Russia, 63, 112, 200

Partisan affiliation, 103
  effect of electoral rules on, 104–6
  effect on campaign strategies, 174–5
  the effect of resources on, 107–11
  uncertainty and, 106–7
Party of power, 90
Pochinok, Alexander, 92
Poland, 34
Political elites
  incorporation into democratic regime, 4, 8–10, 15, 21–2, 27–8

Index

Political parties, 21, 39
  brand name, 57, 59, 61, 104, 107–9, 127, 161, 180
  candidate recruitment, 82–4
  as gatekeepers, 80–1
  party in the electorate, 38–9
  party in government, 77–8, 89, 111–12, 129–30, 169, 181, 189, 193, 198, 200–2
  party organizations, 40
Polity, 16
Presidentialism, 26, 30, 33, 89, 194, 230
Przeworski, Adam, 8, 21, 25, 36, 209
Putin, Vladimir, 2, 14, 64, 87, 90, 101, 114, 129, 189, 198, 200

Rashkin, Valery, 73, 75, 86, 90, 94, 99
Redistricting, 141–2
Regional governors, 85–6, 129, 201
Rokkan, Stein, 188
Rose, Richard, 23
Russia's Choice, 63, 135, 173, 200

Saratov oblast, 66, 72, 73, 79, 86, 90, 93, 99
Schattschneider, E. E., 39
Schlesinger, Joseph, 102, 188
Schmitter, Phillippe, 6, 72
Shugart, Matthew, 50
Shvetsova, Olga, 89, 207
Skach, Cindy, 26

Smyth, Regina, 10, 62, 193, 206
Stepan, Alfred, 6, 9, 23–6, 67, 115

Taagapera, Rein, 50
Tretyak, Vladislav, 73, 76, 90, 94, 99

Udalov, Dmitry, 93, 99
Ukraine, 41, 79, 82, 210
Uncertainty, 4, 6, 10, 36–7, 56, 84, 99, 128, 163, 189, 195, 208
Union of Right Forces, 96–8, 139, 170
United Russia, 62–3, 77, 102, 114, 129, 135, 164, 166, 169, 200–1
Unity, 63, 83, 195, 199

Volga Germans, 66, 143

Way, Lucan, 25
Whitefield, Stephen, 23
Women of Russia, 64
World Values Survey, 29

Yabloko, 76, 83, 97–8, 112, 136–7, 170, 185–7
Yaroslavl oblast, 138–40
Yeltsin, Boris, 92, 94, 141, 143, 199, 200
Yuzhakov, Vladimir, 77

Zhirinovsky, Vladimir, 7, 64

Other Books in the Series *(continued from page iii)*

Valerie Bunce, *Leaving Socialism and Leaving the State: The End of Yugoslavia, the Soviet Union, and Czechoslovakia*
Daniele Caramani, *The Nationalization of Politics: The Formation of National Electorates and Party Systems in Europe*
Kanchan Chandra, *Why Ethnic Parties Succeed: Patronage and Ethnic Headcounts in India*
Ruth Berins Collier, *Paths Toward Democracy: The Working Class and Elites in Western Europe and South America*
Donatella della Porta, *Social Movements, Political Violence, and the State*
Gerald Easter, *Reconstructing the State: Personal Networks and Elite Identity*
M. Steven Fish, *Democracy Derailed in Russia: The Failure of Open Politics*
Robert F. Franzese, *Macroeconomic Policies of Developed Democracies*
Roberto Franzosi, *The Puzzle of Strikes: Class and State Strategies in Postwar Italy*.
Geoffrey Garrett, *Partisan Politics in the Global Economy*
Miriam Golden, *Heroic Defeats: The Politics of Job Loss*
Jeff Goodwin, *No Other Way Out: States and Revolutionary Movements*
Merilee Serrill Grindle, *Changing the State*
Anna Grzymala-Busse, *Redeeming the Communist Past: The Regeneration of Communist Parties in East Central Europe*
Frances Hagopian, *Traditional Politics and Regime Change in Brazil*
Gretchen Helmke, *Courts Under Constraints: Judges, Generals, and Presidents in Argentina*
Yoshiko Herrera, *Imagined Economies: The Sources of Russian Regionalism*
J. Rogers Hollingsworth and Robert Boyer, eds., *Contemporary Capitalism: The Embeddedness of Institutions*
John D. Huber and Charles R. Shipan, *Deliberate Discretion? The Institutional Foundations of Bureaucratic Autonomy*
Ellen Immergut, *Health Politics: Interests and Institutions in Western Europe*
Torben Iversen, *Capitalism, Democracy and Welfare*
Torben Iversen, *Contested Economic Institutions*
Torben Iversen, Jonas Pontusson, and David Soskice, eds., *Unions, Employers, and Central Banks: Macroeconomic Coordination and Institutional Change in Social Market Economics*
Thomas Janoski and Alexander M. Hicks, eds., *The Comparative Political Economy of the Welfare State*
Joseph Jupille, *Procedural Politics: Issues, Influence, and Institutional Choice in the European Union*

David C. Kang, *Crony Capitalism: Corruption and Development in South Korea and the Philippines*
Junko Kato, *Regressive Taxation and the Welfare State*
Robert O. Keohane and Helen B. Milner, eds., *Internationalization and Domestic Politics*
Herbert Kitschelt, *The Transformation of European Social Democracy*
Herbert Kitschelt, Peter Lange, Gary Marks, and John D. Stephens, eds., *Continuity and Change in Contemporary Capitalism*
Herbert Kitschelt, Zdenka Mansfeldova, Radek Markowski, and Gabor Toka, *Post-Communist Party Systems*
David Knoke, Franz Urban Pappi, Jeffrey Broadbent, and Yutaka Tsujinaka, eds., *Comparing Policy Networks*
Allan Kornberg and Harold D. Clarke, *Citizens and Community: Political Support in a Representative Democracy*
Amie Kreppel, *The European Parliament and the Supranational Party System*
David D. Laitin, *Language Repertoires and State Construction in Africa*
Fabrice E. Lehoucq and Ivan Molina, *Stuffing the Ballot Box: Fraud, Electoral Reform, and Democratization in Costa Rica*
Mark Irving Lichbach and Alan S. Zuckerman, eds., *Comparative Politics: Rationality, Culture, and Structure*
Evan Lieberman, *Race and Regionalism in the Politics of Taxation in Brazil and South Africa*
Pauline Jones Luong, *Institutional Change and Political Continuity in Post-Soviet Central Asia*
James Mahoney and Dietrich Rueschemeyer, eds., *Historical Analysis and the Social Sciences*
Doug McAdam, John McCarthy, and Mayer Zald, eds., *Comparative Perspectives on Social Movements*
Scott Mainwaring and Matthew Soberg Shugart, eds., *Presidentialism and Democracy in Latin America*
Isabela Mares, *The Politics of Social Risk: Business and Welfare State Development*
Isabela Mares, *Taxation, Wage Bargaining, and Unemployment*
Anthony W. Marx, *Making Race, Making Nations: A Comparison of South Africa, the United States, and Brazil*
Joel S. Migdal, *State in Society: Studying How States and Societies Constitute One Another*
Joel S. Migdal, Atul Kohli, and Vivienne Shue, eds., *State Power and Social Forces: Domination and Transformation in the Third World*

Scott Morgenstern and Benito Nacif, eds., *Legislative Politics in Latin America*
Layna Mosley, *Global Capital and National Governments*
Wolfgang C. Müller and Kaare Strøm, *Policy, Office, or Votes?*
Maria Victoria Murillo, *Labor Unions, Partisan Coalitions, and Market Reforms in Latin America*
Ton Notermans, *Money, Markets, and the State: Social Democratic Economic Policies Since 1918*
Roger Petersen, *Understanding Ethnic Violence: Fear, Hatred, and Resentment in Twentieth-Century Eastern Europe*
Simona Piattoni, ed., *Clientelism, Interests, and Democratic Representation*
Paul Pierson, *Dismantling the Welfare State? Reagan, Thatcher, and the Politics of Retrenchment*
Marino Regini, *Uncertain Boundaries: The Social and Political Construction of European Economies*
Lyle Scruggs, *Sustaining Abundance: Environmental Performance in Industrial Democracies*
Jefferey M. Sellers, *Governing from Below: Urban Regions and the Global Economy*
Yossi Shain and Juan Linz, eds., *Interim Government and Democratic Transitions*
Beverly Silver, *Forces of Labor: Workers' Movements and Globalization Since 1870*
Theda Skocpol, *Social Revolutions in the Modern World*
Richard Snyder, *Politics After Neoliberalism: Reregulation in Mexico*
David Stark and László Bruszt, *Postsocialist Pathways: Transforming Politics and Property in East Central Europe*
Sven Steinmo, Kathleen Thelen, and Frank Longstreth, eds., *Structuring Politics: Historical Institutionalism in Comparative Analysis*
Susan C. Stokes, *Mandates and Democracy: Neoliberalism by Surprise in Latin America*
Susan C. Stokes, ed., *Public Support for Market Reforms in New Democracies*
Duane Swank, *Global Capital, Political Institutions, and Policy Change in Developed Welfare States*
Sidney Tarrow, *Power in Movement: Social Movement and Contentious Politics*
Kathleen Thelen, *How Institutions Evolve: The Political Economy of Skills in Germany, Britain, the United States, and Japan*
Charles Tilly, *Trust and Rule*

Joshua Tucker, *Regional Economic Voting: Russia, Poland, Hungary, Slovakia, and the Czech Republic, 1990–1999*
Ashutosh Varshney, *Democracy, Development, and the Countryside*
Stephen I. Wilkinson, *Votes and Violence: Electoral Competition and Ethnic Riots in India*
Elisabeth J. Wood, *Forging Democracy from Below: Insurgent Transitions in South Africa and El Salvador*
Elisabeth J. Wood, *Insurgent Collective Action and Civil War in El Salvador*